In the Company of Men

KRITIK: GERMAN LITERARY THEORY AND CULTURAL STUDIES

Liliane Weissberg, Editor

A complete listing of the books in this series can be found online at http: wsupress.wayne.edu

$\mathcal{I}_{n\ the}$ Company $_{of}$ Men

CROSS-DRESSED WOMEN AROUND 1800

 Elisabeth Krimmer

Wayne State University Press   Detroit

08 07 06 05 04   5 4 3 2 1

Library of Congress Cataloging-in-Publication Data

Krimmer, Elisabeth, 1967–
    In the company of men : cross-dressed women around 1800 / Elisabeth
Krimmer.
        p. cm.—(Kritik)
Includes bibliographical references and index.
    ISBN 0-8143-3145-9 (alk. paper)
    1. German literature—18th century—History and criticism.   2. Male
impersonators—Germany—18th century.   3. Gender identity in litera-
ture.   4. Women authors, German—18th century.   I. Title.   II. Kritik
(Detroit, Mich.)
    PT289.K75 2003
    830.9'353—dc21

                                                    2003002255

The paper used in this publication meets the minimum requirements of
the American National Standard for Information Sciences—Permanence
of Paper for Printed Library Materials, ANSI Z39.48-1984

FOR MARK

Contents

Illustrations

Acknowledgments

The debts of gratitude that I have accumulated in writing this book are considerable. I would like to thank the interlibrary loan staff at the University of Massachusetts, the University of Missouri, and at Mount Holyoke College. Both the University of Massachusetts and Mount Holyoke College granted research stipends that eased the burden of hunting down obscure material.

Several essays contained in this book have appeared as separate pieces. My interpretation of Caroline de la Motte-Fouqué's work was first published in *Studies in Eighteenth Century Culture* 30 (2001): 165–181, and is reprinted with the permission of Johns Hopkins University Press. A part of chapter 3 appeared in *Germans at Their Best: Making Use of Material and Mass Popular Culture*, Special Issue of the *Journal of Popular Culture* 34.3 (2001): 209–227, edited by John Plews and Chris Lorey, published by Bowling Green State University. My analysis of Kleist's *Die Familie Schroffenstein* appeared in *Body Dialectics in the Age of Goethe*, edited by Holger Pausch and Marianne Henn, published by Rodopi Press. A part of chapter 5 was adapted from my essay in *Unwrapping Goethe's Weimar: Essays in Cultural Studies and Local Knowledge*, edited by Susanne Kord, Simon Richter, and Burkhard Henke, published by Camden House. My analysis of Bettina Brentano-von Arnim's *Clemens Brentanos Frühlingskranz* first appeared in *Conquering Women: Women and War in the German Cultural Imagination*, edited by Hilary Collier-Sy-Quia and Susanne Baackmann, published by the Center for International and Area Studies at the University of California.

Further thanks go to several colleagues who have contributed greatly to the development of the ideas outlined in this book. First and foremost I would like to thank my editors at Wayne State University Press, and in particular Liliane Weissberg, for their guidance and willingness to support this project. I have benefited greatly from critical responses to my essays from Susanne Kord, Jeannine Blackwell, Sara Lennox, Maria Sieira, and Shilpa Raval. I am most grateful to Susan Cocalis, my Ph.D. advisor, and to Laura Callanan for inspiring conversations, insightful comments, and encouraging words. For moral support I would like to thank Gerda Kilgore. Finally, I wish to thank my husband, Mark Nitzberg, for his patience and his support.

INTRODUCTION

⁂

> "The soul is the prison of the body [. . .] I would like to write the history of this prison, with all the political investments of the body that it gathers together in its closed architecture. Why? Simply because I am interested in the past? No, if one means by that writing a history of the past in terms of the present. Yes, if one means writing the history of the present."
>
> MICHEL FOUCAULT, Discipline and Punish

In 1721 the officials of the German city of Halberstadt brought charges against Catharina Lincken for wearing men's clothing.[1] According to the court records of her case, Lincken—alias Anastasius Lagrantinus Rosenstengel, alias Cornelius Hubsch, alias Peter Wannich—served as a soldier in several regiments and deserted her unit a number of times. It seems that s/he changed her name and religion as often as her clothing, converting from Catholicism to Lutheranism and back. She joined the Inspirants, a mystic Christian sect, and traveled through the German countryside until she settled down and married a certain Catharina Mühlhahn. When charged, Lincken defended herself with a reference to the fact that numerous women before her had worn men's clothing. Even though Lincken's defense strategy did not help her case in the end—she was condemned to execution by sword—it bears testimony to an awareness of a tradition of female cross-dressing which, though widespread in the eighteenth century, is no longer part of our historical consciousness of the time.

Catharina Lincken's story is about clothing. But it is also about more than that. Stories about cross-dressers are about bodies in history, bodies in culture.[2] In the late eighteenth and early nineteenth centuries, stories about cross-dressers were employed to work through competing concepts of the body and to imagine different

1

models of gender identity. The strategies, vagaries, and victories of this re-negotiation are the subject of this book.

In recent years, the interrelation of body and gender has become the subject of many heated debates. The separation of a biological entity called sex from a social construct designated as gender—central to second-wave feminists—has become increasingly problematic. Many theorists now criticize the assumption that sex is a clearly distinct and purely physical entity onto which society inscribes its practices (Fausto-Sterling; Butler, *Gender Trouble*).[3] However, as theorists argue that both sex and gender are discursively constructed, we live with numerous practices in which the body and gender identity have been torn apart. Technological and scientific innovations accompanied by societal changes have put in question our everyday understanding of what it means to be a woman. It is not necessary to refer to measures as drastic as sex reassignment surgery. New reproductive technologies that redefine the role of the body in motherhood have become widely accessible. The internet is another case in point. Chat rooms, avatars, and cybersexuality all but efface the importance of the body in social interactions. It seems that around 2000 the confusion surrounding the concept of gender identity and its relation to the body became greater than ever.

I believe that in order fully to understand our current discursive quandaries regarding sex and gender we need to investigate the eighteenth-century heritage on which they are built. In fact, one might claim that with respect to body politics the years around 1800 present the mirror image of the time around 2000. During the late eighteenth century, gender entered the body and became "natural"; during the late twentieth century, the naturalness of nature itself was put in question and the body was theorized as a social construct. In other words, whereas around 1800 the social category of gender was naturalized and conceived of as inseparable from the body, around 2000 the body itself was denaturalized and conceived of as inseparable from ideology.

Unfortunately, most current research on cross-dressing and the body is marked by a strong focus on the literature and culture of the Anglo- and Francophone realms. I believe that it is necessary to expand this debate to include the contributions made by late-eighteenth- and early-nineteenth-century German authors. Cross-dressing and androgyny were not only very popular motifs in German Idealism and Romanticism that deserve attention in their own right; rather, German portrayals of the body and gender also exerted a strong influence on European and American writers of the Germanophile nineteenth century and thus influenced the way we think about gender today.[4]

In late-eighteenth-century Germany, fascination with gender and the body is evidenced by a surprisingly large number of texts that portray characters whose outward masculine identity stands in stark contrast to their biological bodies. A central claim of this book is that the preponderance of this motif is closely connected to the contemporary re-negotiation of what it means to be a woman. I will argue that the cross-dressers in these texts must be understood as strategic interventions in a debate that concerned the female body, the meaning of gender, and the range of actions available to women. They serve to embody two different conceptualizations of the relation between clothing and identity: one paradigm, which I will call the performative model, is based on the assumption that appearance creates identity; the other essentialist model is based on the belief that appearance expresses identity. In the first case, identity is "immanent" in appearance; in the second case, the body is the bearer of a person's "true" identity even though this identity may by hidden behind deceptive appearances (Entwistle 113). In many literary works, cross-dressers functioned as linchpins that kept these diverse constructs together. But they also became the site at which they fell apart.

I propose that female writers responded differently from male writers to these two models of the relation between body and identity. My analysis will demonstrate that most female authors of the late eighteenth century used their fictional cross-dressers to refute a theory that conceives of female anatomy as destiny. By re-negotiating the discursive demarcations of gender, women writers were engaging in a battle to redefine the boundaries of their lives. To male writers, on the other hand, the body was not the bearer of civic exclusion. Free from the weight of a devalued biology, they sought to institute the body as an anchor of truth. But even as their texts are marked by the desire for a body that serves as guarantor of nature, authenticity, and stability, they also betray an awareness that "the body over which [. . .] the question of truth is negotiated and confirmed is itself the product of pre-cisely the discourse for whose legitimation it is constructed" (Bronfen, *The Body* 116).

My choice of primary texts for this study reflects my convic-tion that, in order to gain a full picture of the contemporary dis-course on gender and the body, one must juxtapose texts by female and male authors. However, in doing so, I do not intend simply to add female contributions to an already existing corpus of knowledge. Rather, female and male authors must be understood as agents who, though not equally powerful, are equally invested in the discursive re-negotiation of cultural categories. Texts by male authors respond to and challenge those of their female con-temporaries and vice versa. By listening to both male and female voices, we will not only change our views about women writers but also transform our understanding of the literary canon itself.

Secondary literature on novels and dramas by German women writers of the eighteenth century often stresses that these texts are thematically limited to the realm of home and family. Lydia Schieth, for example, claims that "the portrayal of a reality outside of the home and of alternative life choices constitutes a taboo for novels by women writers" (220).[5] According to Karin Wurst, nei-ther the female protagonists nor their authors were able to "imag-ine adventures outside of the house" (54). Dagmar von Hoff writes that "controversy, deviation, motion, the Other" are sacrificed in dramas by women writers: "They chose confinement, final forms, stagnancy, death" (71). It cannot be denied that these analyses are adequate representations of a large number of novels and dramas by eighteenth-century women writers. But they do not do justice to many other such texts. By undertaking an investigation of the motif of cross-dressing, this work joins the endeavors of feminist scholars who have sought out everything that is negated by the above statements: the portrayal of adventures and alternative life choices, of deviation, motion, and the Other. The assumption that female characters in fiction of this period are victims, incapable of acting on their own, will have to be modified. As we turn our attention to literary cross-dressers, we will come to realize that female writers were not confined to "women's" themes.

Fundamental to such an approach to literary texts by women writers is the idea that "the simplicity of the action and the conciliatory happy ending often conceal explosive 'revolutionary' situations" (Blackwell and Zantop 6). The historical reception of women's literature demonstrates only too plainly that wild, bizarre, and inconsistent elements of these texts often faded from view behind a screen of conformity. However, the authors' vociferous declarations of their supposed adherence to established notions of femininity should not blind us to the joy with which these writers kicked over the traces, nor to the artfulness with which they circumvented internal and external censorship. Every interpretation of texts by eighteenth-century women writers should take into account the internally contradictory and uneven nature of such material. In order to be able to read these texts with pleasure, we will have to learn to accept polyphony as one of their integral constituents. Every attempt to render women's contributions visible and to remove the stain of marginality from texts by women writers will be doomed to failure if it does not teach us how to read these works with pleasure (see Kord, *Namen* 173).

However, focusing the discussion on women authors only would necessarily produce a lopsided result. Women's literature in its conception and argumentation is inseparably linked with men's literature. I agree with Wurst's contention that, when interpreting cultural products by women, one should not strive for "a seamless integration which is tantamount to a devaluation of its specificity, nor [for] a separate female culture." Rather, Wurst recommends a third approach "which analyses the relations between valorized

and non-valorized discourses" (17). Thus, feminist scholars who
are aware of the dialectic of canonical and non-canonical texts
conceive of works by male writers as only one side of the coin. In
doing so, their work re-contextualizes and thus relativizes familiar
positions by male authors. Male authors responded to literary contributions by women and to challenges presented by the women
in their lives. An investigation that links Johann Wolfgang von
Goethe to Charlotte von Stein and Heinrich von Kleist to his sister Ulrike Kleist, that takes into account that Friedrich Schiller
was familiar with texts by Amalie von Imhoff, Sophie Mereau, and
Karoline von Wolzogen, and that Friedrich Schlegel relied on the
work of his wife Dorothea Schlegel is likely to discover new and
enlightening facets that add to our understanding of some of the
most discussed works of our literary canon.[6]

The goal of the following chapters is to delineate the discursive
formations which female and male writers employ when they
attempt to redefine the relation between body and gender.
However, since such individual reconfigurations are situated within
and influenced by their respective historical context, I will begin
by introducing the contemporary discourse on gender identity.

I.

The second half of the eighteenth century was characterized by
far-reaching cultural, social, and philosophical paradigm shifts.
The normative authority of theology was replaced by that of philosophy and science, and the unity of the "entire household"
(ganzes Haus), the combined family home and workshop, was dissolved as capitalism gradually became the dominant mode of production. The endeavors of the bourgeoisie to establish itself as a
political force were accompanied by a complete restructuring of
the public and private spheres. Interlaced with these changes was
a radical reinterpretation of the meaning and implications of the
category of gender.

In German literary criticism, this emerging concept of gender is generally captured with the term "gendered character" (Geschlechtscharakter). According to Barbara Becker-Cantarino, the concept of gendered character is based on the claim that women possess "certain psychological and moral qualities which are said to correspond to their biological disposition" ["(Sozial)geschichte" 247; see also Duden 23]. In other words, the body prescribes how social and moral tasks are to be distributed between the genders (Honegger ix). In order to achieve the desired ideological effect, the concept of *Geschlechtscharakter* performs two operations. First, it groups together a certain cluster of character traits, such as passivity, emotionality, and lack of independence. Then it defines these traits as inherently "female" by claiming that they are direct "emanations" of woman's nature. Dotzler notes discerningly that this constitutes an astute attempt to shift "the subjection of woman from the outside to the inside" (352).

Recent research has pointed out that, in spite of its increasing importance, the model of gendered character—presented in texts such as Wilhelm von Humboldt's *About the Difference between the Genders and Its Influence on Organic Nature* [Über den Geschlechtsunterschied und dessen Einfluß auf die organische Natur, 1795] and in Friedrich von Schiller's poetry—had not yet become the dominant paradigm by the end of the century (Kord, *Namen* 36–42). It is this undecided state, the coexistence of two different models, that interests me.

My investigation of gender constructs in literary texts is based on Thomas Laqueur's and Claudia Honegger's research on the historical evolution of concepts of gender and the body. However, while Laqueur's and Honegger's analyses of the defining traits and socio-political context of these models are highly insightful, I propose that the notion of paradigm shifts on which their works rely needs further elaboration. Historical evidence suggests that the relation between these competing models of gender identity is not one of successive substitution, but rather one of uneasy coexistence. Though there is a general agreement as to which concept is dominant at a particular time, one often forgets that such dominance must be understood as locally circumscribed and perpetually contested.[7]

In his study of gender constructions from the Greeks to Freud, Thomas Laqueur postulates the existence of two different models of gender identity, the earlier one-sex model, and the later two-sex model. In the one-sex model, the difference between male and female is interpreted as one of degree, not of kind. Men and women were not considered to be essentially different. Rather, the female body was seen as a less perfect, but substantially isomorphic version of the male body. The existing anatomical differences were thought to have been caused by the lack of heat in women, which had resulted in "the retention, inside, of structures that in the male are visible without [. . .] In this world the vagina is imagined as an interior penis, the labia as foreskin, the uterus as scrotum, and the ovaries as testicles" (Laqueur 4). In sum, woman is man turned outside in.[8]

According to the one-sex model, it was absolutely conceivable for a woman to turn into a man (cf. Laqueur 123). There are a number of stories of women who sprouted a penis; for example, that of the shepherdess Maria Garnier, later Germain Garnier (cf. Orgel 20). One day Marie was chasing after some pigs when she jumped over a ditch. The heat, generated by the strenuous exertion, propelled her internal vagina/penis outside, and Marie became a man. Although this story suggests that the physiological boundary between the genders was thought to be permeable, the social stratification associated with femininity and masculinity was decidedly rigid. In the pre-Enlightenment model, social categories themselves, along with their respective tasks and cultural roles, were considered God-given, that is, natural and immutable.

Laqueur claims that in the eighteenth century the one-sex model was abandoned in favor of a binary structure that defined the two genders as discrete and incommensurable. The two-sex model was born. This change was not brought about by an increase in anatomical or physiological knowledge, but by epistemological and political developments.[9] In the Age of Enlightenment, references to transcendental and traditional systems of order could no longer provide sufficient legitimation for social inequalities. As political thinkers began to question the metaphysical foundations of societal hierarchies, the subjection of woman to man could no longer be justified as divinely ordained. However, all attempts to extend the universal claim for freedom and equality to the female gender were foreclosed as women's bodies became the primary anchors of woman's underprivileged position. With biology bolstering the new gender order, women were relegated to house and home while the newly created public sphere became the domain of men.

The work of the Swiss sociologist Claudia Honegger has affirmed Laqueur's theses for the German realm. For Honegger, too, the second half of the eighteenth century was a time of radical changes, during which the body emerged as the Archimedean point of a discursive power struggle. Endowed with the power of "analogical verification" (Scarry 278), the body came to be entrusted with the regulation of gender identities: "It was not until now that gender was fully incorporated into the body and that its 'logical' distribution was determined by the scale of anatomy" (Honegger 8).[10] During the course of the eighteenth century, the social position of women and the relation between psyche and body had remained curiously undecided. At around 1800, however, the new trend solidified as the formula "The body shapes morality" gradually became the central tenet of a new anthropology (Honegger 42).

While Honegger's research is exemplary in many ways, her notion of a paradigm shift is the result of an analysis that privileges texts by male anatomists, male theorists, and male writers. As such, it is apt to produce a linear narrative that cannot do justice to the gender confusion so characteristic of the time around 1800. While Honegger claims that "from approximately 1800 on, one was able to stop all female efforts to achieve autonomy and individuality with references to a rediscovered constant of nature regarding the gender difference" (14), I maintain that the transition was not as clear-cut as that. Interpretations of literary texts around 1800 show clearly that gender was never fully incorporated into the body. A study of women writers provides ample evidence that we must conceive of the relation between these two models of gender identity as of one of competitive coexistence, not of succession and substitution. Though the two-gender model won out eventually, its dominance was never uncontested.[11] I read the contemporary fascination with literary cross-dressers as a symptom of this continuing discursive struggle.

In her study of the motif of women in men's clothing, Gertrud Lehnert claims that the character of the cross-dressed woman "would never again achieve as much popularity as it had enjoyed in the seventeenth century or around 1800" (95–96). It is to be assumed that this cross-dressing epidemic, which touched both canonical and so-called trivial texts, was closely connected to the cultural re-negotiations outlined above. As the two-sex model became dominant, the cultural weight of gender shifted from a person's clothing to her body. "Henceforth the body itself, not merely its clothing, its practiced and customary gestures, its ritual forms of expression, signaled the individual's social position" (Duden 16). Paradoxically, literary cross-dressers might be employed to embody at the same time both the model of "gendered character" and its negation. Authors who wished to deny all possible concatenations between gender and body would emphasize the convincing behavior and looks of the cross-dresser, thus linking gender to appearance and "performance." Those who wanted instead to affirm the priority of the body and to reject a possible connection between clothing and (wrongly) presumed social status would depict the discovery of the cross-dresser's "true" gender. Interestingly, the failed cross-dresser is a recurrent feature in texts by male writers. Many male writers sought refuge in the gendered body. To them, the body becomes a repository of authenticity and truth. Many female writers, on the other hand, dissociate gender from the body. In their works, gendered qualities can no longer be understood as the "natural" truth of the body but must be considered products of social interactions. In order to understand women writers' "performative" concept of gender, it is helpful to turn to the work of Judith Butler.

II.

Butler's seminal contribution to gender studies and body theory consists in her redefinition of the sex-gender divide. According to Butler, any claim that sex is to gender as nature is to culture misunderstands the fundamental fact that both sex and nature are culturally interpreted phenomena, that is, that the idea of "naturalness" is itself a discursive construct. Even personal identity cannot be understood as an expression and causal consequence of an inner core but is continually constructed anew. In Butler's view, this construction of identity takes place within a context of pre-given norms. The relation between subject and normative system is one of mutual dependence and reciprocity. The subject neither precedes nor follows this system but emerges within it through reiterative and citational practices. The normative system, on the other hand, is produced by and derives its force from this citation.

This model of identity construction also holds true for gender identities. For Butler, identity and gender identity are tautological terms because a person is always already a gendered being. Gender identity, according to Butler, comes into existence through performance: "gender is a kind of persistent impersonation that passes as the real" (Gender viii).[12] Butler claims that to insist on the performativity of gender does not imply the denial of the materiality of the body because "to claim that sexual differences are indissociable from discursive demarcations is not the same as claiming that discourse causes sexual difference" (Bodies 1); rather, she argues, "it is to claim that there is no reference to a pure body which is not at the same time a further formation of that body" (Bodies 10).

Like Michel Foucault, Butler does not believe in the possibility of assuming a position outside of the given power structures. Rather, she sets her hopes for social change in a specific form of "citation" of the given normative system, namely in the parodistic appropriation of norms.[13] One such form of parody, which exposes the constructedness of gender, is transvestism. If the transvestite's purported gender identity cannot be told apart from "real" men or women, then one must question the assumption that his/her performance is nothing but an imitation: "in imitating gender, drag implicitly reveals the imitative structure of gender itself—as well as its contingency" (*Gender* 137). The relation between the female-to-male transvestite and the "real" man is not that of copy and original but of copy and copy. The original "man" himself is nothing but a copy of the idea of original masculinity.

Butler's revision of the sex-gender dichotomy has laid bare a fundamental logical flaw that informed most works on gender and the body and has made possible some of the most innovative contributions to gender studies and body theory. But while Butler is right to insist on the discursive nature of the body, the implication of an almost "limitless pliability" of our anatomy must be rejected (Fausto-Sterling 25). Although we will never be able to demarcate the outlines of purely biological bodies, such bodies not only exist but impose their weight on all discursive reconfigurations. I agree with Butler's assumption that the body itself, not just the category of gender, is socially constructed. However, even though Butler herself asserts that such a statement is not tantamount to denying that "real" bodies do exist, her work lacks an awareness of the limits that bodies impose on discourses. Butler is right to claim that "real" bodies are always already discursively constructed and that discursive constructs in turn make their imprint on "real" bodies.[14] She is right when she maintains that discourses have no reality outside of their embodiments and that bodies are not conceivable outside of discourses. But she fails to conceptualize how "real" bodies affect our discursive reconstructions.[15]

However, the most fundamental critique of Butler's work, which has often been accused of ahistoricity, can be effected by situating it in its historical context. I propose that Butler's model of identity corresponds to the dominant values and social conditions of capitalist societies that not only require that "all goods and even personal traits be alienable, marketable, and perpetually up for sale" (Veeser 19), but also need "hollow, empty personalities that resemble money itself" (Veeser 4).[16] Butler's concept of a personal identity that lacks an inner core is congruent with capitalism's need for citizens who are infinitely flexible, adaptable, and mobile. As such, Butler's theories are oddly pertinent to the consumer revolution and emerging market economy of the late eighteenth and early nineteenth centuries. This raises some interesting questions for the German context. For example, one might speculate whether the new gender philosophy acquired a particular urgency in Germany because of the country's industrial belatedness. Since the German process of industrialization lagged behind that of other European nations, Germany was forced to respond to revolutionary rhetoric and the emerging capitalist structures at the same time. My analyses will show that the German conceptualization of gender was affected by this dual challenge.

While such isomorphisms between the performative and the capitalist personality legitimize the use of Butler's theories for this period, they also pose serious questions regarding the liberatory potential of gender performances.[17] Clearly, the evaluation of its liberatory potential is crucial to every interpretation of cross-dressing. Interestingly, the discussion of this question is marked by extremes. While some scholars assume that every instance of cross-dressing is inherently subversive, others claim that cross-dressing reinforces existing structures of patriarchal power. In order to lay out the parameters of this debate, I will first introduce Marjorie Garber's work on transvestites and then discuss Anne McClintock's and Gertrud Lehnert's critiques of Garber's approach.

In her study *Vested Interests*, Marjorie Garber claims that the signifying potential of the cross-dresser is not limited to issues of gender. Often conceptual crises in other societal arenas are transposed onto the gender dichotomy.[18] A transvestite in a literary text may function as a sign of an epistemic crisis elsewhere; that is, questions of social class, ethnicity, language, or morality may be displaced onto the axis of gender. Garber defines an epistemological crisis as the impossibility of arranging phenomena or concepts into a pre-given binary structure: "transvestism is a space of possibility structuring and confounding culture: the disruptive element that intervenes, not just a category crisis of male and female, but the crisis of category itself" (17). According to Garber, transvestites are troublemakers who defy logical-symmetrical patterns of thinking and bring to light hidden social and cultural dissonance. Any destabilization of gender categories, such as is effected by the cross-dresser, is likely to contaminate other binary systems as well.

Garber's notion of the cross-dresser as a sign of an epistemic crisis elsewhere is fruitful for an understanding of the period around 1800. Many of the texts under discussion, though ostensibly concerned with the construction of gender, are in effect using gender as a metaphor to talk about models of politics, truth, and writing. Binaries such as artifice and authenticity that are connected to epistemological questions, and contemporary concepts such as language as the dress of thought that speak to issues of poetology and writing make the figure of the cross-dresser a potent metaphor for numerous categories outside of the realm of gender. However, while Garber's work is important in that it points to the power of the cross-dresser to signify an epistemic crisis elsewhere, it is problematic in its assumption of the inherent subversivity of transvestism, as Anne McClintock points out.

McClintock rightfully asserts that Garber's premise of the quasi a priori subversivity of transvestism is ahistorical and cannot do justice to the diversity of actual transvestites. McClintock also maintains that ambiguity and ambivalence are not necessarily destabilizing. On the contrary, at times social privilege consists precisely in the right to display ambiguity (68). Even though McClintock's own definition of transvestism does not always live up to her ideal of historical specificity,[19] her admonition not to define gender masquerades as universal embodiments of subversion is well taken.

Although McClintock rejects undue generalizations of subversivity, she does not deny that transvestism may at times have a destabilizing effect.[20] The German scholar Gertrud Lehnert, on the other hand, accuses the female cross-dresser of confirming male supremacy:

> The disguise makes the girl invisible as girl without offering any livable alternatives: that is, she is robbed of her identity. Thus, the literary invisibility of women throughout the centuries finds expression in a motif that seems to let woman exist as woman, even seems to grant her a greater sphere of action, which, however, proves to be nothing but a chimera since her disguise was forced upon her and since she is transformed into an imitation of man without granting her the consequences thereof: Essentially, she is a nothing in this role. Il n'y a pas la Femme. (238)

According to Lehnert, the cross-dressed woman is a sign "that can only be administered within an androcentric economy of signs" (349), and that, because of this androcentricity, cannot undermine existing societal conventions. Clearly, Lehnert's concept is based on the assumption that, in order to oppose societal power structures, one must step outside of the boundaries of the given discourse.[21] To this, many would object that it is impossible to transcend the discursive boundaries. In addition, Lehnert herself is guilty of rendering women invisible when she claims that female writers did not begin to portray cross-dressed heroines until the end of the nineteenth century. The following analyses of works by female authors will show that Lehnert's assertion that the cross-dresser is caught within the dominant masculine discourse is closely connected to her exclusion of texts by women writers.

Clearly, all interpretations of literary cross-dressing must proceed with great caution. Not every instance of cross-dressing constitutes a transgressive act. Moreover, even if an act of cross-dressing appears to bear within itself some subversive potential,[22] there is always the possibility that this subversion may itself have been co-opted. The celebration of resistance, the assumption that cross-dressers undermine hierarchical structures, is always threatened by the Bakhtinian paradox that contradiction and deviation might themselves be system-immanent, and hence necessary, conditions for the functioning of ideological constructs (Orgel 124). Furthermore, the fact that the interpretation of literary texts forms the focus of this work makes it liable to the charge of reducing emancipation to an aesthetic accomplishment.[23] McClintock rightfully questions whether it can ever be sufficient to locate resistance and agency in the discursive rifts and cracks of a literary work. However, even though any attempt to redefine abstractions as historical actors is clearly misguided, one should also not deny that discursively constructed concepts do affect social and individual realities.

By analyzing literary cross-dressers we gain insights in the conceptualizations of corporeality and social status, of gender and the body around 1800. It is a central premise of this book that such conceptualizations are culturally constructed and historically specific. In order to grasp this historical specificity, it is necessary to gain a clear understanding of the fundamental difference between contemporary notions of transvestism and eighteenth-century practices and fantasies of cross-dressing.[24] The following historical overview delineates the parameters of this difference. In addition to describing the cultural specificity of late eighteenth-century cross-dressing, it is also motivated by the conviction that any isolation of a text from its historical context must be detrimental to our understanding of both. My decision to intertwine historical and literary cross-dressing is not guided by the intention of "reading a text against its historical background or using the text to illustrate an already-formulated account of a historical moment" (Montrose 3). Rather, it strives to do justice to what Montrose has called "the historicity of textuality and the textuality of history," that is, the fact that every cultural expression is connected to and conditioned by its context even while it in turn shapes and transforms this context.

III.

Until the twentieth century, male-to-female cross-dressers were the exception rather than the rule. Today, of course, the situation is diametrically inverted. The modern medical definition of transvestism all but excludes female-to-male cross-dressers. The origin of this lopsided model can be traced back to the German researcher of human sexuality, Magnus Hirschfeld, who coined the term transvestite in 1910. Thus, one might claim that Germany is not only "the forge in which modern sexuality was constructed," as Robert Tobin proposes (*Warm Brothers* 195), but also the home of the transvestite. Notwithstanding some modifications, today's standardizing definition of the term, set forth in the Diagnostic and Statistical Manual (DSM-IV-R) of the American Psychiatric Association, is essentially based on Hirschfeld's insights. According to the DSM-IV-R, a transvestite is a man who derives sexual pleasure from wearing women's clothing.[25] Transvestites are to be distinguished from transsexuals, who conceive of themselves as female souls trapped in male bodies and ultimately seek to undergo sexual reassignment surgery. Unlike transsexuals, transvestites hold on to their male identity and are mostly heterosexual (Woodhouse xi). The DSM-IV-R considers transvestic fetishism a sexual disorder which calls for treatment. Both transvestism and transexualism refer to gender preference; sexual preference is denoted by the term homosexuality.[26]

One (among many) reasons to be skeptical of the DSM-IV-R is its refusal to include women in the category of the transvestite. The assumption that women wear male clothing for purposes of comfort or fashion effectively denies the possibility of female fetishism.[27] On the other hand, the modern claim that all female transvestites are to be subsumed under the category of transsexualism is based on the even more questionable premise that all women ultimately want to be men. Typically, such psychological theories are unwilling to concede the possibility that female transvestites may want to adopt a male appearance while still holding on to a female gender identity, a combination which is essential to the definition of male transvestism. Furthermore, the pertinent literature maintains that, in a male-dominated society, the desire to be a man does not bear the mark of pathology but must be considered rational behavior. From this vantage point, female transvestism is neither perverted nor psychotic but rather a suitable strategy for dealing with unfavorable conditions.

To the modern feminist sensitivity, postulating fundamentally different motivations for female and male transvestism clearly constitutes discrimination. However, demanding equality for today's gender-benders should not lead us to transpose today's standard onto historical cross-dressers of both genders. In their study of female cross-dressing in the seventeenth and eighteenth centuries, Dekker and van de Pol emphasize that historical cross-dressing is intrinsically different from its modern counterpart. If we level such differences, we fail to do justice to the specificity of a historical epoch nor do we take into account the historically conditioned power dynamics between the two genders.

One of the factors that differentiates historical cross-dressing from its modern counterpart is that cross-dressers throughout the eighteenth century were free of the restrictions imposed by modern forms of identity control such as passports. But while they were not forced to document their identity and gender, they faced other inhibitions, such as sumptuary laws (Boehn, *Mode* 198).[28] These laws were motivated by two considerations: protection of the domestic textile industry through trade restrictions and stabilization of class hierarchies. An example of the former is Frederick William I's prohibition of the import of colored cotton fabrics from England. By outlawing foreign products, the soldier king intended to shield the domestic textile manufactures from unwelcome competition (Boehn, *Mode* 140; see also chapter 3). Socially motivated sumptuary laws were often directed at the lower classes. A Bavarian prohibition from 1749, for example, forbade the wearing of gold and silver fabrics. In addition to prohibitions of particular fabrics, there were also numerous regulations regarding the length of one's train or the wearing of crinolines.

The fact that such proscriptions had to be renewed on a regular basis may well indicate their inefficiency. But this should not lead us to assume that such rules were not enforced. During a quasi-raid in Bavaria, for example, the authorities confiscated gold and silver fabrics from a couple of women who were on their way to church (Boehn, *Mode* 198). The wearing of crinolines constituted the ground for legal action against two farm girls from the Saxon town of Dennschütz in 1743, and against two Dresden farm girls in 1751 (Boehn, *Mode* 122). Johanna Schopenhauer relates that in Danzig ducal officers were responsible for the observance of sumptuary laws (Schopenhauer 76). Interestingly, all these cases concern the demarcation of class, not gender, distinctions. It would appear that until the late eighteenth century gender differentiation was less crucial than class differentiation (see Entwistle 180). Furthermore, it is important to keep in mind that clothing has a substantially different symbolic potency in a society in which it is legally regulated in every detail. In modern societies the symbolic value of dress is altered by the fact that its members base their sartorial choices on financial prowess and social propriety, not on the observation of a given legal code.

No investigation of cross-dressing may neglect the meaning and function of clothing within a particular society, nor should it fail to take into consideration the social position of women in a specific historical context. With regard to the eighteenth century, it is of particular relevance to note the exclusion of women from all forms of higher education and the fact that very few professional venues were open to the female gender. In fact, it is because of such restrictions that Susan Gubar likened female-to-male cross-dressing to the behavior of female prison inmates who—unable to change their environment—transform themselves with the help of make-up and other accoutrements (478). But while such considerations suggest a connection between female cross-dressing and restrictive social conditions, they do not necessarily exclude other possible motivations. Although extant sources do not support the thesis that women derived fetishistic pleasure from wearing men's clothing, we cannot infer that such pleasure did not exist. In the following, cross-dressing will often be interpreted as a rational decision based on the desire for professional or personal advancement. It hardly bears mentioning that such an interpretation reflects the scope of what is historically documented, not a demarcation of what was socially possible.

In the eighteenth century, the large number of women in men's clothing is complemented by the relatively small number of men in women's clothing. Historically verifiable male-to-female cross-dressers were often members of the socially privileged classes. One need only think of the infamous Roman emperors Nero, Caligula, and Elagabalus, or of potentates of later centuries, such as the Abbé de Choisy (1644–1724), the Chevalier d'Eon (see Chapter 4), Henri III, Philippe d'Orléans, Edward Hyde (the governor of colonial New York from 1702 to 1708), or, in German lands, of Duke Emil-August of Saxony-Gotha and Altenburg (1772–1822). In addition to these high-ranking gender-benders, cross-dressers could also be found in the theater—for example, as castrati singers, who dominated European opera houses up to the eighteenth century—or in social sub-groups such as the British "molly-clubs," whose guests often met in women's clothing.[29]

In recent years, historians have begun to investigate the phenomenon of female-to-male cross-dressing, which reached its peak in the seventeenth and eighteenth centuries. The most comprehensive study of original documents is that of Dekker and van de Pol, who traced 119 cases of female cross-dressing in the Netherlands between 1550 and 1830 (xi). A large percentage of these 119 were foreigners who came from the German harbor cities of Bremen and Hamburg and from Westphalia (10). The number 119 is surprisingly high given the limited availability of documented sources and probably represents only the tip of the iceberg. Furthermore, as Dekker and van de Pol's study was based mostly on evidence found in court records, it was most likely to capture those instances of cross-dressing in which the intended deception failed. Unlike the study of Dekker and van de Pol, that of Bullough and Bullough presents a mixture of literary and historical findings. Their evidence largely confirms Dekker and van de Pol's claim that, throughout the course of history up to the second half of the twentieth century, the number of female-to-male cross-dressers exceeded those of male-to-female by far (ix).[30] This proportion is mirrored in the literary texts of the time which also portray far more female-to-male cross-dressers than male-to-female ones.

The occasions and motivations for female-to-male cross-dressing were manifold. Then as now, the carnival provided a socially acceptable occasion to wear the clothing of the opposite sex. Empress Elisabeth I of Russia (1741–62), for example, organized weekly masquerades for which all ladies had to dress like men and all men like women.[31] In the German realm, princess Amalie of Hessen-Homburg (1774–1846) arranged festivities during which all ladies were disguised as men. Like-minded dinner parties took place at the court of the prince of Prussia (Boehn, Mode 230). However, not only aristocrats possessed a predilection for gender masquerades. Carnivalesque gender-bending was also practiced by the lower classes. In his description of the Roman carnival, Goethe initiates the reader into the erotic allure of such mummery. In addition to encouraging sexual licentiousness, carnivalesque cross-dressing also posed a threat to the status quo. Often it evolved into popular protests against social injustice and the abuse of political power.[32] The boundaries between festivity and riot could be very fluid (Dekker and van de Pol 7; Ackroyd 54). In particular, bread riots were linked to a tradition of cross-dressing (Ramet 6).

Riots were not the only events that suggest that the crossing of gender boundaries might be conducive to illegal actions. Some female cross-dressers were members of a gang of thieves. The bride of the much-romanticized bandit Schinderhannes was among the few whom we know by name; equipped with weapons and with men's clothing, she participated in the nightly robberies committed by her beloved (Küther 85). Trijin Jurriaens, a native of Hamburg, was obviously so successful as a man that she felt inspired to embark on a career of bigamy (Dekker and van de Pol 37). Her compatriot Isabe Bunkens, a disguise artist of equally

Anne Bonny op Jamaica Gevangen.

ANNE BONNY, the female pirate. By permission of the Houghton Library, Harvard University

great talent, was indicted for the murder of her landlady in 1701 (Dekker and van de Pol 44). Isabella Geelvinck, born in Germany in 1643, worked as a cook for a military regiment for ten years before she set fire to the house of her new employer (Dekker and van de Pol 36). In England the infamous cross-dresser Mary Frith, alias Moll Cutpurse (1584–1659), a well-known pick-pocket and heroine of the London underworld, gained literary notoriety because of her portrayal as *The Roaring Girl* by Dekker and Middleton (1601).[33] While Cutpurse ravaged London, the cross-dressed pirates Anne Bonny and Mary Read roamed the oceans until they were captured and tried in 1720. There was even an eighteenth-century German witch whose "crimes" were compounded by the fact that she wore men's clothing.

While the cases described above suggest a link between cross-dressing and criminal behavior, other documents establish a connection with sexual licentiousness and prostitution (Orgel 119). Venetian prostitutes, for example, wore plus-fours (Holtmont 14). Anti-theatrical pamphlets of the English Renaissance directed against the supposed immorality of the stage often associated cross-dressing with a lack of self-mastery and depravation. However, it would be wrong to conclude that cross-dressing positions its practitioners at the utmost fringe of social respectability. The numerous instances of gender-bending criminals are complemented by an equally large number of cross-dressing saints.[34] One need only think of saints Thecla, Pelagia (Pelagius), Marina (Marinus), Hildegund, and Athanasia of Antiochia (Athanasius); also of Saint Margaretha, who put on men's clothing in order to escape from her bridal chamber during her wedding night (Bullough and Bullough 51; Dekker and van de Pol 45). Joan of Arc and the legendary female Pope Joan must also be mentioned in this context. An interesting subspecies of the cross-dressed saint are those holy women who actually grew a beard, such as Saint Galla and Wilgefortis/Saint Uncumber, whose facial hair enabled her to avert an unwanted marriage. In these instances, cross-dressing was by no means an opprobrious endeavor. Rather, it was considered an honorable enterprise in that it represented a laudable striving to better oneself, that is, to become a man (cf. Hotchkiss 12). However, a positive evaluation of the cross-dressed saint was contingent on her presumed chastity. Wheelwright has appropriately characterized this trade as an exchange of sexuality for social privilege (116).[35]

Vacillating between criminality and saintliness, cross-dressers seem to cover the entire spectrum of social valuations. But our fascination with such glamorous cases of gender-bending should not obscure the fact that there were also numerous instances of rather mundane cross-dressing. One such example was the female traveler, to whom a male appearance offered protection from the dangers of the road. Several female pioneers of traveling, such as Lady Mary Montague, wore men's clothing on their journeys (cf. Pelz 68). Queen Christina of Sweden traveled under the pseudonym "Count Dohna" after her abdication in 1654 (O. P. Gilbert, *Women* 95–134). The poetess Sidonia Hedwig Zäunemann wore men's clothing when traveling on horseback (Brinker-Gabler 60). The German Maria Anna Steinhaus, a courtesan who skillfully enticed a chamberlain of the Prince of Orange into marrying her, also traveled and hunted in male clothing (Dekker and van de Pol 8), and the Bavarian countess Amalie sported a combination of green trousers and a white wig on her hunting outings (Boehn, *Mode* 238).

In addition to such leisure-time cross-dressers, who wore their gender masquerades for a short period only, one encounters numerous others who were motivated by economic considerations. For a few working women, trousers were actually the normal and required outfit. Eighteenth-century dairymaids in the German Alps, for example, wore pants as a matter of course. More often, however, cross-dressing opened up fields of employ which were otherwise inaccessible to women—a description which, in the eighteenth century, applied to most occupations.[36] Surprisingly, female cross-dressers preferred the occupations of sailor and soldier even though these two professions offered a minimal degree of privacy, thus exposing the cross-dresser to a proportionally larger risk of discovery.[37] The fact that female cross-

HANNAH SNELL, a cross-dressed British soldier. *Courtesy of the Director,*
National Army Museum, London

Angélique Brulon, a soldier in the Napoleonic army. *Musée de la Légion d'honneur, Paris*

dressers aspired to these careers in spite of such substantial obstacles suggests that they were not only interested in securing a livelihood but also in exchanging a monotonous existence for one that promised excitement and adventure.[38] Financial incentives should not be underestimated, however. Almost all historically traceable cross-dressers were of lower-class origin. For them, adopting a male identity may well have provided the only alternative to a life of poverty or prostitution.

While we may be left with doubts as to why women chose to enlist in a regiment, we do know that they did so with great frequency. Cross-dressed soldiers participated in almost all major wars from the French Revolution (Wheelwright; O. P. Gilbert, *Women*, Chapter 2), to the German Wars of Liberation (O. P. Gilbert, *Women*, Chapter 2), the American Civil War (approximately 400 women according to Wheelwright, 27),[39] and World War I. At times female cross-dressers continued to be tolerated even after their gender had been discovered. Thérèse Figueur (1774–1861) and Angélique Brulon, for example, both veterans of the Napoleonic Wars, stayed with their units even after they had been found out.[40] Among the German women who joined the military were Maria van Antwerpen, alias Jan van Ant (1719–1781), and Catharin Rosenbrock of Hamburg, who worked as a soldier and sailor for twelve years (Dekker and van de Pol 23). In 1799, the German cross-dresser Antoinette Berg followed her English regiment to the Netherlands, where she fought against the French. She then joined the English navy and sailed to the Caribbean.[41] Even though one must assume that many of these female sailors and soldiers were motivated by economic and personal reasons, their official declarations of intent always contained some reference to patriotic ideals. One suspects, however, that oftentimes such fervent avowals were nothing but empty formulas. Strategically employed, they bestowed respect and honorability on a disguised woman, whose economic constraints and thirst for adventure inspired but little compassion and understanding.[42] The combination of patriotism and chastity, on the other hand, called for a maximum of admiration, as the reception history of Joan of Arc demonstrates so clearly.

The fact that some women cross-dressed for professional and economic reasons suggests that they attempted to appropriate male privileges by switching over to the other side. One of the male privileges that female cross-dressers acquired for themselves was the right to desire women. Dekker and van de Pol assume that, in the eighteenth and nineteenth centuries, the adoption of a male persona functioned as a psychological "makeshift" construction that made it possible for a woman to legitimize her sexual relationship with another woman (55). Identifying with the male role enabled these gender-benders to categorize and accept their feelings even in the absence of a lesbian subculture. But again, this explanation cannot account for the entire spectrum of possible actions and motivations. Women also cross-dressed in order to embark on searches for their missing husbands or to accompany their husbands on journeys from which women were excluded.[43] Some women disguised themselves to secure passage on ships to the East Indies, a popular destination precisely because the prohibition of women aboard ship made for a surplus of eligible bachelors on the Isles. Others, however, donned their disguises in order to flee from abusive husbands. Thus, if anything can be stated with certainty about the motivations of female cross-dressers, it is that they made up a colorful palette ranging from financial necessity, professional aspiration, patriotism, romantic love, criminal intent, and divine inspiration to a penchant for masquerades, a passion for journeys, and a striving for independence and adventure. In addition, one must not forget that arena of cross-dressing which is most closely related to the realm of literature: the theater.

The trousers' role is a fairly recent phenomenon when compared to the deeply rooted tradition of men in women's parts which defined theatrical practice for almost two thousand years (Möhrmann 7). It was only after women had proven themselves as actresses in the commedia dell'arte that they also began to play men's roles on stage. Even the Shakespearean drama, which had relied on boy actors for all female roles, eventually yielded some breeches' parts.[44] After women had begun to populate the stage around 1550, Hamlet and Romeo developed into popular trousers' roles. Later on, even such "unfeminine" characters as Falstaff (played by Mrs. Webb in 1786) or Richard III (Sarah Siddons in 1775) might be performed by women (Slide 53).[45] Mme Vestris (1797–1856) went so far as to take on the ultra-masculine role of Don Giovanni.

In German lands, actresses were admitted to the stage from approximately 1650 on. But even though the participation of both genders allowed for "realistic" casting, theatrical cross-dressing remained very popular in the eighteenth century (Boehn, *Bühnenkostüm* 251).[46] Karoline Jagemann (Oberlin), Mme Schönberger-Marconi, Mme Schröder-Devrient (Romeo), Mme Ohlin, Mlle Beck, Mme Reinecke, Mlle Döbbelin, and the Viennese singer Josefine Schmeer were widely acclaimed for playing men's parts (Bullough and Bullough 227; Holtmont 168 and chapter 5). Astonishingly, it is Johann Christoph Gottsched (1700–1766), infamous for his rigid poetology and strict morality, who bears witness to the enthusiasm that such displays were apt to inspire. Gottsched describes the impression made by a performance of the young Neuberin in the play *Realm of the Dead*, in which the actress takes on not one breeches' role but four:

> And above all, four young men of the famous Saxon academies were characterized so incomparably that I have not seen anything more beautiful in my entire life [. . .] and that these four different people, namely a hoodlum, an admirer of Oriental languages, a termagant and a galant homme were portrayed wonderfully by a woman in a fourfold disguise so that nothing was missing but a rougher, more masculine voice.[47]

Modern scholars such as Garber have assumed that such fascination with thespian gender-bending is grounded in the fact that cross-dressing expresses the nature of theater in exponential form. Since theater itself consists of the adoption of ever-new identities, that is, of the wearing of masks and disguises, cross-dressers as the ultimate gender performers can be said to embody its very essence. According to Kristine Hecker enthusiasm for the theater is always also

> enthusiasm for the ability of the performer to transform herself [. . .] [An actress, EK] can discard the identity of her role from one moment to the next just so she can adopt many others. Situations of liminality such as androgyny or madness during which differences are blurred and emphasized at the same time, visualize for the audience with perfect clarity a phenomenon which should remain one of the essential concerns of the theater: to stake out the narrow line between appearance and reality, between dissimulation and authenticity (46).

Although spectators were fascinated with such transformations, the public enthusiasm for trousers' parts may have been dampened by the lack of respectability that still adhered to the theater as well as by the deep anxiety that such transgressions aroused:

> Actors were obviously allowed to transgress the boundaries of class, status, and age, to which human beings everywhere else are subjected, without having to fear sanctions because of it. But above all, they could—and this was the reason for the deepest of reservations against them—overstep the difference between the genders [. . .] For if women could be portrayed by men, then this could insinuate the dangerous conclusion that men were really like women, that is, basically no real men at all, whereas women, on the contrary were also men. (Laermann 131–132)

Laermann refers to a text by Kant which gives voice to the idea that performance may ultimately turn into reality: "For if human beings portray these roles, the virtues, whose semblance they have created artificially for some time, will at last be awakened in reality and will blend into their minds."[48] To today's readers, the exchange between person and role that Kant took for granted may seem far-fetched. But a similar concatenation between literature and reality can actually be detected in the lives of historical cross-dressers. Emma Edmond's participation in the American Civil War, for example, was inspired by and patterned after a fictional role model, namely the heroine of Murray's novel *Fanny Campbell or the Female Pirate Captain* (1815). Of course, the reverse is also true. Stories of literary cross-dressing were influenced by the adventures of actual cross-dressers. Fictional gender-benders, just like their historical counterparts, traveled, became soldiers, and used their disguises to flee from importune situations or to be with their beloved husbands. Just like their historical models, they were often single women whose parents had died or who had dissociated themselves from their relatives.[49] In fiction as in reality, these women were mavericks. They were not interested in improving the socio-political situation of a gender with which they no longer identified. Feminist declarations were not part of their repertoire. It is because of this attitude that feminist scholars have at times questioned the ethical (and strategic) validity of cross-dressing. According to their argumentation, donning the clothes of the other sex is equivalent to selling out, to an opportunistic conformity that is ultimately a betrayal of one's own gender.[50] The price for male privileges is the denial of one's "true" gender. Thus, cross-dressing is condemned as a purely individualistic and apolitical strategy that confirms existing stereotypes while it leaves structural problems untouched.[51]

However, one might also argue that such criticism fails to acknowledge that cross-dressing was one of very few empowering strategies available to eighteenth- and nineteenth-century women. Moreover, in literary texts, cross-dressers often carry metaphorical meaning. They embody categorical instabilities and poetological crises. It is only to be expected that the eighteenth century—a society plagued by epistemological uncertainties—would be mesmerized by the ambiguous "nature" of the cross-dresser.

Around 1800, female cross-dressers were all but omnipresent in German literature. The eighteen texts that this work discusses are only a small segment of a much larger corpus.[52] My selection of these particular works was guided by their relevance for a trajectory that traces the emergence and implications of the new definition of the female body. Chapter 2: "Liberty, Equality, Travesty: The Female Soldier and The French Revolution" lays the groundwork by exploring the relation between gender, the body, and woman's exclusion from the public sphere. It contrasts two novels that portray cross-dressed heroines who fight in the revolutionary wars: Therese Huber's *The Seldorf Family* and Caroline de la Motte-Fouqué's *The Heroine from the Vendée*. Building on research about cross-dressed female soldiers who fought in the French Revolution and the German Wars of Liberation, I investigate how women authors dealt with a discourse that referenced the body to legitimize woman's exclusion from the public sphere. Interestingly, both writers experimented with a performative concept of gender. Huber's advocacy of freedom and equality for all is echoed by her rejection of the construct of a naturally given femininity. But in order to free her heroine Huber removes her from all familial and societal contexts. Excluded from the new republic, Sara Seldorf faces an isolated life among ruins. Fouqué, on the other hand, is a supporter of feudal structures but portrays a heroine who frees herself from the limitations of her "natural" place in this hierarchy. The contradictory position of her heroine is not only symbolized by her cross-dressed body, it also finds its resolution in her body. Fouqué's protagonist dies in combat. Though both writers set out to defy the boundaries imposed by the female body, neither succeeded in reconciling her concept of the female body with that of the body politic.

Chapter 3, "Trans-Gender/Trans-Nation: Trojan Horses in Women's Literature," analyzes how Friederike Helene Unger and Karoline Paulus succeeded where Huber and Motte-Fouqué failed. By introducing a third variable, that of national identity, Unger and Paulus managed to create a sphere of female agency. Chapter 3 also demonstrates that such portrayals of "imported" models of femininity in fiction coincided with the development of international trade in textiles. Building on research on the contemporary textile industry and Mosse's and McClintock's work on the interrelation between constructs of nation, ethnicity, and gender, I investigate how discourses of nationality were employed to subvert German gender codes. The literary interpretations focus on three novels, Unger's *Rosalie and Nettchen* and *Albert and Albertine* and Paulus' *Wilhelm Dumont*, all of which feature foreign cross-dressers. "Trans-Gender/Trans-Nation" demonstrates how the exotic gender-benders in these novels function as enabling devices, facilitating both the expression of forbidden desires and a critique of German gender norms. By displacing gender transgressions onto a national Other, Unger and Paulus break the established narrative pattern in which the heroine pays for her spiritual self-determination with the renunciation of her body. The limitations of this strategy are apparent: it does not solve the inherent conflict but merely exports it abroad.

While chapters 2 and 3 are concerned with female agency, chapter 4, "The Death of a Cross-Dresser: Epistemologies of the Body," focuses on the metaphoric potency of cross-dressing. It analyzes the motif of the death of a cross-dresser in order to gain a deeper understanding of the interrelation between the body, gender, and truth. Building on the stories of the Chevalier d'Eon and of Catharina Lincken and on work by Lacan and Bronfen, I argue that the death of the cross-dresser often functions as a turning point that puts an end to an epistemologically unstable and morally "dubious" situation. When the exposure of the cross-dresser occurs at the moment of his/her demise, death is defined as a privileged moment of truth. But death may also be a means of moral retribution meted out as punishment for the cross-dresser's transgressions. Consequently, eighteenth-century German authors could rely on the motif of the dead cross-dresser to solve by proxy the epistemological and ontological instabilities that plague their texts. Friedrich Schiller's *Fiesco's Conspiracy at Genoa*, for example, presents the female body as a vessel of truth and identity. *The Family Schroffenstein* by Heinrich von Kleist also seeks to anchor truth in the female body but ultimately deconstructs its own agenda. In *Mora* and *Darthula according to Ossian* by Karoline von Günderrode, on the other hand, bodies are arbitrary signs, and the gender order is dissociated from both truth and morality.

Chapters 5 and 6 focus on two literary movements whose conceptualizations of gender exerted a particularly strong influence on European and American literature: German Classicism and Romanticism. Chapter 5, "Classic Amazons: Performing Gender in Goethe's Weimar," investigates the interrelation between gender and social order in the context of Weimar Classicism. It integrates the literary analyses with a discussion of social practices, especially the masked ball at the Weimar "Redoutenhaus" and theatrical cross-dressing on the Weimar stage. My analysis shows that "real life" gender transgressions in Weimar were highly orchestrated and carefully contained whereas the realm of literary imagination allowed for fantasies of female power. In von Stein's *A New System of Freedom or Conspiracy Against Love*, for example, the flexibility and adaptability of the gender-bender is the only remedy against a social hierarchy whose odds are stacked against women. Von Stein's cross-dressers outwit their opponents through their perfect imitation of masculinity. Interestingly, some of Goethe's texts also lay bare the arbitrariness of the body-gender connection and introduce a performative concept of identity. But unlike von Stein, who delights in the playful dissolution of gender roles, Goethe is troubled by the social anarchy that comes in its wake and ultimately moves to contain the gender-bender's disturbing potential. In *Wilhelm Meister*, his portrayals of cross-dressing relocate gender in the body.

Chapter 6, "Female Fantasies: Poetology and Androgyny," offers new readings of texts by German women Romanticists. I discuss two female writers, Dorothea Schlegel and Bettina Brentano-von Arnim. My analysis establishes a connection between their models of gender and their "underground poetology" (Kord), that is, the poetological and aesthetic concepts implicit in their texts. Both Schlegel and Brentano-von Arnim employ the motif of cross-dressing to defy dichotomies and to introduce new poetological models that favor openness and ambiguity. "Female Fantasies" argues that by insisting on para-

dox and internal contradiction, by refusing to provide closure
while staging a capricious play with polar categories, Schlegel
and Brentano-von Arnim were able to cope with the constraints
that threatened to stifle women writers of the eighteenth and
nineteenth centuries.

My analyses show that, though male and female authors portray cross-dressed characters in distinctly different ways, there are
also remarkable similarities. Although texts by male writers often
attempt to tighten up the borders, they are ridden by the same
gender indeterminability that characterizes the literary products
of their female contemporaries. Though they may set out to prove
that gender transgressions are pernicious, they end up demonstrating that they are possible. Though they intend to depict
"passing" as impossible and celebrate the natural and authentic
body, their texts are subtended by the clandestine anxiety that
gender boundaries are unstable after all. Women writers, on the
other hand, often imagine cross-dressers whose surface masculinity is uncannily reminiscent of postmodern ideas of gender performance. Paradoxically, however, such performances also harken
back to an older gender model in which the body is a mannequin
adorned with clothing that carries information about the social
status of its wearer. In this older model, prevalent until around
the middle of the eighteenth century, "appearance was not seen
to express the self, but instead to be a performance at a distance
from the self" (Entwistle 73).

All these texts, irrespective of the gender of their authors, seek
to come to terms with the as yet undecided contest between two
different models of the body: one that defines the body as a neu-
tral surface whose gendered meaning derives from its clothing,
and an authentic body whose gender truth shines forth through
its apparel. Gradually, the bourgeois model of an authentic body
as the primary site of identity emerged as the winner of this contest. One might speculate whether the power of this paradigm
resided in the fact that it allowed the new bourgeois class not only
to shed the feudal past and its heritage of the body as mannequin
but also to repress the capitalist future with its need for "hollow,

empty personalities that resemble money itself" (Veeser 4). Certainly, the reasons why the model of the "natural" gender inherent in an authentic body prevailed have as much to do with economic developments as they have with political changes. However, it is not the ultimate triumph of this model that is interesting. Rather, it is its failure to achieve complete dominance that is so fascinating to modern readers; the fact that within the mold of a natural gender is hidden the knowledge of the instability of both nature and authenticity. It is in this sense that the late-twentieth-century deconstruction of sex and gender already exists within the late-eighteenth-century creation of a natural gender, and it is because of this dialectic that an analysis of the "specific and concrete failures" (Jameson 209) of the late-eighteenth-century discourse on gender and identity will yield some insight into our own ongoing gender quandaries.

Chapter 1

EQUALITY, LIBERTY, TRAVESTY:
The Female Soldier and the French Revolution
ॐ

It all begins with the French Revolution, and it all ends with the French Revolution. The watershed event of 1789 marks a beginning because some inspired women demanded that the ostensibly universal claim for freedom and equality be applied to their sex as well. As the culminating point of the Age of Enlightenment, the revolutionary movement put into practice the realization that the transcendental truth on which traditional systems of order were based no longer provided sufficient legitimation for social inequalities. Consequently, as political thinkers began to question the metaphysical foundations of societal hierarchies, the subjection of woman to man could no longer be justified as divinely ordained. But while the revolutionary era inspired the declaration of the rights of woman, it also gave rise to a massive backlash. Almost from the moment of their conception woman's claims for equality were refuted through a redefinition of the female body. Thus, for women the revolutionary era was a time of dashed hopes and broken promises, of paradoxes and contradictions. In short, it was a time in which cross-dressers thrived.

It is hardly surprising that woman's shifting status, caught between the restrictions of the past and the hopes of the future, called forth a surprisingly large number of female cross-dressers intent on conquering the male domains of politics and warfare. These gender-benders embodied women's demands for participation in all civic affairs, but they also signified that, as women, they were not welcome in the public realm. Cross-dressers express the paradox inherent in woman's new, uncertain status. They prove that, notwithstanding the female body underneath the clothes, a woman can do a man's job. But in order to be successful in the male domain, cross-dressers hide their female anatomy. Thus, they unwittingly direct attention to the new ideology of the body that emerged as the main opponent of woman's rebellion against her traditional role.

Beginning with Joan of Arc, the woman-to-man cross-dresser had a long history in France as "the image of female heroism" (Marina Warner). While the eighteenth century boasts an especially large number of amazons, it is not the first period in French history that witnessed the bravery of female soldiers. Cross-dressed noblewomen participated in the Fronde insurrection of 1652–53, in which the independent aristocracy pitted itself against Louis XIV. The Princess of Condé marched to Bordeaux in soldier's garb and persuaded its inhabitants to defend the Frondeurs against their king. The Duchess of Longueville led the Spanish army in Paris and disguised herself as a man in order to escape imprisonment by Cardinal Mazarin (1602–61). Male clothing also saved the Duchess of Chevreuse from incarceration, and the cross-dressed Grande Mademoiselle (Mme Montpensier) conquered Orléans by storming the only gate whose fortification had been neglected.[1]

Late eighteenth-century France also experienced a wave of politically inspired cross-dressing. Many women used the societal turmoil of the French Revolution to foray into the masculine territory of politics. Some participated in public uproars and marches, others joined the armed forces. Théroigne de Méricourt (1762–1817), for example, who led the women's march to Versailles, felt that male clothing enabled women to participate in public events more directly.[2] For female Revolutionary Republicans, cross-dressing and political action went hand-in-hand. During the May 1793 ousting of the Girondists from the legislative assembly, these women— wearing red pants—assisted their male comrades, the Jacobins, by guarding the exits with swords.[3]

Cross-dressed women also served as soldiers in the armed forces of the republic. Some women joined the National Guard as early as 1789. Female officers were among the members of the Societé fraternelle des patriotes de l'un et l'autre sexe. According to Levy, dozens of women enlisted in the revolutionary army (*Women* 221). Often, female soldiers were not only tolerated but received warm welcomes. The sisters Félicité and Théophile Fernigh, for example, who fought along with their father and brothers at the eastern front, were widely praised for their courage in defending the fatherland. Other female soldiers whose names have come down to us are Thérèse Figueur ("Sans-Gêne"), Madame Poncet ("Breton Double") and Angélique Marie Josèphe Brulon, who joined the 42nd infantry regiment after the death of her husband and received the cross of the Legion of Honor for her courage in combat.[4]

In this shifting social climate, it is hardly surprising that courageous women demanded the implementation of laws for armed service for the female sex. On March 6, 1791, 300 women signed a petition which was brought before the French legislative assembly by Pauline Léon, the future president of the Club of Revolutionary Republicans. In this petition, the women of the Revolution demanded nothing less than the right to bear arms and to participate in warfare.[5] But as much as the male members of the national assembly supported natural rights in other instances, this petition was rejected. A similar petition by the women of the Hôtel de Ville-district, submitted on July 31, 1792, met with the same fate. The rejection of these petitions, however, did not lead to the removal of women from the armed forces. As late as 1793, dozens of female Parisians donned male clothing and enlisted in regiments. There was even a plan to form a battalion of amazons to be named after the sisters Fernigh.[6]

Other Frenchwomen, aware that men had better chances of employment, cross-dressed in order to make a living. Catherine Louise Vignot, for example, who was arrested for instigation of public unrest in Year III of the Revolution, had cross-dressed in order to work as a coal carrier (Levy et al., *Women* 299). Anne Grandjean, alias Jean Baptiste Grandjean, found work as a carpenter (O. P. Gilbert, *Women* 136–139). The Archives Nationales document the case of a woman who had been taught cobbling by her husband. When her husband died, she cross-dressed to keep working as a cobbler. A revolutionary committee discussed the moral validity of her action and demanded "that the citoyenne be sent home [. . .] It was also requested that the citoyenne wear women's clothing or incur the penalty required by the rigor of law" (Archives Nationales MSS Comité Revolutionnaire Section Droits de l'Homme F7+ 2497, qtd. in Petersen 53).[7]

The stories of the sisters Fernigh, of Pauline Leon, and of the female cobbler suggest that, while there was great tolerance for the heroic virgin in the tradition of Joan of Arc, women who wanted to compete economically and women who insisted on their femininity while demanding masculine rights could not be accommodated within the existing gender dichotomy. Eventually, even the acceptance of the cross-dressed soldier would fade away.

The year 1793 is generally considered the turning point for women's involvement in the Revolution. Since the subsistence crisis in France was a major factor in sparking the revolutionary uprisings, and since women were most immediately affected by the scarcity of supplies, women played an important role in the early phase of the Revolution, for example, in bread marches. Building on these early experiences, women organized themselves during the course of the Revolution. Their activity reached its peak between the spring and autumn of 1793. The ban on women's clubs, which was passed in October of 1793, must be seen as an attempt to contain the growing political power of the other sex. It was also in 1793 that a law was passed which excluded all women from service in the army. This was due to a report by J. F. Delacroix, a deputy of the revolutionary government, who attributed the deplorable state of affairs of the armed forces to the presence of women, that is, female soldiers, sutlers, and prostitutes (Opitz, "Die vergessenen" 292). In practice, this ban was inefficient in expelling women from the army. We know, for example, that Thérèse Figueur participated in battles as late as 1806, and that Angélique Brulon's retirement in 1799 was due to wounds received in combat, not to administrative instructions (Wheelwright 91). Women also participated in the uprising in the Vendée which began in March 1793 and ended in July 1796.

The peasant Renée Bordereau, for example, who masqueraded as a man, became known as the Vendean Joan of Arc. Francoise Després served the royal army as a messenger, provisioner, and troop leader, while the Vicomtesse Turpin de Crissé is remembered as a peacemaker.[8]

The important role that French women played in revolutionary events captured the attention of the European public. Reactions and comments were generally disapproving and apprehensive, and the German intelligentsia rallied its forces to fend off the specter of the public woman. The following statement by Joachim Heinrich Campe, a German who witnessed these events first-hand during his journey to Paris, is representative of the general sentiments about women's involvement in the French Revolution. Campe thinks "that the women of Paris and, as it seems likely after several events in the provinces, the entire female sex in France is inferior to the male sex in terms of culture, moderation and moral, and, almost always excels in bloodthirstiness and cruelty, when violence occurs."[9] Given such opinions, it is hardly surprising that even the few staunch German Republicans opted against the participation of women in their revolutionary activities. The Jacobins of Mainz, for example, did not accept female devotees of liberté and egalité into their circle (cf. Schmidt-Linsenhoff 498).

However, even in Germany there was a time for amazons. Interestingly, it was the service for the fatherland, not the ideals of liberty and emancipation, that provided the justification for female participation in warfare.[10] Numerous German women enlisted in the army during the Wars of Liberation against the Napoleonic threat. In the heated atmosphere of national enthusiasm, references to a woman's patriotism served to justify her "unwomanly" conduct. The patterns of this discourse are manifest in contemporary documents, such as Friedrich Rückert's poems about Eleonore Prochaska or the speech of the Prussian general Tauentzien before the senate.[11] They continued to dominate the scholarly discourse until the twentieth century, as is evident in the following quote from Major Noel, the author of a book

ANNA LÜHRING. *By permission of the Focke Museum, Bremer Landesmuseum für Kunst und Kulturgeschichte*

about the heroines of 1807–1815: "What deep sorrow these sim-ple, modest, and quiet female souls must have felt about the fatherland which is trampled upon by the enemy, that they left their household and family in order to fight for their country."[12] The idiosyncrasies of such peculiar rhetoric speak to the specific demands of the German political and cultural context. Rather than perceiving cross-dressed soldiers as warrior women, the Napoleonic wars gave rise to a new German conservatism that transformed patriotic warfare into a feminine activity. However, notwithstanding such celebration of female patriotism and self-sacrifice, it is likely that the dearth of volunteers also contributed to the acceptance of female soldiers.

Among the cross-dressed officers of 1807 were such impressive characters as Rosalie von Bonin, who was in command of a cavalry unit of seventy men and who captured a French general. Another amazon, the famous Anna Lühring (1796–1866), donned her brother's clothes and joined the "Lützower Jäger" as Eduard Kruse. She participated in the war against Napoleon and concealed her gender successfully. The final discovery of her womanhood was brought about by a letter by her father, not by suspicious behavior or appearance on her part. According to Cyrus, Lühring is a perfect example of "how easily one was taken for a man if one had a uniform, gun, and perky behavior" (33). Even after the discovery of her sex, Anna Lühring was accepted and well liked in her regiment. That her position was precarious all the same is demonstrated by the fact that every document relating to her case is deeply concerned with her chastity. Obviously, renouncing her sexuality was the price that the female hero had to pay.

Yet another female Lützower Jäger, Eleonore Prochaska, alias Jäger Renz, managed to hide her gender until she died. During her last battle in 1813, Prochaska seized the drum of a French drum major and drove her comrades to attack until she herself was fatally wounded by a bullet. Her heroic death inspired numerous male contemporaries to artistic creations. Friedrich Rückert, for example, wrote a poem about her,[13] and Beethoven composed the music for the tragedy Leonora Prochaska, written by Friedrich Duncker, the privy councilor of Friedrich Wilhelm III.

Neither the adventures of the French cross-dressers nor those of their German successors remained unnoticed by women writers of the time. Both Therese Huber in The Seldorf Family and Caroline de la Motte-Fouqué in The Heroine from the Vendée

Eleonore Prochaska fällt im Gefecht an der Göhrde   *(Carl Röchling)*

ELEONORE PROCHASKA dies in combat in the battle at the Göhrde. *Painting by Carl Röchling. From Benno Bode,* Die Schlacht bei der Göhrde, 16. September 1813: ein Heimatbuch und eine Festgabe, dem Hannoverlande, zum Jubelfeste 1913 *(Hannover: Geibel, 1913)*

wrote novels that feature cross-dressed heroines. But while both writers focus on the same subject matter, the Vendée uprisings, their political viewpoints are entirely different. Therese Huber's Sara Seldorf fights for the republican cause, whereas Caroline de la Motte-Fouqué's Elisabeth de la Rochefoucault exerts herself for king, God, and fatherland. Furthermore, Fouqué's novel uses the Vendée events as a vehicle that allows her to discuss problems related to the German resistance against the French occupation.

The following analysis of these two novels at opposite poles of the same spectrum sheds some light on the concatenation of political views and concepts of femininity during this historical period. I am especially interested in the modes of political participation that these authors propose, in the strategies with which they justify their plea for civic inclusion, and in how they define the relation between gender and the body. Both writers were trapped in a discourse in which revolutionary change and demands for civil lib-

ELEONORE PROCHASKA. *Anonymous woodcut. From Benno Bode*, Die Schlacht bei der Göhrde, 16. September 1813: ein Heimatbuch und eine Festgabe, dem Hannoverlande, zum Jubelfeste 1913 *(Hannover: Geibel, 1913)*

erties were interlaced with a conservative redefinition of femininity. But while both were forced to negotiate the same dilemma, their responses are diametrically opposed. Fouqué's identification with the patriarchal order prompts her to adopt the ideology of patriotic sacrifice to justify her heroine's "unwomanly" conduct. She creates a protagonist whose purportedly feminine essence is at war with her masculine appearance. Fouqué maintains that gender is located in the body, but her surreptitious redefinition of terms empties the category "femininity" of its meaning. Huber, on the other hand, rejects the construct of a naturally given femininity. In her novel, identity is a performance, not an essence, and a woman's body does not dictate the scope of her actions. Ultimately, however, neither Huber's nor Fouqué's heroines prevail: Elisabeth Rochefoucault dies a heroic death, while Sara Seldorf faces an existence amongst ruins.

SURVIVAL TRAINING:
The Seldorf Family BY THERESE HUBER

In recounting the events of the French Revolution, Therese Huber[14] did not have to rely on fantasy only. Her first husband, Georg Forster, was a member of the Jacobin club of Mainz, which founded the first republic on German territory. Therese Huber left Mainz in 1792 when French troops occupied the city. In addition to participating first-hand in these historical events, Huber was intimately acquainted with French culture and thought. Her second husband was of French descent, and Huber also spent some time in Neuchatel befriending French intellectuals such as Benjamin Constant.

Like many other works by Therese Huber, *The Seldorf Family* [Die Familie Seldorf, 1795–96] was published under the name of her second husband, Ludwig Ferdinand Huber.[15] It is set in revolutionary France. The heroine Sara Seldorf, whose mother died young, is raised by her father in the countryside. Her neighbor, the virtuous Republican Roger Berthier, loves Sara, but his feelings remain unrequited. Sara's brother Theodor leaves home to join the counter-revolutionaries in Paris. Deprived of her brother's friendship and guidance, Sara succumbs to the charms of Count L**, a shady character, who hides his royalist convictions from his bourgeois lover. Sara's situation worsens when the Seldorf estate is destroyed by an insurrection. Her father dies, and Sara, now pregnant, lives as L**'s mistress in Paris as the city is ravaged by civil war. There she gives birth to L**'s son. On the day of the Tuileries fighting, Sara, worried about L**'s safety, betakes herself to the center of the action. L**, who does not recognize Sara in the throng, shoots his own child. When Sara, who is already strained by the death of her child, learns that L** is married, she falls sick and is in danger of going mad. When she regains consciousness after a long illness, she swears revenge, cross-dresses, and joins the revolutionary army as Captain Verrier. In the end, all of Sara's relatives and friends are dead. Sara lives amongst ruins and devotes her life to the education of L**'s legitimate child. Roger, the only other survivor, still loves her but is rejected again.

Huber's novel weaves a complicated net in which gender and class discourses are intimately connected. The liberation of underprivileged farmers and the emancipation of the bourgeois woman are depicted as integral components of the same agenda. Huber portrays a society divided into three tiers. Aristocracy and bourgeoisie are pitted against each other in an irreconcilable conflict, while the peasantry is exploited and manipulated by both of these privileged groups. The aristocrat L** and the bourgeois Roger are prototypical members of their respective social classes. L** is elegant, eloquent, sophisticated, and smooth, but highly corrupt. Roger is honest, courageous, and virtuous, but lacks refinement and beauty. In these portrayals, Huber's novel reflects the values and self-evaluation of the rising bourgeoisie. Aesthetic refinement is associated with moral depravity, and virtue is portrayed as coarse and uncultured. In his attempt to assert himself against the aristocracy, the bourgeois references his moral superiority to justify his claim to power. But the bourgeois' pride in his own virtue is undermined by his unacknowledged envy of the cultural achievements of the nobility so that repulsion and attraction complement each other. Huber's novel fails to reconcile these differences, as it is precisely Roger's uncouth behavior that constitutes his virtuousness. His straightforward honesty ill qualifies him for the sophisticated intrigues and hypocrisies at court. Roger's rough naturalness is his protection against the refined temptations of aristocratic vice.

However, the situation is different for the female protagonist. For Sara, naturalness is inseparably linked with "natural" gender, that is, with strictly delimited gender roles. Hence, it is only logical that Sara, wishing to escape her confinement, would be attracted to L**, who represents culturally created distance or even alienation from nature. But L**, and implicitly the entire aristocracy, is also the epitome of immorality. He is portrayed as the source of every ill that afflicts bourgeois and peasant alike.[16] Aristocratic greed and "most cruel self-interest" (I: 66) are responsible for the material and social misery of the farmers. Clearly, bourgeoisie and peasantry share a common lot in that they both suffer from aristocratic oppression. But unlike the peasant whose "poor mind" and "sad simplicity" (I: 66) prevent him from comprehending his own misery, the bourgeois is called upon to help and save his social inferior. Interestingly, Huber's novel suggests but does not state explicitly that this purportedly altruistic striving is employed to lend legitimacy to the bourgeois fight for freedom and equality and to obfuscate other motivating factors that are not quite so noble. The reader wonders whether bourgeois help for farmers, though it ameliorates material misery, is designed to solidify the social hierarchy that causes the unequal distribution of property in the first place.[17] Seen in this light, the bourgeois concept of equality is revealed to be nothing but the attempt to substitute a good (bourgeois) master for a bad (aristocratic) one. Neither the aristocrat nor the bourgeois are willing to accept the "coarse, pathetic peasant" (I: 58) as their equal. For the third estate, the transition of political power from the aristocracy to the bourgeoisie is a relative improvement at best. Where the peasant used to be the subject of a despotic feudal master, he is now the target of the educational zeal of the bourgeoisie. Thus, Sara's failure to choose Roger over L** might be attributed to a preconscious knowledge of the dubious merits of a bourgeois master.

Huber's novel does not depict the social misery of the peasantry as an isolated phenomenon but rather highlights the similarities between the plight of the farmers and that of bourgeois women. Both groups are portrayed as dependent and vulnerable to seduction. Huber's astute insight—that there is no "good master" because even a good master, due to his being a master, cannot but "make despotic use even of the means to do good" (I: 145)—holds true for both peasants and bourgeois women, who are subjected to the sovereignty of their husbands. In the following quote, Seldorf's wife gives voice to Huber's criticism of the autocratic position of the bourgeois husband: "Self-interest and the desire to domineer were the sources of your good deeds: I was supposed to be your creation, and the happiness that I did not receive at your hands, was taken for a crime."[18] Just as dependency is the common destiny of bourgeois women and peasants irrespective of their class differences, so are bourgeois husband and aristocrat alike in their self-interested need for mastery in the private sphere. Thus, L**'s seemingly bourgeois yearning for the comforts of a home, in which Sara as his "bourgeois wife" (II: 81) compensates for the strenuous activities of a tumultuous political life, is actually desire for a feudal arrangement. After all, in his home the bourgeois husband, too, is a king.[19]

Even though Huber's novel is explicit in its rejection of every form of mastery, it retains traces of a deeply ambivalent attitude toward class differences. Forgetful of her own critique of oppressive power relations, she appears at times to champion the benevolent sovereignty of bourgeois over the peasant.[20] Huber's depiction of gender relations, in contrast, lacks such internal contradictions. The structure of The Seldorf Family suggests that the guardianship of the bourgeois husband over his wife will ultimately bring about his own downfall. Sara's destiny exemplifies how the sheltered upbringing of the bourgeois daughter results in a lack of experience and self-reliance that makes her an easy prey to the seductive charms of the aristocracy. That the seduction of its weakest member may set off the destruction of an entire household is reiterated throughout Huber's novel. The disintegration of the Seldorf family, which culminates in Sara's affiliation with the aristocratic villain L**, was set in motion by the moral pessimism of Sara's father, itself brought on by his wife's affair with an aristocrat. Furthermore, Sara's destiny is mirrored in that of

Nanny, another victim of aristocratic debauchery, whose loss of innocence caused the ruin of all her relations.

In Huber's novel, woman emerges as the Achilles heel of the bourgeoisie. By taking possession of the bourgeois woman and thus cutting her suitor off from a male heir, the aristocratic villain drains the lifeblood of the bourgeoisie. One might object that the vulnerability of the bourgeois woman represents the omnipotence fantasies of the bourgeois male which displace the susceptibility to aristocratic temptations onto the other sex.[21] But even so, Huber's novel still draws attention to woman's strategic power because it portrays women as the key to the demise or survival of the bourgeois world. By granting or refusing her consent to enter a marital union, woman controls the ability of her social class to propagate itself.[22] In choosing between two potential guardians, Sara opts for L** against the unattractive bourgeois Roger. Roger, the last male heir of his house, remains unmarried and without progeny. His situation is paradigmatic for that of all bourgeois families in Huber's novel.[23] The siblings Martha, Nanny, and Joseph, the last generation of another bourgeois family, also die without children. The children of the patriotic Raimond lose their lives in the turmoil of the Revolution, and his wife succumbs to her grief. Babet and Mathieu, Sara's companions in the fight for freedom, are killed in the war. Given these circumstances, it is even more astonishing that Sara, the sole survivor of the Seldorfs, decides to devote the remainder of her life to the education of L**'s legitimate son from his marriage to an aristocratic woman. The fact that Sara's teaching is likely to be guided by bourgeois values cannot change the fact that it is bestowed upon the sole heir of an aristocratic family, the only surviving child in Huber's novel. In the figure of this child, the struggle between bourgeoisie and aristocracy is perpetuated.

The question of whether Huber replicates or deconstructs the gender stereotypes of her time, such as that of the vulnerable bourgeois maiden, is also central to the following analysis of the motif of cross-dressing. Becker-Cantarino, for example, has interpreted Sara's male clothing as her "adaptation to and absorption by the destructive, patriarchal society" ("Revolution" 251). However, one might also ask with Judith Butler whether Sara's effortless imitation of masculinity dramatizes "the signifying gestures through which gender itself is established? Does being female constitute a "natural fact" or a cultural performance, or is "naturalness" constituted through discursively constrained performative acts that produce the body through and within the categories of sex?" (*Gender* viii) Seen in this light, Huber's portrayal of a cross-dressed heroine effects a deconstruction of precisely those eighteenth-century discourses that define gender as a natural derivative of the female body. Huber's novel suggests that Sara's femininity is not "natural" and unchangeable but rather the product of societal conventions and thus likely to be transformed if society itself is overturned by revolution and war. The devastating dissolution of all human bonds, according to Huber a consequence of the fight for freedom, is both liberating and destructive. Sara's tragic fate, her existence in isolation, is inseparably linked with her desire for freedom as it expresses itself in her rejection of the constraints of a marriage of convenience. Her defeat is also her victory.

Huber's narration of Sara's socialization in her paternal home paints a vivid picture of the intense efforts necessary to produce "the most tender femininity" (I: 131), which is ostensibly the "natural" product of the female *Geschlechtscharakter*. Clearly, Huber suggests that bourgeois ideology itself contains some secret knowledge that nature alone cannot be trusted to en-gender human beings "correctly." A curious episode sheds some light on this problem. When an angered Sara complains about her brother Theodor's lack of empathy, the latter justifies his callous behavior with a reference to his maleness.[24] Sara rejects his argument by calling upon her own, differing experience, but her father intervenes with a generalization about the social desirability of gender-specific behavior: "One day when you're older, you will learn that it would be effeminate if boys and men loved and gave comfort in a manner that is appropriate for your gender."[25] What is first presented as an anthropological given is now revealed to be the effect of societal norms. Even though many of Huber's casual remarks about "true" femininity and masculinity conform to the dominant contemporary expectations, and even though she is always eager to stress that Sara's behavior and character are "true" models of proper femininity, her text betrays a choreography that runs contrary to these assertions.[26]

The most dramatic exemplification of the artificiality of gender concepts is Huber's depiction of Sara's life as courageous captain Verrier. As soon as she puts on her uniform, Sara is transformed into a paragon of masculine spirit and strength. Gender becomes a masquerade whose attributes can be put on or off along with one's clothing. Moreover, Huber does not rest contented with Sara's new rank as a soldier but elevates her heroine to the position of leader. Verrier is the most courageous warrior of his troop, a model for everybody else, and a fearless leader of his subordinates. It is the perfection of Sara's performance of masculinity that casts a shadow on the validity and originality of that which it is said to imitate. By reproducing masculinity so convincingly, Sara's cross-dressed captain Verrier personifies the social constructedness of gender.[27] Because Huber's fictional copy of a man cannot be distinguished from the other men around her, the primacy of their claim to superiority becomes doubtful.

If Sara's performance as Verrier is interesting, so are the circumstances that make her transformation possible. Sara is not divested of her femininity until all of its concretizations—daughter, sister, wife, and mother—have become obsolete because of the death or absence of the respective partner. It is only after her father and the father-substitute Berthier have died, and her brother Theodor, the brother-substitute Roger, and her "husband" L** have left her, that she joins the army. Given this pattern, it comes as no surprise that the rediscovery of Sara's femininity coincides with her reunion with her brother. In this constellation, the often invoked complementarity of the genders acquires a new significance. Just as a term can be defined only in relation to its opposite, so is the societal gender game predicated on the reciprocity of female and male social roles. If one player exits, the game falls apart.

While the absence of male friends and relations is the precondition for Sara's gender change, a much more urgent concern is offered as its justification. Sara's decision to revenge herself by becoming a soldier is compared with and presented as an alternative to the story of Nanny, one of Sara's neighbors in Paris. Sara's outcry that "woman, too, knows and needs revenge and law" (II: 147) stands in stark contrast to Nanny's passivity. Nanny, like Sara a victim of aristocratic debauchery, chooses silent suffering. Madness is her protection against pain; death is her redemption. Sara does not succumb to the same fate because she is determined to fight and avenge herself, a behavior that is uniquely effective in preserving her sanity and health; as Nanny's brother Joseph explains: "Poor lunatic, he cried, one drop of the craving for revenge into your childish heart, and you would be restored to consciousness!"[28] A further case in point is Frau Raimond, another neighbor of Sara. Like Sara's child, Frau Raimond's children perish in the revolutionary turmoil. Frau Raimond, who cannot overcome her loss, dies of grief. When Sara wants to join Herr Raimond in his fight, the latter establishes a connection between the death of his wife and the necessity of Sara's revenge: "And her death seemed a call to his tense brain to permit Sara to follow her destiny" (II: 159). Sara's refutation of the ideal of female peaceableness and silent suffering is a survival technique. Her foray into the public-political sphere may well be a violation of dominant gender concepts, but it is, first and foremost, a choice that leaves Sara as the only female survivor in Huber's novel.[29]

Interestingly, it is the chaos of the Revolution that makes Sara's agency possible. The disorder that the revolutionary turnover occasioned is both the origin of Sara's misery and the reason why she is able to take matters into her own hands. Deprived of fatherly and brotherly protection, Sara's newly gained independence enables her to make her own choices. Where "all ideas of law and duty depend on the perspective of every single individual" (II: 225), societal conventions lose their binding force. Huber knows that the claims and ideologies of the revolutionaries, according to which humanity and maleness remain identified, hold no liberatory promise for women. Rather, it is the dissolution and devastation which follow in the wake of the Revolution that bring freedom to women; such a freedom, however, can never shake off its association with ruin and destruction. Both Seldorf and Roger are crippled by the fight for liberty. Sara, while physically unharmed, is spiritually "dead for happiness, for humanity" (II: 329).[30]

Huber's refusal to present to her readers the classical happy ending of marriage has been criticized repeatedly.[31] Sara's rejection of Roger, the courageous Republican and virtuous companion of her youth, has been interpreted as fateful internalization of the norms and values of her father. Becker-Cantarino, for example, claims that Sara, by rejecting the given reality as unsatisfactory while setting her hopes on illusory ideas of perfection, remains caught in the idealism of her father ("Revolution" 247). Sara stands accused of sacrificing substance for surface appeal (Kontje 22) because she chose the attractive and enigmatic L** but turned down the "egalitarian offer of friendship" (Becker-Cantarino, "Revolution" 247) from the solid, yet unattractive and unrefined Roger. I believe that such partisanship for Roger deserves critical investigation.

Even though the corruption of female innocence is closely correlated with the aristocrats' seduction of the peasantry, Roger's republican convictions should not be taken as proof of his egalitarian attitude in the private realm. Ignoring the fact that Sara has rejected him repeatedly, Roger continues his courtship with confident persistence. When he happens upon Sara as she nurses her child, he cannot control his passion any longer: "Just for one moment he would have wanted to possess, hold—then kill her" (II: 30). Proclaiming that it is done for her own good, he attempts to keep Sara away from her father's deathbed and locks her up in her room: "He treated her like a child" (II: 2), Huber comments.

But even if we decided to ignore Roger's inappropriate behavior towards Sara, if we believed in the nobleness of his intentions, we would still be confronted with Huber's unwillingness to sub-

ordinate female desire to the dictates of virtue.[32] Huber's novel
not only dissociates the female body from female gender roles, it
also uncouples erotic desire from the bondage of moral conventions. Huber—who admitted that her first husband, Forster, "had
never possessed my love, never my senses" (to Caroline Böhmer,
February 25, 1794, *Freiheitsliebe* 70) and who endured her marriage "like one of those unhappy ones who surrenders her body so
as not to die of hunger" (to Johann Gotthard von Reinhold,
February 24, 1806, *Freiheitsliebe* 148)—imagined a heroine who
did not give in to the dictatorial demands of enlightened reason
but insisted on her right to her own desires—even when confronted with her dying father.

Huber's novel is extraordinary and unusual. It foils many of the
expectations that we bring to eighteenth-century literature by
women writers. Virtue is not rewarded. The heroine does not suffer patiently and humbly but becomes the agent of her own
revenge. Huber's novel does not end with the formation of a new
family but with the dissolution of almost all familial bonds. The
existing societal norms are not confirmed but dissolved. But even
more astonishing than these thematic choices are the conclusions
drawn from them. A marriage without love is rejected even
though Sara's relationship with L**, which is based on love, is
doomed to failure. Sara is a positive character in spite of all her
violations of the codes of proper femininity. The freedom to
which the revolutionaries aspire constitutes "the happiness of
France" (II: 219) in spite of the heavy toll of so many lives. It is
remarkable that Huber espouses the cause of the Revolution even
though she is fully aware that freedom may lead to loneliness and
revolution to violence and destruction. But, as she declares, freedom is "preferable to slavery in spite of all pain about its infinite
misery" (II: 241).[33]

Huber's novel draws our attention to an interesting period of
transition. The remnants of old traditions coexist with modern
forms as society slowly builds a new order on the relics of the old.
In the cracks and gaps of this changing edifice, whose building
blocks are still ungrouted, there is room for a new femininity

embodied in the character of Sara Seldorf. However, in spite of
its temporary splendor, Sara's respite is brief. As the edifice of the
new state is completed, the new woman must dwell in ruins.

AN ANGEL FOR GOD, KING, AND FATHERLAND:
CAROLINE DE LA MOTTE-FOUQUÉ'S
The Heroine from the Vendée

In her time, Caroline de la Motte-Fouqué was a widely known
and well-liked author.[34] She wrote more than 60 stories, 20 novels, and numerous essays on education, fashion, mythology, and
many other topics. Among her friends were prominent artists and
writers, such as Rahel Varnhagen and her husband August
Varnhagen von Ense, Jean Paul, August Wilhelm Schlegel, and
Ludwig Tieck. Today, Fouqué is either forgotten altogether or
remembered as an addendum to the biography of her husband,
Friedrich de la Motte-Fouqué, the author of the popular *Undine*
tale. It seems that Fouqué must be counted among those female
authors who are subject to a twofold bias. While traditional scholarship considered her texts trivial, feminist scholarship ignored
Fouqué because of the conservative agenda of her work.[35]

Fouqué's predilection for cross-dressing, disguises, and masquerades is evident in her work and life. As a regular at the Berlin
court, Fouqué attended numerous masked balls, some of which
she described in her *Letters about Berlin in Winter of 1821* [Briefe
über Berlin im Winter 1821]. Some aristocrats even formed a plan
to model the costumes for one of these balls after the characters
of her novel *The Duchess of Montmorency* [Die Herzogin von
Montmorency, 1822].[36] Several of Fouqué's novels feature cross-
dressed heroines. There are Jeanne d'Arc figures in *Memoirs of an
Unnamed Person* [Memoiren einer Ungenannten, 1831], *The Blind
Leader* [Die blinde Führerin, 1821] and in *Feodora* (1814).[37] A
number of Fouqué's female characters cross-dress in order to
escape from a pernicious intrigue (*The Duchess of Montmorency*
and *Heinrich and Marie*). Some wear men's clothing at a ball

(*Edmund's Paths and Wanderings*, Edmunds Wege and Irrwege, 1815).[38] Elisabeth de la Rochefoucault, Fouqué's heroine from the Vendée, performs her feats in revolutionary France. But unlike Huber's novel, which was published shortly after the Revolution, Fouqué's *The Heroine from the Vendée* [Das Heldenmädchen aus der Vendée] did not appear until 1816. Thus, even though the plot evolves in the context of the Vendée events, the date of publication and letters by Fouqué suggest that the actual frame of reference for this novel is not the battles of the French Revolution but the German Wars of Liberation, in which German volunteers fought to fend off Napoleonic occupation.

The Heroine from the Vendée tells the story of Elisabeth Rochefoucault, an orphan, who is staying with her uncle, the Duke de la Tremouille, in the Vendée when the uprising against the republic starts. Elisabeth first remains at home with an unmarried relative, the marquise de Robillard, while her uncle and his son, the brave and radiantly beautiful prince Talmont, lead the royalist forces. But when the republicans attack the castle, Elisabeth decides to don male clothing and join the war. Together, Elisabeth and the prince go through victory and defeat as they discover their love for each other. The first part of the novel reaches its turning point when the Vendée troops attempt to conquer the coast in order to secure a base for auxiliary forces from England. Their endeavor fails, Elisabeth is wounded, and the prince dies.

In the second part, Elisabeth goes to England in order to contact French aristocrats who are in exile there. After initial difficulties, a fleet is raised which is supposed to come to the aid of the Vendée royalists. In spite of good preparations, the attack fails because of the egotism and thirst for glory of some of the officers. After having led the troops one last time, Elisabeth dies a heroic death under the crucifix.

The decision to feature a protagonist who belongs to the party of the historical losers casts a dark shadow over the entire novel.[39] From the very beginning, there is an atmosphere of somber resignation laden with numerous premonitions of illness and death.[40] In addition to the certainty of defeat, the political perspective of the author gives rise to yet another failure. Fouqué's royalist opposition to the revolutionary demands for freedom and equality for all runs counter to her attempt to secure the equality of her female heroine. This predicament, which remains unresolved to the end, causes multiple internal contradictions.[41] But while such contradictions are detrimental to the aesthetics of the novel, they are also a striking testimony to the author's struggle with contemporary notions of femininity. One might therefore argue that it is precisely these contradictions, as well as Fouqué's futile attempts to reconcile them, that make this text so fascinating even today.

Fouqué takes recourse to patriarchal values in order to justify her heroine's warrior-like behavior. It is only the dire situation of the fatherland, along with the heartfelt wish to serve her country, that motivate Elisabeth to leave her traditional place in the house. Instead of serving one husband, Fouqué's heroine is now subordinated to God, king, and fatherland. Thus, Fouqué argues for a violation of the patriarchal order and its gender-specific division of work by referring to this very order.[42] She takes traditional stereotypes, such as female self-sacrifice and self-denial, and utilizes them for her own purpose by infusing them with patriotism. In doing so, Fouqué employs the same argumentational structure that was applied to female soldiers during the Wars of Liberation. In destroying the enemies of God and the king, Elisabeth hopes to annihilate the "unwomanliness" of her own transgression. It is a sign of Fouqué's sophisticated strategy that she has a male character—Elisabeth's uncle, the duke—explain the connection between female self-sacrifice and patriotism in his eulogy to Elisabeth after the first battle: "Thus, he praised the women and their pure self-denial, and how this heavenly shield laid itself on their breast so firmly and protectively that they defy grievous danger without particular efforts. Certainly, he added full of emotion, their weapons are not from this world."[43] Through religious stylization and a reevaluation of her combative behavior as sacrifice, Elisabeth's militancy is simultaneously confirmed and negated. Even when Fouqué portrays battle scenes, Elisabeth is never directly involved in any kind of violent or aggressive behavior. She is reduced to the status of symbolic figurehead rather than acknowledged as an equal participant in the fight. She may carry a sword and a pistol, but she must not use them. Furthermore, in participating in the war, Elisabeth is not acting according to her own volition and strength but as an instrument of "higher" powers:

> Not conscious of herself, neither thinking nor wanting,
> Elisabeth had seized the white flag from one who stopped
> beside her. Like an arrow she divided the lines. Magnetically,
> she was drawn to where the plume of the prince waved back
> and forth in the throng [. . .] Do not leave your flag, people
> from the Vendée, she shouted with her pure angelic voice.
> Save the honor of France.[44]

Fouqué emphasizes her heroine's purity and "angelic voice" in order to set her apart from the self-interested fighters. Elisabeth becomes an empty vessel whose pure nature guarantees the precarious bond between the troops and their aristocratic leaders. This bond was endangered because the prince—unlike his affable and popular father, the old duke—is alienated from the crowds. It is precisely this rift between troops and officers which, again and again, is cited as the cause for the inferior combat strength of the royalist forces. Without leadership, Fouqué argues, these troops—which consist mostly of peasants—are disorderly and weak-willed. An inept leader, even though better than no leader, will not succeed in mobilizing his followers. Only perfect harmony between feudal lord and vassal can guarantee the victory. And who better to provide such harmony than Elisabeth? Her eyes directed towards the prince while calling the Vendée forces to battle, Elisabeth functions as the "missing link" between the duke and his people. Thus, Fouqué has her readers convinced that it is woman's participation in the war that makes victory possible.

Fouqué's double-speak, with which she tries to normalize her heroine's transgression as a necessary consequence of her "true feminine" nature, is inevitably discredited by her own argumentation. For in a society where the imitation of masculinity can never be justified, the donning of male clothing becomes a test of courage. As Elisabeth puts on the "unfamiliar clothes that repel her unwillingly," "her new dreadful attire" (I: 88), she suffers a dizzy spell, she trembles, her knees give in. Clearly, body and clothing are at war. Although Fouqué stresses that Elisabeth is now "an entirely different being, a stranger to herself" (I: 89), she also insists on her "tender, undeniable femininity" (I: 90) that shudders at the thought of her new task. Trying to create a heroine who is both an officer and a lady, Fouqué devises a being that is neither.

The instability of Elisabeth's new identity is evident in the permanent shift of gender identifications. Unlike Sara Seldorf in Therese Huber's novel, Elisabeth is never fully recognized as a man. She is a boy, a beautiful youth, a young sir with the face of a girl, or simply the poor little one. If she is not categorized as a boy, that is, not yet a man, she is not categorized at all. Often Elisabeth is seen as a neuter entity, as "appearance" or "youth" per se. More often, however, her femininity is uncovered altogether. It is of note that it is only after her separation from the prince that her underlying gender is frequently unveiled. It seems that her love for the prince functioned as a guarantee of her femininity. So long as becoming the mate of a powerful man is Elisabeth's highest goal, her femininity remains unquestioned and transgressive actions may be excused. After the death of the prince, however, the pressure on the female soldier to live up to the requirements of the traditional gender roles increases. In this, Fouqué's novel differs from Therese Huber's portrayal of a cross-dressed heroine. Whereas Sara Seldorf's utterly convincing performance of masculinity establishes gender as a social construct rather than as "natural" fact, Fouqué insists on the natural femininity of her cross-dressed protagonist.[45] But even as she insists on her heroine's feminine nature, she continues to describe her "masculine" foray into warfare and politics.

It is not only Fouqué's reluctance to transgress against traditional gender stereotypes that undermines her heroine's adoption of masculinity; Fouqué's political logic does so as well. Elisabeth's flirt with that which is opposed to her nature threatens to discredit Fouqué's political agenda by unwittingly likening her protagonist to the republicans. This dilemma results from Fouqué's attempt to ground her critique of the republican party in the party members' "unnatural" behavior. Especially with respect to Robespierre, but also in connection with Charlotte Corday and the Gironde, Fouqué stresses repeatedly that, in order to perform their heinous crimes, these revolutionaries act against their own blood and even against their own nature. Barbaroux, for example, a member of the Gironde, disguises himself as a crippled beggar, and his companion Cornelius hopes to escape from persecution by dressing up as an old woman. Thus, the fact that Elisabeth, too, acts against her own female "nature" by cross-dressing, obfuscates the political message that Fouqué intends to convey. Since the sole differentiation between the royalist and the republican party is the latter's predilection for disguise and deceit, Elisabeth's own disguise constitutes an unwanted closeness to her ideological opponent. Such unwanted similarities between the pure heroine and the depraved Cornelius make it necessary to stress Elisabeth's virtue and femininity over and over again. But since the heroine's transgression is an indispensable element of the plot, the contradiction cannot be resolved but must be glossed over through the repetition of the same old stereotypes. It is this repetition that is most likely perceived as aesthetic unevenness by a reader whose training is based on canonical texts by male authors. It is therefore reasonable to assume that the gender discrimination that lies at the heart of this conflict has a negative impact on the aesthetics of this text.

One strategy that is employed to cover up the contradiction between the heroine's phallic presumption and her "natural" femininity, is the introduction of a duplicitous structure in which every attempt at dominance and authority is immediately followed by a revocation of all such demands. It is symptomatic that, in starting her new life as a soldier, Elisabeth acquires pistols and a saber but never actually uses them.[46] She is not a warrior or even a soldier, but a good angel. Although initially Elisabeth joined the army out of patriotism, by the end of part I her presence in combat has become redefined as an ardent wish to be with her beloved prince. Throughout the entire novel, Elisabeth has no authority, and, even though an officer, is never in command. Clearly, the price of her phallic presumption is the complete renunciation of power.

But again, the reader wonders whether Elisabeth's lack of authority can also be interpreted as a sophisticated strategy on Fouqué's part. When the troops of the exiles land on the coast of France, the victory is forfeited by individual leaders' desire for glory while Elisabeth's wise insights and plans are ignored. We may assume that victory would have been possible, had Elisabeth been consulted.[47] We might also note that the English take Elisabeth for a German.[48] If we remember again that *The Heroine* was written around the time of the Wars of Liberation, the novel can be read as testimony to Fouqué's conviction that German women should be included in patriotic endeavors.[49]

Caroline de la Motte-Fouqué herself certainly took a lively interest in political events. She contributed by donating money and jewelry to the campaign for the fatherland organized by Princess Wilhelm. Her literary activities also attest to her interest in the patriotic cause. Fouqué composed a *Ruf an die deutschen Frauen,* in which she encouraged her female compatriots to sacrifice for the fatherland. How much the Wars of Liberation preoccupied her is also evident in a letter to Varnhagen in which the author exclaims: "I think of nothing but this great fight" (qtd. in Varnhagen, *Portraits* 145).

However, in spite of such attempts to influence the course of events, Caroline de la Motte-Fouqué's realm of agency was severely limited when compared to that of the protagonist of her novel. While her imaginary heroine participates in the war and enjoys the company of her beloved prince, Fouqué remained at home by herself. Her husband Friedrich enlisted in 1813 and fought in the famous "Völkerschlacht" at Leipzig in October of 1813. Fouqué's two sons also joined the army. While they were engaged in battle, all Caroline de la Motte-Fouqué could do was wait for their safe return. In 1813, French troops took up their quarters in the Fouqué family estate in Nennhausen. In addition to worrying about her loved ones, Caroline now also feared for her own safety, as she tells Varnhagen in a letter from November 1813: "Often we were threatened here, and only recently the Mark was almost ravaged [. . .] During that time I have lived through hours of such despair as nobody can imagine."[50]

De la Motte-Fouqué's desperation and immobility set her apart from her fictional heroine. They do, however, remind the reader of another female character in the novel. Aphrodise, the sister of the Parisian carpenter Duplair—in whose house Elisabeth's relative, the marquise Robillard, finds shelter—suffers from periodically occurring paralysis. From the morning hours until noon, she is mute and paralyzed and yet fully conscious. Aphrodise is the only person to recognize Robespierre's depravity—the latter also a resident in the Duplair household—yet her knowledge remains without consequence. When Aphrodise is briefly liberated from her paralysis, she admonishes St. Just, Robespierre's companion, to speak the truth. But even this last and only action before she dies cannot effect any changes. Unlike in the case of Elisabeth, there is no need to stress Aphrodise's feminine virtues. Her paralysis, however, illustrates drastically the price she pays for her conformity to traditional gender roles.

Although Fouqué's inability to act while she waited for news from her husband and sons reminds one of Aphrodise's paralysis, and though imagining the feats of a fictional heroine may have helped Fouqué to cope with this situation, her intellectuality and vivid interest in the political events of her time are mirrored in the character of the marquise. Just like the author herself, the marquise de Robillard, a single relative of Elisabeth, is a femme de lettres. She reads the newspaper and corresponds with numerous contemporaries. But far from being portrayed sympathetically, the marquise represents Fouqué's fear of female intellect. The

marquise's persistent efforts to convince others of her analysis of
the political situation, and her repeated attempts to direct the
actions of the male protagonists, are in stark contrast to her utter
helplessness in practical matters. Her impracticality is demonstrated at the very beginning of the novel when the inhabitants
of the castle prepare to leave their residence. The marquise, while
ruling entire states in her mind, allows herself to be overwhelmed
by trifles. Under her direction her coach is loaded with so many
mirrors, cases full of essences, a cage for a parrot, and her pet pugs,
that there is no more room for Elisabeth, who ends up riding. The
marquise's solemn vow never to give way to the enemy is forgotten as soon as hostile forces appear at the castle's gate. Her cow-
ardice and helplessness are carried to such extremes that it is only
with the greatest effort that she is finally saved by her people.
Once exiled from the castle, she becomes completely dependent
on her old servant Anna. Left to her own devices, it soon becomes
evident that, in addition to the unbridgeable gap between the
marquise's theoretical insights and her practical abilities, her theories themselves are also utterly inadequate. Due to her limited
understanding, the marquise becomes an instrument in the hands
of the Gironde. The more she is entangled in their plans, the more
she resorts to fainting fits and illnesses until she finally goes mad.

However, in spite of this negative portrayal, there are also
instances where the marquise succeeds in mobilizing the masses.
Her call to free Paris from the revolutionaries and to save the
queen is answered by loud cheering (I: 34), and her attempt to
rouse the masses against her persecutor Cornelius leads to his
death:

> Ha! She cried, rushing to the armed crowd, a traitor! Citizens,
> the mercenary of the convent is in your midst! In a wild
> embrace she kept hold of Cornelius, and violently pulling him,
> she repeated: a traitor! Beat him to death, a perjured traitor.
> Momentarily, a thousand fists were clenched against Cornelius
> [. . .] and before he could move his smooth tongue, he lay dead
> on the ground.[51]

It is undeniable that her demagoguery brands the marquise as a fury. But even though she corresponds to the stereotype of the "female hyena" of the "Goethezeit," in Fouqué's eyes she is fighting for a good cause. Her goal of freeing Paris and saving the monarchy is shared by the positive figures in the novel. Furthermore, her opponent Cornelius must be counted among the most depraved characters of the novel. His punishment and death are justified within the logic of the text. One might also add that the marquise is the only main character in the novel who sees Napoleon and recognizes in him the future emperor of France. This insight immediately followed by her death not only lends her some dignity but might be interpreted as a vindication of her previous political shortsightedness.

As different as these three female characters are, they all share one common fate. Unlike Therese Huber's Sara Seldorf, Aphrodise, the marquise de Robillard, and Elisabeth are dead at the end of the novel. The central contradiction of the novel—the portrayal of "natural" femininity combined with a demand for male agency—can be reconciled only through the death of the female heroine. Elisabeth, already an angel during her lifetime, is transfigured into a supernatural being. In the end, when Sombreuil witnesses her appearance as an angel, she has finally transcended the limits of her gendered existence.

Both Therese Huber and Caroline de la Motte-Fouqué imagine a heroine who dons male attire and leads the life of a soldier. In choosing as their setting a period of political and social turmoil, they make use of the fact that times of radical change—such as the Fronde uprising of 1652–53, the French Revolution of 1789, and the Wars of Liberation against Napoleon—have often brought about greater independence for women and facilitated transgressions against traditional gender codes. Furthermore, by portraying a heroine who makes a vital contribution to the success of a military enterprise, both authors make an argument for including women in the patriotic effort. Both writers suggest that society at large—for example, the bourgeoisie in Huber's case and the German nation in Fouque's novel—will benefit if women are granted equal rights. Their definitions of what it means to be a woman, however, are fundamentally different. For Huber, femininity is an empty formula filled by societal conventions. Masculinity and femininity are performances. Thus, Sara Seldorf's cross-dressing does not violate the laws of nature, and atonement for her transgressions, effected through death, is not necessary. The possibility of survival opens up as Sara ends her complicity with the patriarchal order and begins to pursue her own fight.

Fouqué's explicit adherence to the patriarchal structure of feudal lord and vassal, on the other hand, is coupled with her adoption of traditional gender stereotypes. But even though she keeps referring to the feminine nature of her heroine, for example, to her female body underneath her clothes, she undermines the expectations tied to this "nature" by emptying the traditional concept of femininity of its meaning. The contradictions that mark the entire novel culminate in the death of the heroine which could alternately be read as an act of compliance or of resistance. One might claim that Elisabeth dies because the traditional gender roles prove too inflexible; that Fouqué's walk on the tightrope fails because "natural" gender can be restored only through the death of her cross-dressed heroine. Seen in this light, Fouque's attempt to justify transgressions against patriarchal gender norms with a recourse to these very norms can only go so far. But one might also read Elisabeth's demise as an act of resistance. The death of Fouqué's heroine and her subsequent transformation into an angel, that is, into a genderless being, could be understood as a much more radical erasure of the female body and rejection of the ideologies that are tied to it than that effected by Huber's heroine.

However one chooses to interpret Elisabeth's death, one is left with the question why Huber's and Fouqué's portrayals of cross-dressers are so fundamentally different. Was the concept of *Geschlechtscharakter* so established by 1816 that the portrayal of gender as performance was well-nigh impossible? Or are the differences between the authors the result of ideology rather than chronology? I would like to suggest that there is a connection between each author's political stance and her ideal of femininity. Fouqué's static concept of society does not brook exceptions. Birth assigns every individual to his or her "natural" place in the hierarchy of estates. Not even Elisabeth's privileged position in the social hierarchy, her aristocratic *Übermenschentum*, can provide an excuse for the violation of gender norms. In Fouqué's texts, transgressions against traditional gender roles are haunted by a triple predicament. They do not exist, that is, they are reinterpreted until they conform to the given norms (for example, combativeness and courage become self-sacrifice). They are not convincing, that is, true gender is always visible even when disguised. And, finally, even though non-existent and unconvincing, they are punished with death. Huber, in contrast, champions the abolition of all forms of slavery, whether that of lord and vassal or of husband and wife. Society is not bound by a "natural" hierarchy. The flexibility of this concept allows for the adoption of a male persona but also for the return to femininity. In spite of this progressiveness, Huber's novel, too, is full of contradictions. The survival of her heroine is predicated on an existence among ruins. Although Huber condemns slavery, she seems at times to support the benevolent guardianship of the bourgeois over the peasant. Fouqué, on the other hand, surprises her readers because she creates an audacious and brave heroine in spite of her professed conservatism. She pays lip service to the ideology of a femininity that is rooted in the body, but Elisabeth's impressive heroism contradicts such facile display of conformist ideas. Most of all, informing all these choices is the fact that, as women authors, Fouqué and Huber themselves were transgressing against gender norms. Their novels are attempts to cope with the paradoxes and contradictions imposed on them by their time. By creating cross-dressed heroines they found a fitting symbol of these paradoxes, of women's right to freedom and equality, of the obstacles they faced, and of the travesties necessary to overcome them.

Chapter 2

TRANS-GENDER/TRANS-NATION:
Trojan Horses in Women's Literature

Both Huber and Motte-Fouqué imagined dashing female soldiers whose stories bear testimony to the increasing difficulty to reconcile the female body with the body politic. Ultimately, their heroines pay dearly for their attempts to enter the public sphere: Elisabeth Rochefoucault dies; Sara Seldorf is condemned to a life at the margins of society. Clearly, inside the parameters of Huber and Fouqué's conceptual framework, there is no solution to the predicament presented by the female body. That is, there is no solution as long as one remains confined to the German homeland. By introducing a dynamic of import and export—by adding the variable "nationality" to the equation—Paulus and Unger succeeded where Huber and Fouqué had failed. In order to understand the ideological trade in gender concepts it will be necessary to turn one's attention to the actual trade in textiles as it was practiced in the early stages of capitalism.

The previous chapter has treated the dress of the gender-bender as an insubstantial, textual signifier. This chapter, in contrast, desists from such abstraction and turns its attention to the material roots of cross-dressing. It connects the representation of textiles in texts to their factual existence as products of specific structures of manufacturing, as objects of international trade, as subjects of sumptuary laws, and, last but not least, as clothing that provides the material base for the construction of gender.

It is hardly accidental that the first traces of a performative concept of identity emerged during the early phase of capitalism. In Germany, this curious coincidence may be even more pronounced since, due to the belatedness of the German industrialization process, revolutionary politics, the new gender philosophy, and early capitalism entered the national arena in close temporal proximity. Thus, an analysis of the economic dynamics of the textile industry is likely to shed some light on contemporary models of gender identity. The novels that I discuss in this chapter employed discourses of nationality and clothing to subvert their seemingly conservative representations of femininity. In them, ideology is woven (*textere*, from Latin to weave) and undone. Both Unger and Paulus took advantage of the fact that the international nature of textiles lent itself to a transference from the axis of gender onto that of nationality. It was this transference that enabled women writers to imagine powerful female agents within the restrictive German context.

In the late eighteenth century, the production and consumption of textiles defied national boundaries. Toward the end of the century, textile products accounted for a large part of all international trade (Gutmann 2). Karin Zachmann even claims that the integration of the German economy into the world economy was to a large measure achieved through the exchange of textile products (35). This high degree of internationalization developed gradually over the course of the eighteenth century. The textile industry was among the first to subvert the medieval guild order and to pioneer the factory system (Kisch, *Rhineland* 22). The feudal economy of the past centuries had been based on the principle of subsistence, that is, on local use of locally produced goods. In contrast, the new putting-out system ("Verlagssystem") and the emerging manufactures (cottage industry) produced for the market.[1] The transition from a subsistence to a market economy was accompanied by the concentration of previously widely dispersed production facilities at a few well-suited localities and, subsequently, by regional, national, and international trade among the providers of raw material, the centers of production, and the consumers.[2]

It was not accidental that textiles formed the avant-garde of international trade. The cotton industry was dependent upon importing its raw material since cotton could not be cultivated in the temperate climate of Europe. The products of the textile industry also lent themselves to transportation across vast distances.

Unlike agricultural products, textiles do not perish quickly and are thus not tied to a local market; unlike the products of the mining industry, they are fairly lightweight and relatively easy to transport. Widespread distribution of textiles, in addition to being feasible, was also profitable, since the immediate usefulness of clothing to every consumer guaranteed a large market (Blumberg 17). In Germany, the strong desire for foreign fabrics was equaled only by the strong resistance to them. In fact, what we know about the demand for foreign textiles is often ex negativo, that is, from reading the numerous regulatory codes, import restrictions, and sumptuary laws designed to cut off foreign supply.

Resistance to "outlandish" products operated on a multiplicity of levels, ranging from the economic and national to the moral. It served an economic function by shielding the domestic industry from foreign competition. King Frederick William I of Prussia (1688–1740), for example, hoped to protect the Berlin textile manufacturers by outlawing the wearing of English cotton (von Boehn, *Menschen und Moden* 140). In a war, import restrictions might be used as a weapon. Napoleon's continental blockade (1806–12), directed against the marketing of English products on the continent, led to an artificial boom in the textile industry in the lower Rhine valley.[3] But even in times of peace, numerous German states, including Prussia, chose to sponsor their domestic industries by the imposition of excise taxes on imported cloth (Purdy 16). Import and export restrictions often complemented each other since farmers were prevented from selling raw materials abroad (Purdy 197).

To a large degree, the sovereigns' interest in protecting national textile industries was motivated by the need to ensure a steady domestic supply of uniforms for their armies (Purdy 3, 197). At times, however, the rejection of foreign influences had to be abandoned in favor of other concerns. Thus, protectionist measures were counterbalanced by efforts to modernize the German textile industry, which lagged behind those of England and France. Some sovereigns actively encouraged the immigration of foreign labor and offered incentives to foreign textile workers with the expectation that their superior skills and know-how would stimulate local production (Dascher 83). Often foreigners were hired in order to train the German employees and help familiarize them with the latest technological innovations (Blumberg 54). Textile workers from England were especially welcome since England had forbidden the export not only of the spinning machines but also of construction plans for this important technological innovation. The know-how of English mechanics was therefore of crucial importance for the reconstruction of the jenny on the continent.[4]

The economic considerations that underlay textile laws were bolstered by national and moral rhetoric. Sumptuary laws often appealed to a hostility to the foreign (Hunt 73). Frequently, foreign origin was sufficient grounds for outlawing certain forms of clothing (Greenfield 125). The available sources show that such prohibitions were often driven by a desire to preserve a uniform visual identity both on a local and on a national level. Examples of such attempts to impose or reinforce a particular collective identity via clothing are the prohibition of the national costume of a defeated nation, such as the prohibition of Scottish kilts under English rule (Bulst 40), and efforts to introduce a national uniform in order to unify a heterogeneous nation, such as in Justus Möser's plea for the introduction of a national German dress code (Purdy 180) or Ernst Moritz Arndt's suggestion of a German ceremonial dress ("teutsches Feyerkleid," cf. Boehn, *Die Mode* 148).

In many instances, the argument that foreign attire is detrimental to the preservation of a national identity was complemented by a vociferous campaign that branded imported textiles as agents of moral corruption. Significantly, the mannequin which the French dressed in the latest fashion and shipped to England every month to keep the English abreast of recent trends was called Pandora (Boehn, *Die Mode* 74). Clearly, this name suggests that fashion is the box from which spring all evil and misery, but it also implies that it is impossible to keep this box shut. Unsurprisingly, intellectual denigration of the "outlandish" luxury and profligacy that was feared to penetrate the homeland via clothing could not quench the widespread desire to emulate foreign chic. And, as the figure of

Pandora indicates, not the least among the foreign depravities that were simultaneously feared and desired was a deviant concept of femininity.

Sumptuary laws were especially attentive to issues of gender. The stabilization of gender identities was at the heart of these regulations not only in terms of their design, but also by virtue of gender-biased enforcement practices. Alan Hunt even makes the claim that "insofar as sumptuary laws were enforced, they were enforced overwhelmingly against women" (214). By defining clothes as the visible expression of a person's gender identity, an otherwise elusive concept could be externalized and hence become easily accessible to regulatory measures. The fact that the external trappings of gender were considered valuable objects of legislative intervention implied that gender itself was not yet reduced to a biological entity, but rather was conceived as a social phenomenon. However, if gender is a social fact, not a biological essence, misrepresentation and transgression are to be expected.

One of the severest transgressions against traditional gender roles is the adoption of the appearance, behavior, and privileges of the opposite sex by cross-dressing. Interestingly, in fictional portrayals of cross-dressing the destabilization of gender is closely associated with the crossing of national and ethnic boundaries. By importing sartorial deviance, the literary cross-dresser from abroad subverts domestic codes of femininity and thus effects a redefinition of gender through the detour of nationality.

Post-colonialist research has demonstrated that constructs of nation, nationality, and ethnicity are inextricably connected with constructs of femininity and masculinity (cf. McClintock; Mosse; Pratt; Zantop, *Fantasies*).[5] Marjorie Garber and Anne McClintock have shown that the transgression of gender roles is often intertwined with the crossing of national (and social) boundaries so that "cross-gender is imagined as cross-culture" (Garber 336). In this complicated dialectic of discourses, nationality and ethnicity may function as both excuses and explanations for gender deviance.[6] By referencing nationality or race, an author may downplay or even blot out transgressions against traditional gender roles.

Examples of how gender bending is hidden underneath the blurring of national categories are manifold. In her discussion of female
coal miners in nineteenth-century England, McClintock investigates the overlapping discourses of gender and colonialism. She
demonstrates that the transgression of female miners against gender codes, made visible by the wearing of pants, was accounted for
by conceptualizing these women as belonging to another race
(115–118.). But while British society resorted to an ethnic discourse to distance itself from its cross-dressed miners, Hannah
Cullwick (1833–1909), the maid and lover of the Victorian lawyer
Arthur Munby (1828–1910), relied on the alienating effect of race
to draw attention to the strangeness of British gender codes.
McClintock shows that Cullwick's gender politics—that is, her
struggle for "the social recognition of women's domestic work"
(140)—was accompanied by ethnic drag, such as her wearing of a
slave's wristband or having herself photographed dressed up like a
male slave (136–139). A similar interweaving of ethnicity and gender is evident in Marjorie Garber's analysis of an episode in the life
of the French socialist and feminist Flora Tristan (1803–1844).
Dressed up like a Turkish man, Tristan used her ethnic guise to gain
access to the English parliament. One might also mention Isabelle
Eberhardt (1877–1904), who wore the traditional clothing of an
Arab man during her stay in the North African desert. In all these
instances, national and ethnic transgressions served either to hide
gender deviance or, conversely, to draw attention to the iniquity of
dominant gender codes.

Some gender-benders seem to have been very aware of the
obfuscating effect of nationality on other binary categories and
cleverly employed it for their own ends. In the case of the
"transvestite nun" Catalina de Erauso (1592–1650), for example,
the transgression of gender boundaries was completely blotted out
by the celebration of her nationality. De Erauso, who had escaped
from a Basque convent by cross-dressing, embarked on a ship to
South America. In the New World, she stole, gambled, fought in
duels, and killed numerous opponents, including her own brother.
Shrewd references to her Basque nationality, however, sufficed to

CATALINA DE ERAUSO, the "transvestite nun." *Portrait by Daniel Vierge. From Catalina de Erauso [supposed author]* The Nun Ensign, *tr. James Fitzmaurice-Kelly (London: T. Fisher Unwin, 1908)*

save her from imprisonment. Later on, de Erauso participated in fights against the Native American population, always eager to stress the chasm between her own Basque roots and these "cannibals," as she called the Natives. During a visit to the Pope in Rome (following the discovery of her biological gender), some cardinals remarked that being a Spaniard was de Erauso's only flaw, thus nonchalantly ignoring the biblical "abomination" of cross-dressing! Clearly, for de Erauso questions of gender were obscured by national identification.[7]

If for de Erauso matters of gender receded behind questions of nationality, for the Spaniard Eleno de Céspedes (c. 1545–?) ethnicity provided an explanation and excuse for gender ambiguity. De Céspedes had been living the life of a man for twenty years when she was arrested in 1587. Under her male guise, she earned her living as a doctor and was married to Maria del Cano (Burshatin 105). In defending herself when she was brought to trial, she referred to the hybridity of her origin in order to justify the hybrid nature of her gender. The descendant of an African slave, de Céspedes alluded to the fact that her brown skin and a branded mark on her cheek made her easily identifiable as a foreigner and slave. Claiming to be a hermaphrodite, she followed an argumentation by Pliny who asserted that hermaphrodites lived at the margins of the known world, also the home of people with dark color (Burshatin 114).[8] Even though her defense strategy proved unsuccessful (de Céspedes was condemned both as a cross-dresser and, because of a prior marriage, as a bigamist), it provides an interesting model and an argumentation that is also at the heart of Friederike Helene Unger's and Karoline Paulus' novels. Both Unger and Paulus not only link the transgression of gender boundaries to the crossing of national borders but attempt to justify gender deviance with references to national differences. In their writing, nationality functions as a distancing device that enables fantasies of transgression.[9] Moreover, both authors employ a discourse of nationality in order to draw attention to the "strangeness" of eighteenth-century gender codes.

Although Unger's and Paulus' novels both employ discourses

" In charge of ten thousand sheep of burden, and over a hundred Indians."

CATALINA DE ERAUSO "In charge of ten thousand sheep of burden and over a hundred Indians." *Illustration by Daniel Vierge. From* The Nun Ensign, *tr. James Fitzmaurice-Kelly (London: T. Fisher Unwin, 1908), facing p. 66.*

of nationality to undermine the German ideal of female propriety, their narrative investment in the gender-bender differs. In *Albert and Albertine* [Albert und Albertine, 1804], the foreign amazon gives voice to Unger's critique of German gender ideology. Furthermore, the distancing device that projected transgression onto the French gender-bender made it possible for Unger to hint at the possibility of a lesbian love which could not yet leave the closet. In *Rosalie and Nettchen* [Rosalie und Nettchen, 1801], Unger splits the female heroine into a German maiden and a Spanish amazon. While the non-German "madwoman in the attic" is ultimately punished for her transgressive cross-dressing, her parasitic German counterpart reaps all the benefits and eventually marries a prince. The portrayal of a French cross-dresser in Karoline Paulus' *Wilhelm Dumont* (1805) follows a different rationale. Paulus' Frenchwoman, who exhibits traditionally feminine virtues and yet insists on her right to her own desires, implicitly questions the value of German female self-sacrifice. German masochism can no longer hold its own when faced with the jouissance of the foreign cross-dresser.

I propose that the textile trade and its complicated dynamic of hoped for innovation and dreaded corruption through foreign influence provided a model for Unger and Paulus' strategy. This, however, does not explain why they chose to employ such a distancing device in the first place. In order to understand why Unger and Paulus felt compelled to locate their cross-dressing heroines in a non-German realm, we must again take into account the precarious position of the woman as author.

For an eighteenth-century woman, the very acts of writing and publishing constituted a transgression against traditional gender codes. In fact, one might argue that, because of the uneasy combination of femininity and authorship, women writers themselves were transformed into androgynous hybrids. It is thus not surprising that female literati often tried to mitigate the transgressive act of their authorship by portraying heroines who conformed to conservative notions of femininity. But even so, such a display of conformity on the surface of the text was often complemented by hidden subversive messages. It seems as though many women authors clandestinely transformed their corset of virtue, which they needed in order to gain access to the public sphere, into a camouflage battle dress.

Alluding to such clandestine subversion, Susanne Zantop has compared novels by women authors of the eighteenth century to Trojan horses (Zantop, "Aus der Not" 134). Interestingly, the image of the Trojan horse suggests that the defeat of the target culture is effected by an import from abroad. Consequently, in Unger and Paulus' novels, the subversion of traditional notions of femininity is achieved by pairing off the modest German maiden with an exotic cross-dressed heroine. Just as German factory owners relied on the superior technical skills of English migrant workers for the modernization of domestic production, so Unger and Paulus depended on the French cross-dresser for the reformation of German womanhood. But drawing on a discourse of nationality is but one strategy to negotiate the challenge of developing female individuality within a restrictive environment. Another such strategy is the heroine's renunciation of her sexuality.

In 1806, Johann Wolfgang von Goethe (1749–1832) wrote a review of Friederike Helene Unger's *Confessions of a Beautiful Soul: Written by herself* [Bekenntnisse einer schönen Seele: Von ihr selbst geschrieben, 1806]—whose title alludes to Goethe's own chapter *Confessions of a Beautiful Soul* in the sixth book of his novel *Wilhelm Meister's Apprenticeship* [Wilhelm Meisters Lehrjahre, 1795–96]. His analysis draws our attention to an interesting form of gender discordancy in Unger's work. Goethe first expresses that Unger's heroine truly deserves the epithet "beautiful soul," but then qualifies his praise in the following sentence: "The heroine of this novel truly ought to be called a beautiful soul as her virtues spring from her nature and her education derives from her character. However, we still would have preferred to entitle this work *Confessions of an Amazon* [. . .] For a she-man truly manifests herself here."[10] Even though Unger's *Confessions* contains no accounts of cross-dressing, Goethe's perceptive eyes do not fail to see the amazon who lurks beneath the beautiful soul in Unger's novel. But Goethe not only recognizes the "unfeminine character" of Unger's beautiful soul, he also understands that the amazon is the solution for the book's most pressing problem: "The main question that this book is concerned with is: how can a woman save her character, her individuality against the circumstances, against her environment."[11] According to Goethe, Unger answers this question by introducing the mannish maiden. Sigrid Lange comes to a similar conclusion when she writes that Unger's protagonist relies on a male socialization in order to be constituted as a female self (*Spiegelgeschichten* 78–83). But, according to Lange, the price that such a heroine pays for her spiritual self-determination is the renunciation of her body. Only by desexualizing her life can the beautiful soul achieve identification with an ideal of selfhood that was not meant for her gender.[12]

In this chapter, I argue that both Unger and Paulus employ discourses of nationality to avoid the desexualization of the female protagonist. By focusing her readers' attention on a foreign woman whose masculine attire flaunts her gender deviance, Unger and Paulus hid the more subtle transgressions of their German heroines behind the pants of their exotic friends. In doing so, they could draw on an already established discourse that associated imports from abroad with both modernization and moral depravity. However, at least in Unger's case, this solution is problematic since it relies on a process of "Othering" that does not completely eliminate the necessity of renunciation but merely exports it abroad.

A Spaniard in the Attic: Friederike Helene Unger's *Rosalie and Nettchen* and *Albert and Albertine*

Unger's *Rosalie and Nettchen*, published in 1801, was strongly influenced by the model of the *Prüfungsroman*, or novel of virtue, whose most famous example is Samuel Richardson's *Clarissa* (1747–48).[13] The heroine, Rosalie Linden, is a lady-in-waiting at the court of Princess Amanda. Rosalie's beauty catches the eye of the aristocratic villain Count Silberbach, and he kidnaps her. But

due to Rosalie's delicate feminine nature, this insult to her virtue
plunges her into a desperate rage that threatens to destroy her
good looks. Dreading such a grave loss, the count reacts quickly
and removes Rosalie to his country estate, where he also keeps
the Spanish Seraphina, another victim of his debauchery. The
two women together plan their escape, for which Seraphina cross-
dresses as a man. In the country inn where they take refuge,
Seraphina experiences a spiritual revelation which incites her to
attack the Count, the cause of her undoing, with a dagger. Finally,
the Count, whom she has wounded only slightly, is killed by
Seraphina's brother. Seraphina herself goes mad and retires to a
monastery, while Rosalie, after several other intricacies of plot,
marries princess Amanda's brother.

Unger's narrative strategy is based on the doubling/splitting of
the female heroine. Throughout their common ordeal, Seraphina
is described as Rosalie's alter ego. Like Rosalie, she was deceived by
the Count, who by staging a sham marriage lured her away from
her family and fatherland. Just as in Rosalie's case, he abandoned
her when an illness, smallpox, threatened to disfigure her. And, like
Rosalie, she too is held captive on his country estate. "She spoke
every word of my own part" (186), says Rosalie after their first
encounter. But while this shared experience makes the Spanish
woman a mirror-self of the German one, important differences bear
witness to the fact that Seraphina embodies wishes and desires that
Rosalie has repressed. For unlike her German counterpart, who
transforms her anger into self-destruction and melancholy, the
Spanish woman refuses to succumb to misery and plots her escape
and revenge. She is Rosalie's "madwoman in the attic."[14] Underneath the protective layer of distancing exotics, Unger hides the
German woman's craving for power and revenge. By introducing
the Spanish woman, Unger replaces the uncomfortable association
of aggression and German womanliness with the more tolerable
one of violence and foreignness. As the actual assault is committed
by the doppelgänger figure, Rosalie enjoys the sweetness of revenge
without facing the punishment of madness that is inevitably connected with a violation against gender norms.

In *Rosalie and Nettchen*, Seraphina performs the part of the mannish maiden. And it is not only her dagger that makes her a phallic woman; repeatedly, Unger calls her "a female master"; her character is described as "unspeakably proud." Unlike Rosalie, she is not willing to passively accept the humiliation and betrayal from which she suffered: "The Spaniard will avenge herself, her honor requires it" (192). Moreover, Seraphina's spiritual empowerment is buttressed by the possession of ample financial means. Her money and her gold are essential to the success of the escape.

However, in spite of the distancing device that locates the female fury in a southern realm, Seraphina's lack of submissiveness constitutes a danger to her mental health. Innumerable times the adjective "wild" is used to describe the Spaniard. Her black eyes are either flaming or gloomy. Seraphina's clothing also expresses her fiery temper and her foreign origin. Her strange ("sonderbar") costume is adorned with a fire-colored ("feuerfarben") ribbon, interwoven with gold (181–182). While the precious material indicates her noble standing as a Spanish aristocrat, the flammability expressed by the color forebodes the madness to which she finally succumbs.

But Seraphina's wildness seeks yet another outlet through her clothing. After discarding the emotional and spiritual qualities of her own sex, Seraphina assumes the physical appearance of the other by cross-dressing. Interestingly, she helps herself to the clothes of her oppressor. Though Unger provides no description of the Count's clothing, we may assume that in his choice of attire, like in everything else, Silberbach was influenced by the French. We can be certain that he would have preferred tight knee breeches and stockings to the long trousers which were despised by many aristocrats because of their revolutionary connotations and were not generally used until 1815. Silberbach would have worn a waistcoat, buttoned across his breast, and a coat with skirts that swung outward at hip level (Hollander 83). His clothing would have been made of colorful silk or velvet, even though toward the end of the century these precious materials began to give way to brown or blue cloth and leather (Boehn, *Die*

Mode 140). Clearly, by putting on the Count's clothing, Seraphina would have assumed the appearance of an aristocrat. Paradoxically, it is only by imitating the persecutor that she is able to escape from persecution. And, as so often in these cases, her mimicry is a success. Her new outfit suits her perfectly well (197).

The ease with which Seraphina assumes a male persona demonstrates that, in Unger's novel, gender is not a natural essence but a social construct. Clearly, the contemporary concept of *Geschlechtscharakter* does not apply here. In *Rosalie and Nettchen*, biology is not the foundation of the social order, nor is a woman's character a result of her physical constitution. Rather, it is Seraphina's behavior and looks which have everybody convinced that she is a man. In Unger's novel, gender is not a biological given but "a kind of persistent impersonation that passes as the real" (Butler, *Gender* viii). As Judith Butler would argue: "There is no gender identity behind the expressions of gender" (*Gender* 25).

This hypothesis is strengthened when one considers what happens to the "real" count. For as one pole in the dichotomy is destabilized, the other too must tumble and fall. Parallel to Seraphina's muscling up is the emasculation of the count. When Seraphina starts to wear his suit, the count is reduced to donning an effeminate nightgown. Though Unger does not describe his gown, we may assume that Silberbach wore the standard long, white shirt whose cut more closely resembled a female dress than the common male outfit of jacket and breeches (Loschek 362). Clearly, Unger designed the count's new clothing in accordance with his new shameful position: "Count Silberbach was not particularly impressive in his nightgown and the dress of infirmity [. . .] The nightgown humiliated him unspeakably."[15] Along with his impressive outfit, the count loses his power to charm women as well as his social superiority and attractiveness. In the beginning of the novel, Silberbach is loved and appreciated by the whole court. As the novel progresses, he becomes the object of ridicule and contempt. His scheme to pass himself off as an ingenious author at a reading at court is thwarted as Amanda recognizes the real authors of his fairytale and his poems, namely herself and

Rosalie. Not even the Count's purported talent is really his own. Humiliated by the court, the Count never regains his former status nor does he ever again put on his former clothing. Shortly before his death, he is still wearing his nightgown (266).

On the basis of Unger's depiction, one might think that, like gender, social status is on loan and can be stripped off together with a suit. Indeed, Unger leaves no doubt that social power adheres to clothing. When Rosalie's mother visits Silberbach to plead for her daughter, the count is taken aback by her stately outfit. Her black satin dress with its long train and splendid laces lends her dignity and makes it difficult for the count to treat her like a commoner (68–72). In Unger's text, bourgeoisie and aristocracy are separated by a thin thread. When Rosalie's little sister Nettchen goes to court to seek the help of Princess Amanda, she is confused and misled by the outer trappings of status. She bows to a servant, whose feathered hat tricks her into believing that he is a nobleman, and recognizes her mistake when she sees the pink ribbon of the lackey (138). In the chamber of the Princess, Nettchen pays her respects to the lady with the most beautiful dress, who turns out to be an actress. Though Nettchen's blunders are partly due to her inexperience, they are only possible because in Unger's texts identity and authority do not flow from an inner core but are the result of an interplay between society and individual. Power does not emanate from the body, power comes from pants.

However, there is also a less salubrious way of conceiving of the power of clothing. One might well argue that, even though a performative concept of gender liberates women from the dictate of biology (and the bourgeoisie from that of birth), it subjects them to the logic of the new market system. After all, it was the textile industry that pioneered the capitalist mode of production. Thus, when Unger stresses the performativity of gender and hence its "emptiness" as a category, she aligns herself with the same capitalist economics that had begun to dominate European textile production, an economics that not only required that "all goods and even personal traits be alienable, marketable, and perpetually up for sale" (Veeser 19), but also needed "hollow, empty personalities that resemble money itself" (Veeser 4). By creating characters whose gender and class performances revolve around empty cores, Unger contributed to the formation of the capitalist personality in its infinite capacity for mobility, flexibility, and adaptability.[16]

One might even take this one stitch further. If performativity is personality, then there is nothing that resists the impact of one's clothes. Consequently, clothes not only endow their wearer with power and status, they also determine his behavior and personality. Certainly, in Seraphina's case, the adjustment does not remain limited to her wearing of the clothes of the unfaithful. Rather, as Oscar Wilde said, the influence of the costume penetrates to the very soul of the wearer, and Seraphina becomes unfaithful herself. Clandestinely, she runs away at midnight and leaves poor Rosalie all alone in the country inn. In the neighboring city, rumor has it that "a young rich rascal eloped with a girl and jilted her" (201). Paradoxically, Seraphina's escape from the original story of female victimization results in the reduplication of this story. Or does it result in the parody of the reduplication, meaning that there is "the possibility of a repetition of the law which is not its consolidation, but its displacement," as Judith Butler suggests (*Gender* 30)?

If Seraphina's performance of masculinity is a "subversive operation" (Butler, *Gender* 30) that denaturalizes gender categories,[17] this subversion itself is interrupted in *Rosalie and Nettchen*. The possible story of lesbian love between the "rascal" Seraphina and the girl Rosalie is disturbed by and displaced onto a story of revenge. Seraphina, the substitute count, runs off to kill the "real" count, and the revenge of innocence is blotted out by the elimination of the rival. Tellingly, her weapon is a dagger. But in the same way Seraphina abandons Rosalie without finishing what she started, she also does not kill the Count, choosing simply to wound him. And as Seraphina's brother carries out the killing of the Count, Amanda's brother consummates marriage with Rosalie. Seraphina, deprived of her substitute body, enters the spiritual realm. She retires to a monastery.

This ending demonstrates drastically why Unger deemed it necessary to displace transgressive behavior onto a foreign other. By splitting the female self, Unger manages to wear two hats. Seraphina, the Spanish mannish woman, the agent of desire and revenge, sacrifices her body. Rosalie, however, the parasitic German, enjoys the pleasure of a well accomplished escape and marries a prince in the end. In this unequal trade, the Spaniard is left with the burden of agency and renunciation while the German woman reaps all the benefits. It is important to remember that it is Seraphina's punishment that makes Rosalie's integration possible. Significantly, it is Seraphina's clothing that bears witness to this. After Seraphina's disappearance, the impoverished and humiliated Rosalie is reunited with her sister and asked to assume her former position at court. Threadbare herself, she can only join the courtly society with decency ("Anstand") because Seraphina had taken the precaution of presenting the German woman with her own cloth-ing. Attired in the Spaniard's dress, Rosalie resumes her former life of leisure and wealth. Clearly, in order to portray transgressive behavior without punishment, a woman writer of the early nine-teenth century needed to have a Spanish woman in the attic and her clothing in the closet.

But Unger did not stop at redressing the ills of German wom-anhood by introducing a foreign "Other." In her novel, German women are absolved of every guilt; even their faults are not of their own doing but are imported from abroad. Interestingly, Seraphina's Spanish passion is the remedy for misfortunes which were brought about by the French; it was the Count's French connection that caused the deformation of his character in the first place. He was spoilt by Voltaire's freethinking: "In his gallantry and agility he was superior to everybody, and in worldly and courtly insincerity and perfidy he found no equal. He had gathered the ingredients to this commendable character with difficulty and at great cost from all countries and all courts."[18] In Unger's novel, moral vice and sexual decadence are imports from abroad. They belong to another nationality as well as to another social class ("from all countries and all courts"). By associating aristocratic corruptibility with French culture, Germany becomes the homeland of a virtue with a specific social coding, the virtue of the bourgeois middle-class. In addition to introducing different models of femininity, the discourse on nationality serves yet another purpose. It seeks to establish a political alliance among the forming bourgeoisie.[19]

But we should not assume that it is always the French who are decadent and the Spanish who avenge themselves. Rather, every nationality is an empty screen for projections which can be employed in every possible way. Aside from French decadence, we also find a surprisingly large number of sympathetic French cross-dressers, such as Rosalie in Paulus' *Wilhelm Dumont* and Adelaide in Unger's *Albert and Albertine*.

Like Huber's and Fouqué's novels, Unger's *Albert and Albertine* (1804) contains the story of a woman whose cross-dressing is motivated by the turmoil of the French Revolution, and like *Rosalie and Nettchen*, it relies on the distancing device of a foreign nationality to hint at lesbian desires. Albertine, the female protagonist, has been married for only one year when her husband Louis of Lindenhain leaves their home in order to join the royalist forces in France. After a brief stay at her brother's country estate, where she is bored by the monotony of rural life and annoyed by her sister-in-law's peevishness, Albertine moves in with her uncle, the banker Dämmrig. Falsely believing herself to be widowed, she has accepted the offer of marriage from her devoted friend Albert von Ulmenhorst when her long-lost husband Louis suddenly returns from France. Severely wounded Louis survived the war because of the selfless care of the Frenchwoman Adelaide, who has come to Germany with him. Louis and Albertine are reunited, but their marriage is increasingly perturbed by the presence of Adelaide and Albert. The alienation between the two spouses reaches a climax when Albertine is disfigured by smallpox. Louis, who is now given to wild rides to escape from his domestic misery, dies in a riding accident, and Albert and Albertine are married after all.

At first glance, a reader might conclude that *Albert and Albertine* reproduces the dominant gender stereotypes of its time. Almost all female characters are subject to Unger's biting sarcasm.

Albertine's aunt Elise, who throws herself at Albert in spite of her old age, is ridiculed for her romantic delusions. Elise's fanatic Goethe cult and Antonie's literary ambitions are easy targets of Unger's wit. Unger delights in decrying the maliciousness of Albertine's cousin Laurette and pokes fun at the loose morals of Rosamunde, her uncle's mistress. But again, even though Unger mouths the misogynistic platitudes of her time, the hidden choreography of her text betrays a different agenda.[20] Not only must her male characters weather equally rough treatment,[21] but Unger also portrays a female character who is exempt from the scathing criticism that she reserves for the rest of her sex.

In *Albert and Albertine,* Unger devises a plucky heroine whose less than spotless virtue is not the subject of authorial reprimands. In fact, the frequency and magnitude of Albertine's transgressive acts are quite impressive. Albertine, hopelessly addicted to gambling, finances her ever-more-costly escapades by pawning her valuables. Amazingly, this highly reprehensible behavior is not punished but rewarded as her faithful admirer Albert settles her debts and redeems her pawned possessions. While Albert is busy clearing up the monetary mess of his beloved, Albertine frequents the local masked balls—a privileged symbol of transgression and sexual license in eighteenth-century discourse—and enjoys herself in the company of the trickster baron Weißensee. The fact that Albertine was completely oblivious to Albert's warnings of Weißensee's debauchery does not keep Albert from saving her from a malicious kidnapping plotted by the aristocratic knave. Susanne Zantop has rightfully pointed out that Albert suffers and tolerates far more than Albertine before he wins the object of his affection ("Beautiful Soul" 44).[22] It is astounding that Albertine is not punished for her numerous transgressions but marries the hero in the end. Thus, rather than interpreting her illness and subsequent disfigurement as narrative retribution, one might claim that they are no more than much-needed symbols of Albertine's moral catharsis and as such represent Unger's minimal concession to the contemporary definition of female propriety.[23]

Juggling her conflicting objectives dexterously, Unger constructs a heroine who does not renounce her desires for virtue's sake and yet manages to create at least the semblance of conformity to the gender codes of her time. Again, the figure of the foreign cross-dresser is crucial to this operation. While Unger's German protagonists do lip-service to the ideals of conventional feminine propriety, the female foreigner stands up for her oppressed gender. Cleverly, Unger manages to have it both ways. She endows the Frenchwoman with youth, beauty, talent, inner nobility, and altruism, and thus insinuates that Adelaide's opinions are grounded in reason and morality. However, by designating her as non-German and by freeing her from familial ties, Unger capitalizes on Adelaide's splendid isolation in order to express her gender critique. Significantly, it is Adelaide who insists on the importance of education and points out that woman's inferiority is the result of human culture, not of woman's natural disposition:

> Adelaide sided with her gender and claimed that one could not hold it accountable if its views about the world and its conditions do not have the force and urgency of the male gaze. "Consider, mademoiselle, in which light the world must appear to us as our minds have been educated to the infiniments petits only, and how every proper wife who wants to be useful to her husband and her family has to consent to perform the most ignoble details of the household. She who has to see like this will certainly become a moral myopic at last."[24]

That Adelaide's pronouncements should be taken seriously is evidenced by the fact that at times the narrator herself expresses her dissatisfaction with the conventional gender roles of her time. Thus, when Louis reprimands Albertine because she neglects her household duties in favor of her aesthetic interests, the narrator accuses him of undue expectations:

> He [Louis, EK] was not aware that it is in the nature of things, and that it is unfair to demand from a woman what only very few men can do: to satisfy all. Would not female talent

develop less inhibited in competition with the male if woman
were not simultaneously obliged to devote herself to a hundred
time-splitting works? And cross your heart, you female artists
and women writers, if you put down the brush, if a rhyme or
lively image is at the tip of your tongue just now, do you then
go to the kitchen or the linen closet with the same lively
interest as you sit down at your desk or at your easel? I say no!
and the man who demands of you that the delight of the mind
be subordinated, is an unjust one.[25]

While Unger's protagonist struggles to live up to the expectations
of her husband, the narrator comments on the injustice of his
demands.[26] Seen in this light, Unger's conspicuous display of
misogynistic opinions might not reflect the author's uncritical
adherence to patriarchal values but serve as a camouflage technique designed to hide her subtle subversion of these norms.

However, while the narrator limits herself to a criticism of the
unfairness of woman's lot, the Frenchwoman calls for action. In
accordance with her belief in the preponderance of nurture over
nature, Adelaide is also convinced of everyone's innate right to
better his or her position in life: "If nature had left me with a defi-
ciency I would try to redress it without any second thoughts"
(256).[27] Unsurprisingly, Adelaide's proactive nature, indicated by
this quotation, finds its most pronounced expression when she
escapes certain death by cross-dressing. Because of their kindness
to Louis, Adelaide and her father are suspected of treason. When
her father is guillotined, Adelaide puts on men's clothing so as
not to incur a similar fate. Accompanied by an unknown lady she
travels to southern France where she meets with Louis and offers
her services to him: "One day I [Louis, EK] came home from a
walk; I was told that a young, beautiful boy had inquired after me;
he had gone to the nearby church to wait for me. Who could
inquire after me here! After half an hour there appeared a cleanly
dressed boy in the attire of a servant; in whom, at the first sound
of his voice, I recognized Adelaide."[28] In introducing the foreign
cross-dresser, Unger relies on an excess of positive signals.

Adelaide's dress is clean, her figure beautiful, and her appearance is dignified by its sacral environment. Like in Huber and Fouqué's novels, the turmoil of war is reason and excuse for Adelaide's cross-dressing. Just as in Sara Seldorf's case, the death of her father and the lack of other relatives justifies the heroine's recourse to disguise; a disguise, moreover, which is so convincing that it is not her appearance but her voice that betrays Adelaide's identity. Why is it then that such a positive character does not share the fate of all conventional heroines who are invariably destined to marry in the end? Considering the floweriness of Unger's plot, it would not have been beyond the scope of her novel if Albertine's first marriage had proven invalid, thus enabling a union between Louis and Adelaide. But as it is, Adelaide's supposed passion for Louis is rather unconvincing. When Adelaide first moves in with Louis and Albertine, she is conspicuously uninterested in the German veteran. Throughout her stay at the Lindenhorst estate she barely notices Louis—who, moreover, is increasingly por-trayed in a negative light.[29] Consequently, the reader is quite sur-prised when, towards the end of the novel, Adelaide proclaims all of a sudden that her devotion to the dead Louis prevents her from ever entering another engagement, and subsequently declares her intention to dedicate the rest of her life to the education of Albertine's children. Adelaide's professed but bloodless attach-ment to Louis, dead or alive, is even more suspect if contrasted with her intimate friendship with the unmarried artist Henriette Euler, to whom she is bound by inseparable ties ("unzertrennlich gekettet," 262), and with her love for Albertine herself. When Albertine is sick with smallpox, Adelaide lies down next to her to share her affliction and disfigurement. Throughout her stay at the Lindenhorst estate, she is much more interested in Louis' wife than in Louis himself. Even the ring, which she braided with her own hair and gave to the departing Louis, was destined for the latter's wife: "pour la charmante Albertine" (244). Furthermore, while the destiny of Adelaide's cross-dressed journey is Louis, the companion of her adventure is a lady. Adelaide may don the trap-pings of the other sex, but her desire is firmly rooted in her own.

Thus, one might claim that, in addition to opening up a new sphere of agency and adventure, the wearing of men's clothing also functions as a synecdoche for Adelaide's "masculine" desire for her own sex. In *Albert and Albertine*, just like in Unger's *Confessions of a Female Soul Written by Herself* (1806), the dead male beloved serves as a moral placeholder for the missing heterosexuality of the female protagonist. In order to unprime its explosive potential, lesbian desire is not only projected onto a foreign other but appears under the guise of intimate friendship. However, it is precisely the overload of justifications and motivations that draws attention to the underlying transgression. Not satisfied with Adelaide's national Otherness and her supposed heterosexual, though dead, partner, Unger adds the topos of "the romance between conqueror and conquered" (Zantop, *Fantasies* 121). In Adelaide, who is supposedly so fascinated by the Germanic soldier Louis that she becomes a traitor to her country and risks her life to save that of the enemy, Unger plays out the old "myth of the women's natural surrender to the colonizing force" (*Fantasies* 121). In doing so, she manages to hide the sexual non-conformity of her character beneath her appreciation for Germanic heroes, and then turns the surplus sympathy, garnered through patriotism, into the license to criticize German gender norms.

Savoir Vivre in Karoline Paulus' *Wilhelm Dumont*

In 1805 Karoline Paulus published her epistolary novel *Wilhelm Dumont* under the pseudonym Eleutherie Holberg.[30] The title of her work is quite misleading since the real protagonist of Paulus' fiction is not Wilhelm Dumont but the narrator Adelaide,[31] whose story is presented in a series of letters. However, like so many other epistolary novels of its time, Paulus' text only purports to possess the dialogical character that defines the genre of correspondence. Tellingly, the response of Adelaide's friend Clara is reduced to only two brief notes while Adelaide's numerous and elaborate letters are marked by the intimacy of diary entries.

Wilhelm Dumont features a heroine who has no home. Adelaide travels from place to place in order to find her missing brother Gustav and her beloved Wilhelm Dumont. To please her friend Clara, whose impending marriage and stable home furnish a stark contrast to Adelaide's itinerant life, Adelaide agrees to write down her story. She describes how her mother's premature death put an early end to her and her brother's happy childhood. When her ambitious father introduces her to the rich and powerful Eduard, Adelaide is impressed by the latter's superior knowledge and manners. Even though she cannot love Eduard, she agrees to marry him in order to remain close to her brother Gustav. Soon, however, this union proves to be a fatal error. Eduard tortures his young wife with his jealousy and egotism, and Adelaide becomes ever more aware of her deep feelings for Wilhelm Dumont, a friend of her brother. Rendered helpless by Adelaide's firm resolve to stay with her husband, Wilhelm and Gustav embark on a journey. From this point on, all contact between the three is broken off as Eduard wrongfully informs Adelaide's brother and lover of her untimely death. It is only at his deathbed that Adelaide learns of her husband's betrayal and of his illegitimate daughter Marie, who lives with peasants and whom the dying man entrusts to Adelaide's care. Accompanied by Marie and Jakob, the son of these peasants, Adelaide sets out for Paris where she hopes to find her lost beloved. Her eventual reunion with Wilhelm is complemented by Marie's engagement to Gustav.

Among the most moving features of Paulus' novel is its unsparing criticism of the institution of marriage. Even though Adelaide's submissive acceptance of Eduard's cruelty and injustice conforms to the gender stereotypes of her time, any glorification of such female self-sacrifice is missing. On the contrary, Adelaide insists that her ill-advised martyrdom initiated the most unhappy period of her life. Her misery is further augmented by regrets about what she later calls the "insolent hubris" ("Vermessenheit," 165), which caused her to deny the failure of her marriage and stay with her husband. Marriage is described as a form of slavery which cannot but deform a woman's character.

I had been chained [. . .] I am not talking about external freedom; for this is by far the smallest loss in marriage. I am talking about the far more important loss of our moral individuality. A woman, who wants to comply with the nonsensical laws,
the unnatural duties of marriage, must sacrifice on the altar of
prejudice her most beautiful feelings, her most noble sensa-
tions, the freedom of her will which was given to her, like to
every other being, by God. She must strive to resemble her
husband, be he what he may [. . .] And if the better nature of
woman rebels against this, then she must at least strive to
defend the weaknesses of her husband before the world, to
hide his mistakes. Thus, she must become dishonest.[32]

The flaw which attracts the brunt of Adelaide's criticism is
Eduard's selfishness. From the very beginning, when he persuades
her to marry him in spite of her resistance, Eduard is thinking only
of his own gratification, not of the happiness of his beloved.
Eduard's egoism stands in stark contrast to the self-denying love
of Wilhelm Dumont. Dumont, who as a child fled from hard and
unjust foster parents, was raised by a blind Frenchman and his
daughter Margot, both impoverished through the war. Even
though he adores his stepsister and longs to marry her himself,
Wilhelm does not hesitate to sacrifice his happiness for hers when
Margot falls in love with somebody else. Later, when Wilhelm
begins to love Adelaide, he again lives for her welfare only, never
even thinking of his own: "If he only saw me cheerful, he was
delighted, and oblivious to his own wishes, he lived for my apparent happiness only."[33] His "loving sacrifice unto utter oblivious-
ness of his own self" (137) feminizes Paulus' hero. The ideal partner, as Paulus portrays him, is a man who is capable of the
"feminine" virtues of self-sacrifice and patient suffering.[34]

Thus, one might argue that Wilhelm too is a gender-bender. But
while Wilhelm's passivity is limited to matters of the heart,
Adelaide resigns herself to every willful injustice. Though her travels in search of her lost brother and beloved show some initiative
on her part, Adelaide is adamant in her rejection of even an

attempt to influence the course of events. For, as she claims, "which mortal may presume to control his own destiny high-handedly" (309). Repeatedly, she refuses to take matters into her own hands: "I will await in faith and resignation what the laws of a higher power have allotted to me" (309). Contemporary readers were very aware of Adelaide's submissiveness. Goethe, for example, in his review of *Wilhelm Dumont*, claims that the heroine's passivity constitutes a narrative problem: "Adelaide travels too calmly, she makes inquiries only, and retrieves her desired friends more through destiny and accident, than reaching and winning them through effort and actions. What should have been portrayed is a passionate endeavor."[35] With his usual insightfulness, Goethe addresses the central problem of the novel: the question of whether or not it is possible to exercise control over one's own life. But while Goethe's judgement is perceptive in one sense, it is distorted in another. Goethe fails to take into account the gender norms that confine women writers and their female protagonists. If Paulus had portrayed a passionate and venturesome heroine, she would also have incurred the censure of contemporary reviewers. A courageous and defiant Adelaide would have been stigmatized as a she-man. In order to imagine a female protagonist who is both active and sympathetic, Paulus had to resort to a narrative ruse: the figure of the French cross-dresser Rosalie. By overlaying gender-coded character traits with national connotations, Paulus got away with the unfeminine nature of Rosalie's all too active behavior. The initial dichotomy of male heroism and female dependence gives way to the binary of German powerlessness and French self-reliance as Adelaide's failure to control her own life is contrasted with Rosalie's ingenuity.[36]

Rosalie loves Ferno, a Parisian doctor who turns out to be Wilhelm's cousin, but her rich aunt has a former lover, Brancard, for whom she hopes to provide by uniting him with the heiress of her fortune, that is, Rosalie. Rosalie, however, has no intention of going along with this scheme. Cross-dressed and equipped with a false passport, she pretends to be Adelaide's brother and accompanies her to Paris. "A brown wig, eyebrows painted in black and the like will make the blond little face rather unrecognizable. Also, she is tall enough to pass for a respectable gentleman, and a Frenchwoman knows how to adapt herself to every part."[37] Rosalie's talent to play every part, which enables her to exercise control over her life, is contrasted with Adelaide's supposed inability to put on an act.[38] While Adelaide's happiness is dependent on external events, Rosalie takes hers into her own hands. Always mistress of her own destiny, she does not stop at winning her beloved Ferno but secures her inheritance as well. After her first plan has been foiled, Rosalie's amorous aunt attempts to unite her lover Brancard with her other niece and potential heiress, Mme Simonville. But the cross-dressed Rosalie proves her resourcefulness one more time and simply courts her cousin herself. Mme Simonville promptly falls for her and is foolish enough to agree to a clandestine correspondence in which she expresses her disdain for her aunt in the most unkind terms. Her letters supply Rosalie with the hard evidence she needs to convince her aunt of the silliness of her plans. In the end, Rosalie's aunt, now reconciled, agrees to her niece's marriage with Ferno. Brancard receives a small bequest, granted by the rightful heiress, and there is even a little money left over for Mme Simonville. Interestingly, like Seraphina, Rosalie too comes to possess a large fortune. One might wonder whether there is a natural affinity between these characters' flexibility and adaptability, that is, their performative identity, and their ability to gain control over financial resources. Certainly, Rosalie's venturesome spirit, her initiative, and her willingness to take risks, are closer to what one might describe as "capitalist" personality than Adelaide's resigned passivity and willingness to accept a God-given fate.

In addition to her generosity that leads to the conciliatory ending, Paulus adds other character traits designed to win the Frenchwoman the sympathies of the reader. Respecting their differences, Rosalie expects no help from her German friends, who do not approve of her little intrigues. But though she asks nothing of them, she herself does everything in her power to improve Adelaide and Marie's lot. Thus, the reader can easily believe

Adelaide's assurances that the Frenchwoman, in spite of her wan-
tonness and joyous excess, is a "truly good" person (298).

While Rosalie's flamboyant playfulness does not lessen her
virtues, it exceeds the scope of pragmatic necessity. Her willingness to submit "to every seductive mood, to every charming game
of her liking" (298) is motivated by a pursuit of pleasure which
belies every practical justification. The value of German virtue and
righteousness fades before the glittering shine of Rosalie's "fresh,
inexhaustible love of life" (278). Compared with Rosalie's savoir
vivre, the morally inspired suffering of her German friends appears
like foolish masochism. While Adelaide is pained by the memory
of her loss, and Marie—refusing to see her lover as long as Adelaide
is unhappy—rejects present bliss, Rosalie is having a good time in
Paris: "The one is looking for what she cannot find; the other tries
to hide from herself and others that she has found what she was
looking for involuntarily; and the third enjoys what she has without letting that keep her from finding even more."[39] Comments
like this invite readers to draw their own conclusions, and it is
likely that Adelaide's melancholy and Marie's self-sacrifice, signifiers of admirable female virtue in many other contexts, suffer in
comparison. If Rosalie can be both rich and happy, if she enjoys
herself without being callous or selfish—in short, if her morality is
not based on pain—why then the German self-flagellation?

By introducing a French cross-dresser, Paulus undermines the
German morale. But she does so in a clandestine and rather
ambiguous manner since she chooses to weaken the subversive
nature of her message by insisting on "the great difference in character between the two nations" (286) and "the French qualities
which will always repel us Germans" (72).[40] If one attempts to
define this great difference, one is left with only one trait: the ability to act a part, to dissimulate and disguise oneself. The secret to
Rosalie's success is pretense: "Her new part suits her very well.
The most experienced mimic artist could not imitate masculine
movements and gestures more gracefully and faithfully than she.
I am certain that nobody will take this perky, unaffected, fiery
young man for a girl. At times she deceives even me."[41] Rosalie's

performance is so utterly convincing that Adelaide fails to recognize her own brother at a masked ball because she mistakes his
Spanish costume for Rosalie's customary disguise. But even
though Adelaide admires the chutzpah of Rosalie's role-play, she
herself relentlessly assures the reader that she is utterly incapable
of such "falseness" [Unwahrheit]. That this is not entirely true is
proven by the enthusiastic applause which the adolescent
Adelaide received for her participation in an amateur performance of Iffland's *Hagestolz*. Even cross-dressing is not as alien to
the German context as Adelaide would like it to be. Emulating
her brother, Adelaide herself had donned male clothing as a child.
She believed herself a boy, played only with her brother, and
climbed on trees as he did. Even though Adelaide's cross-dressing
episode is relegated to an early phase of childhood, it still exists
as a possibility and thus collapses the seemingly unconquerable
difference between German straightness and French frivolity.

It is of interest to note that Adelaide's cross-dressing is inspired
by the wish to be respected by her beloved brother. As Gustav
cannot empathize with a being different from himself and only
appreciates the qualities of his own sex, Adelaide changes her
gender to please her brother. Unlike Rosalie's cross-dressing,
Adelaide's is not a self-chosen strategy. Rather, like all her other
actions, it too is guided by the desire to conform to the wishes of
others. But even though it is not self-directed, Adelaide's cross-
dressing is still meant to embody a utopian ideal of harmony and
freedom that predates and is terminated by the misery that the
demands of her father inflict on her. In *Wilhelm Dumont*, the heroine's childhood is conceived of as a quasi-paradisical realm precisely because it predates gender differentiations. In contrast, the
male-female dichotomy, with its dissociation of autonomy and
empathy, is portrayed as the source of much human unhappiness
and suffering. However, even though Adelaide's cross-dressing is
presented as a blessed existence beyond the restrictions of gender
("O ihr seligen Jahre der Kindheit," 24), this androgynous childhood idyll is already tainted by the workings of a homosocial order
that reserves recognition for the male gender only. Moreover, it

is an idyll that is confined to the incestuousness of the brother-sister relationship and thus precludes romantic attachments beyond the realm of the immediate family.

Throughout the novel, emotional closeness and opposition to an education that thrives on renunciation are associated with Adelaide's mother. Adelaide's father, on the other hand, takes more delight in order than in intimacy. Consequently, when their mother dies, the intimate relationship between Adelaide and her brother comes to an end. Adelaide's until-then-absent father breaks up the brother-sister dyad and coerces Adelaide into a marriage with the father-substitute Eduard.[42] Thus assured of his legacy, he dies shortly before her wedding. A worthy successor, Eduard too is disturbed by the close relationship between the siblings. It is only after Eduard's death and after Adelaide had teamed up with the "fake" brother Rosalie that she replaces her beloved brother with the brotherly lover Wilhelm.[43] Once all fathers and father figures have been eliminated, Paulus' novel revels in the restoration of a love that is characterized by both freedom and equality.

However, one would be wrong to assume that Paulus' novel is uncritical in its celebration of the motherly realm. For while Adelaide's mother cherished intimacy, she is also responsible for the lack of agency that caused Adelaide's misery in the first place. When Adelaide is torn between her desire to divorce her husband and her obligation to stay with him, an apparition of her dead mother admonishes her to fulfill her duty. Tellingly, Adelaide associates Rosalie's cleverness in worldly affairs with the realm of the father and rejects it as such. The comparison with the Frenchwoman suggests that it is this strict separation of male and female virtues that is at the heart of Adelaide's suffering.

It comes as no surprise that Rosalie's mother and father are long dead when the reader makes her acquaintance. Not confined by filial obligations, Rosalie commands both the "male" politic astuteness and the "female" capacity for intimacy. By laying claim to the *Weltklugheit* and theatricality that Adelaide rejected as attributes of the world of her father and husband,[44] Rosalie becomes the mistress of her own destiny. Thus, as the union of female and male competencies becomes the distinguishing mark of cross-dressing, cross-dressing becomes the emblem of humanism. In creating the French gender-bender, Paulus imagined a world in which active control over one's own life and loving tenderness for others are not mutually exclusive categories. One might call the invention of such a utopian world a truly "passionate endeavor," even if Goethe did not perceive it as such.

Both Unger's and Paulus' novels displace gender transgression onto a national Other. This common strategy, however, should not obfuscate the fact that Unger's foreign transvestites follow a rationale fundamentally different from that of Paulus'. While Unger's Seraphina and Adelaide embody forbidden fruits such as lesbian desire, female power, and revenge, Paulus' Rosalie is a model of human wholeness. While Unger engages in a duplicitous game of conformity and subversion, comfortably reliant on vicarious living and the marginalization of the Other, Paulus' foreigner questions German masochism and passivity. However, even though *Wilhelm Dumont* is not based on the complementary binary of excess and exorcism, its endorsement of cross-dressing is implicit and rather non-committal. While its plot celebrates French savoir vivre, its authorial comments reject it, thus leaving it up to its readers whether they want to follow or ignore the admonitions of the cross-dresser.

Both Unger and Paulus employ a discourse of nationality in order to subvert and resist restrictive gender roles. They were able to do so because the uneasy amalgamation of importation, innovation, and deviance that characterizes their novels had been prefigured in the economic life of their time. Thus, the fact that clothing became such a powerful trope in the arena of gender experimentation has as much to do with an ongoing struggle over gender definitions as it has with the contemporary conditions of manufacture and trade. The structural transformation of the textile market and the growing importance of international trade relationships had given rise to a discourse that was concerned with the demarcation of the dangers and desirability of foreign products. In this discourse, foreignness might be welcomed because of its innovative and modernizing potential or reviled as harmful economic competition and a potent agent of moral corruption. Consequently, Unger and Paulus' attack on French immorality combined with the importation of deviance through the foreign cross-dresser could rely on the eighteenth-century rhetoric of sumptuary and textile law. Furthermore, one might claim that the influence of the contemporary textile industry and its capitalist mode of production on the formation of a performative concept of identity is evidenced by another curious fact. The adaptability, flexibility, and mobility that the cross-dressing characters display might be said to be essential to success in a capitalist market economy. But again, the message is ambiguous. Even though Unger and Paulus rejoice in the resourcefulness of their cross-dressers, they prefer to locate them in a foreign realm.

Unger's and Paulus' novels testify to the liberating influence of the figure of the foreign cross-dresser, even though this liberation is limited and bought at a high price. Spanish and French cross-dressers allowed German women authors to explore different models of femininity while still maintaining the appearance of respectability. Paradoxically, it was by foregrounding the textile transgression of their foreign heroines that these authors were able to hide the transgressive nature of their own texts. But while they must be credited for their successful navigation within a restrictive context, one should not forget that they did not solve the inherent conflict, but merely exported it abroad.

It has become evident that Unger and Paulus' strategies differ from those of Huber and Motte-Fouqué. However, in spite of these differences, all four share one ideologem. Whatever predicament their texts are trying to overcome, whatever crisis they are handling, none of these authors look to the female body as a potential source of resolution. In this, their texts are radically different from those of Schiller and Kleist who display nostalgia for the body as a repository of truth or legitimation.

Chapter 3

THE DEATH OF A CROSS-DRESSER:
Epistemologies of the Body

> I don't know what to tell you about myself, this unspeakable being—I wish
> I could tear my heart from my body, pack it into this letter and send it
> to you—Stupid thought.
>
> Heinrich von Kleist to Ulrike von Kleist, March 13, 1803

In May 1810 a rather peculiar group gathered in the apartment of the widow Cole in London. Ten men, among them a professor of anatomy, two surgeons, a lawyer, and a journalist, had been asked to inspect the body of Mrs. Cole's roommate of fourteen years, a certain Chevalière d'Eon.[1] To their great surprise, they discovered that the Chevalière was anatomically male. Clearly, such a discovery is sensational in and of itself. But it is even more so in the case of d'Eon, whose gender had been the subject of speculation for quite some time. Charles Geneviève Louise Auguste André Thimothée d'Eon was born the son of a Burgundian nobleman in 1728. He served with distinction in the Seven Years' War, was awarded the prestigious Cross of Saint-Louis, and became a diplomat and spy for King Louis XV. His brilliant career took a piquant turn when rumors that the Chevalier was a woman were confirmed by an official declaration of Louis XVI in 1776. For the rest of his life, the Chevalier himself would insist that he was born a woman but was forced by his parents to assume the identity of a boy. But even though d'Eon wanted his contemporaries to believe that he had always been a woman, he continued to puzzle them by refusing to wear women's clothing as the King's orders demanded. For several years, d'Eon's gender was the subject of numerous bets and legal proceedings. But in spite of such keen public interest, his "real" sex remained hidden until his death.[2]

MADEMOISELLE de BEAUMONT, or the
CHEVALIER D'EON.
Female Minister Plenipo. Capt. of Dragoons &c. &c.

CHEVALIER D'EON, eighteenth-century French diplomat and spy. *The Harvard Theater Collection, The Houghton Library, Harvard University*

D'Eon's story teaches us that as long as we live and breathe, the culturally mediated body is an unreliable agent of truth. It took the rigor of death to harden the fluid indeterminacy of the Chevalier's gender identity into an unambiguous fact. And the Chevalier's story is not the only one of its kind. Death also led to the discovery of Mary Lacey—alias Happy Ned—who, as a sailor, participated in the American Civil War. Lacey's anatomical gender remained a secret until she died in 1887. Another case in point is that of Dr. James Barry (1795–1865), who finished his studies of medicine in Edinburgh in 1812 and subsequently worked in the colonies for the remainder of his life. It was only after his death that a newspaper article revealed that the doctor's anatomy was that of a woman.[3] In all these cases as in numerous other stories about cross-dressing, the riddle of a dubious gender identity was only to be solved postmortem.[4]

In fiction as in history, death and cross-dressing entertain a rather intimate relationship. When the exposure of the cross-dresser occurs at the moment of his/her demise, death is defined as a privileged moment of truth.[5] But death may also be a means of moral retribution meted out as punishment for the cross-dresser's transgressions. In both versions—as moment of truth and as punishment—death is not only at the center of the narrative but also imparts authority to the particular interpretations of truth and gender that these stories present. In fact, one often encounters a mixture of these two narrative patterns in which the killing of the cross-dresser becomes the guarantor of an order that defines both truth and gender as newly accessible and unambiguous.

A recurrent element of literary and historical accounts of cross-dressing from the eighteenth century to the present is the murder or legal execution of gender-benders.[6] The most famous example of such draconic punishment imposed on a gender-bender is the sentence of death pronounced against the Virgin of Orléans. The fact that Joan of Arc had put on men's clothing informed almost all accusations leveled against her. Cross-dressing was mentioned in no less than five points of her indictment (cf. Bullough and Bullough 57–58; Garber 215; Hotchkiss 49–68).

Significantly, when Joan of Arc first recanted, she also put on women's clothing. It was her return to men's clothes that brought about her final conviction.

Though Joan of Arc's story seems to suggest the opposite, the wearing of male clothing per se was not generally considered a capital offense by legal authorities.[7] But if a cross-dresser laid claim to the privilege of desiring another woman—especially if a marriage had been performed—capital punishment would invariably be enforced.[8] A well-documented case of this kind is that of Catharina Lincken, who was executed by sword in Halberstadt in 1721.[9] When she entered the bond of matrimony, Catharina Margaretha Lincken—alias Peter Wannich, alias Anastasius Lagrantinus Rosenstengel, alias Caspar Beuerlein, alias Cornelius Hubsch—could already look back on a rather adventurous life. Wearing men's clothing, Lincken joined a group of religious zealots in Halle and traveled through the countryside as their prophet. Following this spiritual interlude, Lincken became a musketeer with the Hannoverian troops, then with the Royal Prussian troops and finally with the Royal Polish regiment. Her subsequent career as a dyer and manufacturer of cotton was crowned by her marriage with Catharina Margaretha Mühlhahn in 1717. To perform her matrimonial duties, Lincken used a "stuffed male member, made of leather, to which a pouch out of a pig's bladder and two stuffed testiculi made of leather had been attached" (F. C. Müller 96). The sexual details of her intimate relationship of four years with Mühlhahn stimulated much interest during the investigation and trial that followed upon her arrest. Lincken was eventually sentenced to death while Mühlhahn got off with a fairly mild penalty.

As different as the story of the death of the Chevalier d'Eon and the account of the execution of Catharina Lincken may seem, they share a common element. Both stories depict the death of a cross-dresser as a turning point that puts an end to a situation that is epistemologically unstable and morally dubious. Over his/her dead body, truth is again knowable and transgressions are again punishable. Both Friedrich Schiller's *Fiesco's Conspiracy at Genoa*

[Die Verschwörung des Fiesco zu Genua, 1783] and Heinrich von Kleist's *The Family Schroffenstein* [Die Familie Schroffenstein, 1803] use the elimination of the gender-bender as a panacea for metaphysical and political uncertainties. However, whereas Kleist's text consciously undermines its own agenda, Schiller's text unwittingly reaffirms what it set out to negate.

In Schiller's *Fiesco*, death and cross-dressing function as privileged topoi for the resolution of a moral dilemma inherent in language and art. This dilemma is rooted in the fact that language is not only a powerful tool to convey truth but also a highly efficient means to conceal it. Linguistic signs are arbitrary since the relation of signifiers to their signified is not determined by inherent similarities, correspondences, or causalities. Because of this arbitrariness language conveys meaning independent of whether it describes "real" facts or whether that to which it refers exists in the realm of language only. It is due to this arbitrariness that language, and thereby literature, lacks any inherent guarantee of truth and thus any inherent moral justification.

Schiller was acutely aware that the creative potential of an author might turn into a dangerous manipulative weapon if not guided by a higher moral authority. His *Fiesco* not only explores the morally indifferent nature of language, it also attempts to do away with it. In Schiller's drama, the cross-dresser, who has transformed gender into an arbitrary sign, becomes a metaphor for language itself. In the figure of the cross-dresser, just as in Fiesco's rhetorical distortions of the truth, signifier and signified have fallen apart. However, the figure of the cross-dresser not only expresses an epistemological crisis, it is also instrumental in solving it. Schiller achieves this by introducing the female body as an immediate and pure sign that defies all attempts at distortion. *Fiesco* suggests that, though clothing (and men) may lie, the truth of the female body will reassert itself in the end, and that signs are as natural as bodies. In the end, so we are to believe, truth and true gender will always triumph over false appearances. It is through re-inscribing gender in the body that the validity of truth and morality is restored.

Like cross-dressing, the motif of death is apt to fulfill this function because it has an ambiguous relation to the body and to language. The French theorist Jacques Lacan, for example, postulated an association of death and language when he defined
language as the "murderer of the soma."[10] Lacan based his claim
on the notion that linguistic signs designate that which is absent.
They constitute substitutes for—are "murderers" of—material
reality. Based on Lacan's theory, Elisabeth Bronfen maintains that
in death the human body becomes its own sign. Because it is in
a state of transition, the corpse can be thought of as an auto-icon.
While it preserves its identity with the living person, it is also
transformed into a sign that points to the absence of this person
(cf. Bronfen, *Dead Body* 96–97). During this liminal phase, in
which signifier and signified are identical, death brings a material
dimension to the realm of the symbolic. Because it is identical
with and yet different from the deceased, the corpse opens up the
possibility of a "true" sign (cf. Bronfen, *Dead Body* 84–85,
314–315).

The question whether truth, especially the truth of gender,
inheres in the dead body is also central in Kleist's *Family
Schroffenstein*. Kleist's drama intertwines the search for truth and
the interrogation of the body with the concept of gender identity.[11] The nature and naturalness of signs are inextricably linked
with the nature and naturalness of gender.[12] But even though it
might seem as though the murder of the cross-dresser is used to
establish identity and to naturalize the gender hierarchy, this is
not actually the case. There simply is no remedy for the metaphysical quandaries that haunt Kleist's text.

The texts of Karoline von Günderrode present a contrasting
model to that of Schiller and Kleist. What Schiller affirms and
Kleist deconstructs, Günderrode rejects offhand. In her texts, the
female body is not used to stabilize cultural norms and values, nor
is it employed to naturalize sign systems. Rather, the death of the
cross-dressed woman is the result of a morally indifferent order
which does not reward good acts nor punish evil ones. In
Günderrode's texts, in which men are feminized while women

possess great courage and strength, the traditional gender dichotomy is invalid, and signs are always arbitrary.

Günderrode's attempt to solve the problems of the woman writer through the dissolution of rigid dichotomies was doomed to failure. This failure, however, was not due to a lack of artistic talent but to the biases of male-dominated scholarship. Her desire to blur the boundaries between fiction and reality was perverted by a reading tradition that defined her life as her "real" oeuvre. Günderrode's attempt to liquefy the male-female polarity was turned against her. Her "manly" work was denied recognition, and the author herself was accused of being unfeminine. In contrast to Schiller's and Kleist's works, Günderrode's texts are still virtually unknown. I believe that discussing Günderrode's work together with two dramas by canonical male authors will shed new light on the interrelation between body, gender, and truth.

FRIEDRICH SCHILLER's *Fiesco's Conspiracy at Genoa* (1783)

Fiesco's Conspiracy at Genoa is often considered inferior among the dramas of the young Schiller.[13] According to August Wilhelm Schlegel, it is "most wrong in its concept, the weakest in its effect" (II: 281); other critics have even called it a monstrosity (cf. Oellers 225). If asked to give reasons for their dislike of *Fiesco*, scholars often refer to the numerous inconsistencies and ambiguities that are said to deform this play (cf. Fowler 2), a problem which is further compounded by the existence of several different versions.[14] One might speculate whether the choice of words ("monstrosity," "ambiguity") suggests the kind of discomfort that is caused by the presence of a cross-dresser. However, even if the cross-dresser is the unnamed center of displeasure, ambiguity characterizes not only the gender order in the play but extends its dreaded influence onto the arenas of art, politics, and even personal identity.

The impossibility to make out Fiesco's "true" character along with his "true" politics forms the core around which the entire drama revolves. Scholars have pointed out that the "motives of role-play, game, mask, person, art, performance and their variants are part of the structural foundation of our drama" (Hinderer 254; see also Hecht 49; Graham; Ueding 40; Janz 39). The master of such performativity is Fiesco himself. Indeed, the most prominent trait of his character is his talent to perform ever-changing roles. He assumes new and discards old identities according to the circumstances and the needs of his respective partners (see Fowler 21; Bolten, *Schiller* 80). Schiller emphasizes Fiesco's chameleon-like nature by turning the readers themselves into victims of his intrigues and deceptions (cf. Meier 131). In the beginning, readers, just like Fiesco's wife, Leonore, are convinced that Fiesco is in love with Julia, the sister of his political opponent Gianettino. After long-winded misinformation and confusion, however, readers realize their error as they learn of Fiesco's love for his wife.

Interestingly, the confusion evident in Fiesco's personal life is replicated in the political realm.[15] Here, the intratextual inconsistencies are exacerbated by an intertextual one. To the contradictory images of Fiesco presented in the version of 1783, the stage version of 1784 adds yet another variant. The existence of two versions of the drama, which differ mostly in the design of the fifth act, has often been connected to Schiller's vacillation between two incompatible concepts of his hero (see Fowler 3). The Fiesco of the first version wants to usurp power and become ruler himself. The Fiesco of the stage version, on the other hand, proves loyal to the republican constitution of Genoa. In the first version, the republican Verrina kills the power-hungry Fiesco in order to prevent an autocracy and then subjects himself to the jurisdiction of the newly appointed ruler, Andreas Doria. Because Doria is re-instituted as legitimate authority, some scholars have wondered whether it is appropriate to classify Schiller's drama as a "republican tragedy" (see Phelps 442).[16] They read Verrina's submission as the reinstatement of an absolutist ruler, that is, as "bankruptcy of the revolution" (Hinderer 233). Opponents of this theory claim that Verrina defers authority to the legitimate political structure of which Doria is but a symbol.[17] But even if one adopts the latter reading, the central contradiction—that the aristocrat Andreas Doria is chosen as embodiment of the republican state—remains unresolved.[18] Moreover, Fiesco's sudden adherence to republican ideals in the stage version has also engendered criticism. His republican fervor in the fifth act is difficult to reconcile with the previous presentation of his character and has therefore been branded as implausible by many scholars.[19] Given this multiplicity of conflicting interpretations, it is likely that all attempts to recover Schiller's "true" politics will fail to produce an unambiguous result. This, however, does not imply that one should read Fiesco's political shadiness as a sign of Schiller's ideological arbitrariness (Bolten, *Schiller* 81). Rather, I suggest that it might be more fruitful to turn one's attention from Schiller's political beliefs to his identity politics. For hidden behind the conflict between republican façade and tyrannical intent is the muddy relation between performativity and self, and ultimately that between nature and art.

The complexity of Fiesco's role-playing becomes apparent when the artificially created surface of Fiesco's masks not only conceals his real intentions—whatever they are—but produces a reality of its own. Paradoxically, the powerful impact of Fiesco's masterfully staged performances surpasses by far the impression made by any authentic action (Graham 11). One need only compare the real and the fake attempt at Fiesco's life. The "real" killer, hired by Gianettino Doria to do away with his rival, fails miserably. But when Fiesco, who wins over the would-be assassin to his side, stages a feigned attack, he manages to reap great political benefit from this subterfuge. Ultimately, the relation between performance and reality is diametrically inverted as Fiesco claims authorship of events that happened without his doing. When the moor Hassan—a character whom Schiller invented freely—betrays Fiesco's planned coup d'état to Andreas Doria, Fiesco quickly regains the initiative. He maintains that he had only pretended to plan a coup so as to test the courage of his fellow citizens and thus lulls his opponents into a false sense of security. In Fiesco's hands, real facts vanish behind constructs even as constructs create real facts. But as Fiesco's artistic imagination triumphs over reality, his performance obscures his self. Though we are goaded on to look for the "real" Fiesco underneath the constructs, the idea of a "real" identity that underlies all performances becomes increasingly questionable.

It is remarkable that Fiesco is able to exercise such tight control over his artificial performances, but it is even more interesting to note precisely where and why he loses control. Though highly sophisticated in the political arena Fiesco has unwittingly—and as it turns out wrongly—counted on the truism that women will always be women. Thus, he is unaware that his wife, Leonore, has donned male clothing and joined the ranks of the conspirators as they fight in the streets.[20] The disappointment over her husband, who does not, as she had hoped, aspire to become Genoa's liberator but wants to be its tyrant, has driven her into a state of mad rapture. When she happens upon the corpse of the tyrannical Gianettino Doria, she puts on the purple coat and the helmet of the deceased.[21] Fiesco, mistaking her for Gianettino, stabs his own wife to death. Schiller's drama suggests that, when the primacy of performance and artifice begins to subvert the realm of gender, nature herself strikes back.

The murder of Leonore is generally recognized as the turning point of the drama, but the accounts of its significance vary considerably. Some scholars interpret Leonore's death as a symbol of Fiesco's self-destruction (Hinderer 272; Graham 32). Others claim that she is the "victim of her own passion" (Mansouri 44). I believe that one misses the importance of this scene if Leonore is reduced to a raging fury or to Fiesco's alter ego. Rather, I would like to suggest that Leonore's cross-dressing and her murder because of her cross-dressing contain in a nutshell the moral message of the drama. Leonore's male attire, as a symbol of the parting of performance and self, of nature and art, of signifier and signified, marks both the illness and the remedy that propel Schiller's *Fiesco*.

Schiller's stage directions, which call for a timid Leonore, who silently sneaks onto the stage, show clearly that the transformation of her outward appearance did not alter Leonore's inner being. Far from parading masculine bravado along with her male clothing, Leonore exhausts herself in wild raging without actually participating in the fighting. Her martial appearance stands in stark contrast to her demeanor, which is still motivated by her love for her husband. The responsibility for this rift between inside and outside, which Leonore embodies to the highest degree, must be laid at Fiesco's door. But while Fiesco's intrigues gave rise to the dissociation of appearance and reality, it is Leonore's death that effectively puts an end to it. Lützeler has suggested that Leonore's tragic end exposes Fiesco as "the uncommitted and egoistic aristocrat whom he pretended to imitate" (17). As she dies, the reader realizes that not even the murder of his wife can put a halt to Fiesco's insatiable craving for power. If, after the initial confusion, readers had started to believe in Fiesco's loving nature and political liberalism, they must witness that what initially seemed to be a performance now appears to be Fiesco's real self. Thus, the death of the female cross-dresser is both the result of and the punishment for Fiesco's web of lies. The "natural" order of signifier and signified, of appearance and reality, is reestablished over her body because, in Leonore's case, the performance has not eroded the self.[22] Schiller's drama seems to suggest that, though men may lie, women's bodies will ultimately tell the truth. But the truth about what? Significantly, the reader never learns whether Fiesco always was what he turned out to be in the end (Lützeler 18) or whether he succumbed to the power of his own performance and became his own role (Kieffer 128). Though death unveils Leonore's true identity, Fiesco's "real" self remains as elusive as it ever was.

Rather than continue the search for Fiesco's true self, we might also retrace our steps and ask why the rift between appearance and reality, between signifier and signified, is so grave an offense to begin with? I believe the answer lies in the fact that Fiesco's love of performance, his fabrication of a false appearance, is uncannily reminiscent of the process of artistic creation (Kieffer 126).[23] One might even claim that Fiesco is a play about art (Graham 13–14). I have already mentioned the overall significance of metaphors of theater and play-acting. Towards the end of the drama this theme is intensified as Fiesco gathers his co-conspirators under the pretext of a comedic performance. He then proceeds to plan the coup d'état like a theatrical production, in which everybody is assigned a certain part.[24] Schiller's revolutionary is a stage manager. Interestingly, Schiller also discusses the similarities between the profession of a politician and that of an artist or author in other texts. In the following description of his own writing, Schiller endows the artist with the traits of a powerful ruler:[25] "Saint and solemn was always the calm, great moment in the theater when the hearts of so many hundreds, as though moved by the omnipotent beat of a magical rod, tremble according to the fantasy of a poet [. . .] where I lead the soul of the spectator by the reins and can throw it as I please like a ball towards heaven or towards hell."[26] Judging from this description, the skills of the demagogue Fiesco, whose rhetorical might holds sway over the hearts of his listeners, are identical to those of the masterful poet, whose magical rod governs the souls of his spectators. Furthermore, the fact that Fiesco's performance is more powerful than any "real" reality also reflects convictions of the author Schiller:[27] "One single great surge of passion, which I bring about in the breast of my spectators through daring invention, in my view offsets the strictest historical accuracy."[28] Such parallels between the author Schiller and the tyrant Fiesco render an inquiry into the reasons for Fiesco's death even more imperative. If we refuse to interpret Fiesco's death as the self-punishment of the author, we must assume that Schiller intends to set his own concept of art off from a "false" art, represented by the performer Fiesco.

Though Schiller's drama is mainly concerned with political intrigues, it contains a scene in which Fiesco and the painter Romano—a character who is not mentioned in any of Schiller's sources—discuss the merits of art. Surprisingly, the "artist" Fiesco, who owes his power to role-playing and rhetoric, is a detractor of art. He attacks Romano for the feebleness of his creations: "You stand defiant because you feign *life* on *dead* cloth and immortalize great actions with little effort [. . .] You overthrow tyrants on canvas—you yourself are a miserable slave? You free republics with your brush—yet cannot break your own chains? (*Full and commanding*) Go!—Your work is an illusion—*appearance* give way to *action*."[29] In his diatribe against art, Fiesco privileges action over appearance even though his own actions consist in the art of creating appearances. Given that Fiesco is so curiously unaware of the source of his own power, it is only logical that he is defeated by his own methods. In the murder of Leonore, reality momentarily gives way to appearance as Fiesco falls prey to the semblance that his own intrigues have unwittingly brought about.[30] Not knowing that he himself is an artist, Fiesco loses control of his oeuvre.

But the scene about art has yet another purpose. By presenting Fiesco's response to Romano's painting as a litmus test of his political probity, Schiller exposes the chasm between Fiesco's and Romano's practices of art. The staunch republican Verrina, who is unsure about Fiesco's true intentions, had hoped that Fiesco would declare his republican convictions when confronted with an artistic depiction of Roman virtue. At first, his plan seemed to fail. While Verrina, carried away by Romano's portrait of Virginia, begins to strike out at the painting in order to vent his hatred of tyrants, Fiesco, unimpressed by the artwork, maintains his cool, Epicurean composure. Later, however, when Fiesco speaks of his plans, Verrina detects his tyrannical intent behind the republican façade and resolves to kill him. Thus, Romano's painting is the site at which Fiesco's true beliefs are exposed after all. By contrasting Fiesco and Romano, Schiller presents the central thesis of the play. While Romano's art grants privileged access to truth, Fiesco's art is separated from virtue and therefore falls prey to the appearance that it helped to create.[31] In this way, Schiller manages to reinstate his claim to the "magical rod" while simultaneously detoxifying its manipulative potential. According to this logic, the power of art cannot but do good. For art, if used for immoral purposes, such as self-aggrandizement and the appropriation of tyrannical power, will necessarily self-destruct.

In order to give the appearance of naturalness to his argumentation, Schiller employs the contemporary gender dichotomy.[32]

The dissolution of Fiesco's moral integrity is accompanied by the disintegration of the traditional gender roles. Leonore's femininity is obscured as Fiesco's depravity reveals itself. The fact that Fiesco turns out to be a wolf in sheepskin, who seeks to overthrow the republican order under the pretext of its restoration, leads to a reversal of all values. But even as Fiesco's performances deconstruct all confidence in the ideas of self and truth, the belief in the stability of identity and truth is re-introduced over Leonore's dead body. At the bedrock of female biology, all lies and intrigues must end.

The reversal of all values is most visible in the perversion of the gender dichotomy, with Leonore's cross-dressing as its crassest manifestation. But reversal of values can also be detected in the transposition of the categories of private and public that permeates the entire play.[33] From the very beginning, the happiness of Fiesco's marriage is identified with the welfare of Genoa.[34] The concatenation of public and private also motivates the behavior of Verrina, whose daughter Berta was raped by the depraved Gianettino. To Verrina, the revenge for the violation of Berta's innocence is synonymous with Genoa's liberation from the yoke of tyranny.[35] Given this close association, it comes as no surprise that the transgressions in the private sphere—the supposed adultery and the rape—bring about the reversal of the gender dichotomy in the public sphere. In the 1783 version, both Berta and Leonore don men's clothing and join the fight.[36] But Berta's fiancé, Bourgognino, who, unlike Fiesco, has not lost his moral integrity, recognizes his beloved in spite of her cross-dressing. By killing Gianettino, he achieves both public and private revenge. Fiesco, on the other hand, whose craving for power signals the absence of a moral consciousness, can no longer see through false appearances and loses his private happiness to his political ambitions. The fact that Leonore wears a purple coat when Fiesco stabs her further emphasizes the perversion of all moral values. Leonore, "the personified republican conscience" (Fuhrmann 335), is bedecked with the symbol of tyranny. Significantly, the purple coat also brings about Fiesco's own demise. Verrina kills

Fiesco by tearing at his coat, thus causing the latter to fall and drown: "Now when the purple falls, the duke must follow" (IV: 120).

In the character of Fiesco, Schiller not only punishes the power-hungry politician, but also the aspiring artist whose work is not committed to the pursuit of truth. By depicting Fiesco's immoral performances and intrigues as the causes of his final destruction, Schiller establishes a seemingly unproblematic harmony of art and truth.[37] By linking art and truth to gender, Schiller employed the naturalized gender hierarchy for the stabilization of societal norms and values. As signifier and signified become one in Leonore's dead body, the harmony of art and truth is presented as natural and unquestionable fact.[38] Or is it? Clearly, the stunning success of Fiesco's previous performances belies the unproblematic nature of this harmony.[39] It is precisely because art as performance and as rhetoric is not inevitably tied to truth that Fiesco's schemes were possible in the first place.

Schiller's proverbially conservative concept of femininity has been pointed out by feminist critics.[40] Other scholars have suggested that the female characters of Schiller's dramas explode the restrictive gender ideology of his epistolary statements (Fuhrmann 333). I believe that it would be difficult to maintain that Leonore is a case in point. Neither Leonore's republican convictions nor her exemplary virtue and loyalty transgress the boundaries of conventional femininity.[41] Rather, these positive qualities turn her into a symbolic figurehead. Moreover, it is by leaving the private sphere, woman's proper place, that Leonore meets an untimely death (see Mansouri 75). The fact that Leonore is wearing male clothing only underlines her inability to act manly.

The same logic, which confirms that, no matter what confusions their male partners bring about, women will always remain women, also informs Kleist's Family Schroffenstein. Kleist, too, employs "natural" femininity for the naturalization of societal norms and values so that "the (only seemingly) accidental is replaced by an ethically founded causality" (Meier 128). But unlike Schiller, Kleist consciously undermines his own agenda.

HEINRICH VON KLEIST's *The Family Schroffenstein*

From his Kant crisis to his preference for "as if" constructions
(Altenhofer 45), the Kleistian trauma of the epistemological inac-
cessibility of the world has become commonplace in scholarship
about this fascinating and unusual eighteenth-century author.[42]
Kleist's textual universe is haunted by the anxiety that all knowledge will ultimately remain uncertain. The fear that the truth not
only about the constitution of the universe and the nature of moral
law but also about the core of one's personal identity can never be
grasped informs many of Kleist's dramas and stories.

To Kleist, however, unattainability does not equal undesirabil-
ity. Even though the Kleistian world is one "where we cannot
decide whether that which we call truth, really is truth, or
whether it merely appears to be so" (to Wilhelmine von Zenge,
March 22, 1801, *Briefe* 163), Kleist's texts are driven by the desperate and often ferocious desire to stabilize cognition and prove
the validity of "natural" moral laws. In order to do so, they attempt
to deduce the moral teleology of the world from its physical facts.
More often than not, the body is singled out as privileged signifier and guarantor of stability, certainty, and truth.[43] One need
only think of the numerous instances of swooning, blushing, and
stammering in which the body seems to promise access to the
truth of the Other. But Kleistian characters are not content to
limit their search for truth to the surface of the body. When in
dire straits, only the sacrifice of the body can restore order and
stability. In *Hermann's Battle* [Die Hermannsschlacht, 1808; published by Tieck in 1821], for example, the bodies of Hermann's
sons are pledged to guarantee the truth of his message, and the
despoiled dead body of the rape victim Wally becomes the instrument with which national unity is restored.[44] As the second
example indicates, it is especially the female body that is called
upon as the last reliable repository of truth. Again and again,
Kleist's "nostalgia for a preverbal, pre-discursive realm" (Cullens
and von Mücke 3), for a truth that has not yet been corrupted by

language, attaches itself to the female body. Thus, one might be tempted to conclude that if Kleist's metaphysical arch does not tumble it is not because all stones are falling[45] but because it rests on the female body of the caryatid.

However, such a conclusion would fail to do justice to Kleist's philosophical sophistication. Just like Kleist is no advocate of a Rousseauistic return to nature (Horn 126), he is also unwilling to endow the body with the task of redemption. My reading of Kleist's *The Family Schroffenstein* will show that, even though Kleist's first drama appears to take recourse to the body in order to stabilize meaning and identity, it is ultimately aware of the futileness of such an endeavor.[46] In the end, the hoped-for naturalness of the body turns out to be nothing but another cultural sign. The empirically given body and the socially constructed body turn out to be inseparable after all (Kelly and von Mücke 3). In order to understand Kleist's epistemological quest, it is again helpful to turn to the motif of cross-dressing. The figure of the cross-dresser, more precisely the death of the cross-dresser, functions as a linchpin in the conflicted relationships between body and text, nature and culture, and truth and gender.

Kleist's first drama *The Family Schroffenstein* has come down to us in three different versions.[47] The first version, entitled *The Family Thierrez* [Die Familie Thierrez] is merely a rough sketch of the plot. The second manuscript, *The Family Ghonorez* [Die Familie Ghonorez], bears traces of several stages of revision. Some of the alterations, even though rejected by Kleist, entered the printed version of 1803, entitled *The Family Schroffenstein*, whose authenticity must thus remain questionable. While some scholars assume that the editors Ludwig Wieland and Heinrich Geßner changed Kleist's manuscript without prior authorization, it is now commonly accepted that the variations are mostly due to mistakes by typesetters and copyists (Wichmann 53).

The Family Schroffenstein is a drama about lovers whose families are engaged in a feud. Kleist's lovers, unlike Shakespeare's *Romeo and Juliet*, belong to different branches of the same clan, the Rossitz

and the Warwand line of the Schroffenstein dynasty. The cause of
the conflict between the families is an old testamentary contract
which decrees that, should one of the family lines become extinct,
the other line stands to receive possession of all property, thus fos-
tering an atmosphere of mistrust between the two households. New
fuel is added to this fire of hatred as two Warwand servants are found
next to the corpse of Peter, the youngest son of Rupert of Rossitz.
Under torture one of the two pronounces the name of Sylvester,
the master of Warwand. Rupert, already convinced of Sylvester's
guilt in the death of his son, sends a messenger to Warwand to
declare war. Sylvester, frightened by the news, suffers a fainting spell
during which his men kill the messenger. Meanwhile a meeting
between Johann of Rossitz and Agnes, Sylvester's daughter, is mis-
interpreted, and Johann is wounded and incarcerated. Rupert now
wants revenge and maliciously kills Jeronimus, a Schroffenstein of
the line Wyg, who had been sent by Sylvester in order to mediate
between the two houses. When Rupert learns that his oldest son
Ottokar is engaged in a clandestine love affair with Agnes, he
makes preparations to kill Agnes. But Ottokar anticipates him. In
order to protect his beloved, he and Agnes exchange their clothes.
Rupert, mistaking his own son for Agnes, stabs Ottokar to death.
Sylvester, wanting to take revenge for Agnes, kills his cross-dressed
daughter. Only Agnes' blind grandfather Sylvius recognizes the true
identity of the two corpses. Finally, Rupert's pain over the loss of
his son Ottokar is aggravated by the news that his son Peter was
not murdered but drowned in a brook in the forest.

A number of critics consider *The Family Schroffenstein* an inferior drama. Peter André Block refers to it as the "product of a
madman" (357) and Peter Szondi calls it a "poetic failure" (97).
Interestingly, many scholars connect this failure with the cross-
dressing scene and the following murders. Hinrich Seeba, for
example, refers to Kleist's attempts to revise the last act as evidence of its failed design (69–70). Such a negative evaluation of
the last act, however, is completely contrary to its importance for
Kleist's own creative process. According to Ernst von Pfuehl,
Kleist wove the entire drama around the exchange of clothes:

One day the strange scene of undressing in the final act came to his [Kleist's, EK] mind, purely as a scene, and as the situation attracted him, he wrote it down like a fantasy without context. Then it occurred to him that he could weave it together with other threads of a story, maybe also with an accidentally discovered plot and so the entire tragedy developed gradually around this scene.[48]

George Howe names Wieland's A *Powder Against Sleeplessness, A Dramatic Story* [Ein Pulver wider die Schlaflosigkeit, in einer dramatischen Erzählung] as a possible source for the "accidentally discovered" plot (150). Wieland later developed this theme in his *Novella Without Title* [Novelle ohne Titel, 1803]. The young Kleist's predilection for Wieland as well as the fact that Wieland ended his story with the remark that it would be an excellent subject for a drama corroborate this assumption. Furthermore, Wieland's story, too, relies on the motif of a cross-dressed woman.[49] Given that Kleist's cross-dressing scene had been written before the rest of the plot, it is possible that it was this common motif that prompted him to adopt Wieland's idea of a testamentary contract as the missing link for his own drama. A comparison with the earlier versions of *The Family Schroffenstein* demonstrates that Kleist's original choice of Spain as location can also be traced to Wieland's story. Following the advice of his friends, Kleist later changed the location to medieval Swabia.

The testamentary contract—and the Rousseauistic concept of the Fall of Man due to worldly properties and possessions (Fischer 480), for which the contract is said to stand—was not Kleist's only or even primary preoccupation in conceiving his drama. Although the contract plays a prominent role in the first act, it is hardly mentioned afterwards. Rather, as the genesis of the drama suggests and as further analysis will bear out, it is the question of personal, and hence gendered, identity that is at the heart of the drama.

That questions of gender are of great importance in Kleist's early drama is even more evident if we remember that Kleist

started working on *The Family Schroffenstein* in 1801 in Paris; he
finished it during his stay on the Swiss Aare-island. His companion on this journey to Paris was his half-sister Ulrike, who was
wont to travel in men's clothing. However, it is not only Ulrike's
cross-dressing that emerges as an important reason for the author's
interest in gender-bending.[50] Rather, his sister's entire being stood
in stark contrast to everything that Kleist deemed proper in a
young woman. Puzzled by his sister's "manly" behavior, Kleist
seeks to reconcile Ulrike's heroic soul with her female body:

> I would have been very happy during the journey on the
> Rhine if—if—oh, madam, there is no greatness in the world of
> which Ulrike is not capable, a noble, wise, generous girl, a
> heroic soul in a female body, and I would have to have no part
> in all of this if I did not feel this with all my heart. But—a
> human being can have much power, give much, it is still not
> always possible, as Goethe says, to rest in his bosom—She is a
> girl who writes and acts orthographically, plays and thinks in
> time, a being that has nothing of woman but the hips, and
> never has she felt how sweet a handshake is—but I hope you
> do not misunderstand me—? O there is nobody in this world
> whom I honor as much as my sister. But what mistake has
> nature committed when it made her a being that is neither
> man nor woman, and vacillates like an amphibian between the
> two genders?[51]

Kleist is both impressed and frightened by Ulrike's courage, level-
headedness, and determination, all of which he considers unfeminine qualities. During their journey to Paris, he tries to fend off
his insecurity by engaging in a frantic search for Ulrike's "feminine" traits. And to Kleist, the privileged site for such an endeavor
is the body. Thus, when Ulrike's actions attest to her "manly"
spirit, when she attends lectures in men's clothing, or when she
is the only one who keeps her cool when a storm turns a family
boat trip into a dangerous adventure, Heinrich recalls Ulrike's
bodily weakness and takes note of the "contradiction between will

and strength" (*Briefe* 202). Again, the body is called upon as the
last resort that can guarantee the gender identity of his half-sister. But the fact that Kleist feels compelled to repeat this manoeu-
vre over and over again is ample evidence of its unsatisfactory
nature. Moreover, what if it is precisely this body, hidden under
men's clothing, that cannot be identified as female?

Kleist's experience with his sister Ulrike's gender obfuscation
certainly contributed to how the author fashioned the cross-dressing scene in *The Family Schroffenstein*. During their journey to
Paris, Ulrike von Kleist and her brother encountered a blind flute
player, who, unaware of her male outfit, was not fooled by Ulrike's
masquerade. The parallel to the blind Sylvius, the first character
to recognize the true identity of his cross-dressed granddaughter,
is obvious. Kleist's fascination with this scene was motivated by
his ardent wish that, by interrogating the body, he could snatch
from it the absolute truth of a person's identity and gender. Thus,
his quest for truth is inseparably linked with an inquiry into the
naturalness of gender. In *The Family Schroffenstein*, Kleist probes
the epistemological consequences of a transgression against the
"natural" boundaries of the gender dichotomy.

From the very beginning, Kleist's drama toys with the idea of
a natural order, from which man's moral order derives its validity.
Both natural and moral order are then linked to the truth of gender. In the first act, Rupert, convinced that his relative Sylvester
is the murderer of his son, believes that this atrocious crime has
destroyed the natural order. He calls upon his wife Eustache to
take part in his revenge. When Eustache refers to her feminine
tenderness, he objects:

> I know, Eustache, men are avengers—
> You are the wailing mourners of nature.
> But nothing more of nature.
> It is a sweet delightful fairytale from childhood,
> Related to humanity by the poets, its nurses.
> Trust, innocence, loyalty, love,
> Religion, fear of the Gods are like

The animals who talk.—The bond itself
The holy one, of blood relation, is torn, [. . .]
And because everything has changed, humans
Have changed their nature with animals, change
You, too, wife, your nature.[52]

Here, the destruction of the moral order is portrayed as inseparable from the disintegration of the gender code. A comparison of
the printed version with its predecessors suggests that the link
between natural order and "natural" gender that Rupert invokes
was of some importance to Kleist. In *The Family Ghonorez*, Elmire,
later named Eustache, is portrayed as a cold, calculating, and
vengeful character—all attributes that do not conform to stereo-
typical notions of proper femininity. Thus, one might claim that
the transformation of the harsh wife into a soft, conciliatory character is connected to the desired concatenation between natural
order and "natural" gender. Seen in this light, Eustache's feminine nature functions as a guarantee for the intactness of the natural order; an order which, as the reader later learns, has not yet
been despoiled by the murder of a relative. Rupert's inability to
appraise the facts correctly would then be a result of his moral
blindness. However, accepting moral blindness as the root cause
of the misunderstanding would be tantamount to falling for
Rupert's flawed logic. Superficially, Rupert's error consists in
the failure to recognize the intactness of the natural order.
Fundamentally and epistemologically, it consists in the problematic assumption that there is such a direct correlation between
nature, natural gender, and moral law to begin with. But Kleist's
first act presents a world in which any such concatenation is conspicuously absent. Indeed, in the first act of *The Family
Schroffenstein*, it is a deviation from the "natural" gender order
that accounts for the intactness of the moral order. Peter was not
murdered precisely because Sylvester is not an avenger—as
Rupert claims all men "naturally" are—but a conciliatory neighbor and concerned father. He might even be characterized as
effeminate. Far from plotting revenge, Sylvester is first introduced

as swatting flies. He occupies himself with gardening and swoons when overwhelmed by his enemy's accusations. Moreover, Sylvester, unlike Rupert, does not confuse natural order with moral law. When Aldöbern wrongly accuses Sylvester of murder, he replies:

> —Look, if you told me,
> The rivers flowed uphill besides their banks
> And collected on mountain peaks
> In lakes, then I would—I would want to believe you;
> But if you tell me that I killed a child
> The child of the cousin—[53]

To the wise Sylvester, the order of nature and the laws of human morality are two distinctly different categories. Changes in one order do not affect the organization of the other.

The second scene in the third act provides a further example of how *The Family Schroffenstein* first posits a connection between gender and truth that it then proceeds to deconstruct. In trying to establish the whereabouts of his messenger and his illegitimate son Johann, Rupert is confronted with contradictory reports. Eustache claims that the messenger was beaten to death, while Santing wrongly informs his master that Johann was killed. As Rupert identifies unfounded rumors with femininity—

> RUPERT: Beaten to death, you say?
> EUSTACHE: Yes so say the people.
> RUPERT: The people—a people of women? [Erschlagen, sagst du?
> EUSTACHE: Ja so spricht das Volk.
> RUPERT: Das Volk—ein Volk von Weibern wohl, 1503–1504]

—the question of truth is again confounded with that of true gender:

> RUPERT: Who of you two is the woman?
> SANTING: I say Johann [was killed, EK]; and if it is the messen-

ger, well, so clothe the woman with an armor and me with a
woman's skirt [. . .]
SANTING: Here is the messenger, master, he can tell you
whether I am a woman or not.[54]

The reader, knowing that Johann is still alive, is called upon to
take Santing for a woman. Thus, unlike Rupert, the reader realizes that the gender dichotomy cannot possibly function as the
foundation for epistemologically correct statements. Rupert, on
the other hand, continues to confuse the gender order with moral
law. Consequently, and in spite of his inquisitive interrogation,
he learns neither that Johann is still alive nor that Sylvester had
no part in the murder of the messenger. Interestingly, both Rupert
and Santing define gender not as a natural entity but as a category that has yet to be determined. Does Kleist suggest that it is
Rupert and Santing's alienation from the "natural" order, manifest in their inability to read gender correctly, that leads to their
distortion of basic facts? Does Eustache's superior knowledge signify that woman is a vessel of truth? Although Kleist teases his
readers with these options, a careful reading of The Family
Schroffenstein suggests that in Kleist's drama truth is not distributed according to gender lines. In the Warwand household, it
is Sylvester's wife, Gertrude, who is full of suspicion and unwilling to face the truth whereas both Sylvius and Sylvester are portrayed as conciliatory and trustful.

The gender confusion reaches a peak in the fifth act when
Ottokar takes advantage of the general chaos in order to protect
his beloved Agnes. Aware that his father is roaming through the
forest in search of Agnes, Ottokar betakes himself to the cave that
has long been his and Agnes' secret meeting place. He finds Agnes
and attempts to calm her nerves by narrating the fantastic tale of
their future wedding. As he describes the wedding night, he takes
off Agnes' coat and wraps his own coat around her. Then, taking
her hat and replacing it with his helmet, he urges Agnes to flee
while he himself dons Agnes' clothes and awaits the arrival of his
father. Tragically, however, Ottokar's plan effects the very oppo-

site of what he had intended. Both Ottokar and Agnes die through the hands of their fathers. Interestingly, it is Ottokar's consciously devised perversion of nature, embodied in the exchange of gender roles, that brings about the final catastrophe. Again, we might be tempted to conclude that for Kleist the illegibility of the gender order must necessarily lead to the impossibility of finding truth. Or does it?

Some critics have interpreted the exchange of clothing as a positive utopia. To Seeba, Kleist's cave transvestism represents "a mystery play of reconciled identity" (92). To Zons, it symbolizes "the political coup of the overthrow of the dynasty- and gender-hierarchy" (92). However, a reading of the cave scene as a positive utopia of a fusion of identities must ignore the fact that Ottokar and Agnes are not equal partners. Ottokar does not share his knowledge with Agnes but uses his poetic fantasies to manipulate her. Similarly, Ingeborg Harms' interpretation that Ottokar and Agnes transcend death in their willingness to sacrifice themselves is problematic (294). A textual reference, that Harms herself points out, suggests that there is no resurrection in Kleist's drama: when visiting the cave where Jesus is buried, the biblical Maria finds the grave empty. Agnes, however, after remarking that "the cave is empty, as you say," discovers Ottokar in it (2553–2554). Far from portraying a positive utopia, the cave scene embodies the martyrdom of self-inflicted alienation. It is "the real and final fall into the difference of reality and appearance" (Schulte 89–90).

The inability to see the truth is taken to its extremes when neither fathers nor mothers recognize the true identity of their disguised children. But while both parents mourn at the site of the wrong body, Agnes' blind grandfather Sylvius realizes that a mistake has been made. Does Kleist suggest to his readers that, in spite of deceitful appearances and in the midst of utter confusion, truth—and truth is again the truth of gender—can be discerned by touching the body? It is of interest to note that the murder of Rupert's younger son is also solved through the truth that his body tells. The old Ursula, a witch-like character, had cut off a finger from the body of the drowned boy. In the last scene, when presented with this severed body part, Eustache recognizes a characteristic pock mark and identifies the finger as that of her son. In fact, allusions to the truth-telling power of the body permeate the entire drama. Rupert, looking at his mirror image in the river, perceives the face of a devil, and Sylvester's swooning indicates that he is innocent of murder. Indeed, one might wonder why Kleist's drama is fraught with so many misunderstandings if the body tells the truth so loquaciously.

Although Kleist's play repeatedly teases its readers with the idea of the body as a vessel of truth, it is never wholly committed to it. In fact, readers are alerted to the problematic nature of bodily signs at the very beginning of the play. The origin of the entire Schroffenstein feud can be traced to the misinterpretation of a bodily state: when the sick Rupert was wrongly taken for dead (188–195), Sylvester laid claim to the estate. All further misunderstandings follow from this. Moreover, even if bodily symptoms are diagnosed correctly, their meaning is anything but straightforward. Agnes' swooning, for example, is caused by fear but is mistaken for a reaction to physical pain. Sylvester's vomiting is a reaction to spoilt food, but is believed to be the result of poisoning. Thus, at the origin of all confusion in the play, and of the split in Kleist's world, is not the psychosomatic dyslexia of the characters but the precarious relationship between signifier and signified.

In his essay on bodily signs and legal codes, Manfred Schneider claims that Kleist has strayed from the tradition of the Christian councils, which was guided by the belief in a strict juridical relation between letter and spirit. Schneider maintains that Kleist is part of a "Jewish" tradition that does not believe in any preordained assignment of signifier and signified. According to this tradition, signs can be read adequately only if put in their proper context. The meaning of signs can never be separated "from the surface of their contiguous relationships" (Schneider 125). Thus, Sylvester's name, pronounced under torture by his servant (235), may signify Sylvester's guilt or a last attempt to exonerate an innocent master. The fact that Sylvester's servants are found near the corpse of Peter also has no intrinsic meaning. Even the finger of the dead child can be interpreted only if inserted into a narrative context.

In Kleist's drama, disjointed signs lead to wrong conclusions. Meaning can be established only if the isolated signifiers are re-contextualized correctly. However, there seems to be one exception to this rule. When Agnes and Ottokar meet in the forest, Agnes accepts water from Ottokar's hands although she believes it to be poisoned. Offering her body as a pledge for the truth of her affection, she is willing to stake her life on Ottokar's word. Thus, one might be tempted to conclude that Agnes' body becomes the new agnus dei that heals the breach caused by Rupert's perversion of the holy communion in Act I. Moreover, whatever its consequences, Agnes' action is the logical result of her general inability to separate body and spirit. Her firm belief in the unity of body and identity is already evident when Agnes first appears on the scene. Mourning the death of her brother, Agnes takes no comfort in the words of the priest, who assures her that her brother is well even though his body is in the grave. For Agnes, such a split of bodily and spiritual well-being is not possible:

> Just as I have to laugh ere I want to if somebody
> Proves to be ridiculous so I must cry
> If somebody dies [. . .]
> Granted the priest says
> He is not in the grave.—No, let me
> Say it right, he is in the grave but—Oh
> I cannot repeat it to you. In short,
> I see where he is, on the hill.[55]

Unwilling to separate her brother's corpse from his soul, Agnes is also prepared to sacrifice her own body in order to answer "Kleist's cardinal question regarding the truth of the feelings of the other" (Neumann, von Klein 160), an act that Hugo Dittberner calls "the

horrible initiation of the future through the sacrifice of a woman"
(17). But if Agnes' sacrifice in Act III initiates the future, what
is the purpose of her death? Should we conclude that it is only
when this child of nature is alienated from her (cross-dressed)
body that the catastrophe can ensue? Does Agnes live in perfect
harmony with her natural gender until she becomes the weak-
willed object of Ottokar's gender manipulation (Stephens,
Dramas and Stories 24)? Does her death restore the "natural"
order? After all, Agnes' alienation, that is, the disassociation of
body and identity, is brought about by the agency of a man.
Ottokar not only induces a trance-like state in Agnes but also
takes off her coat and clothes her with his. And it is precisely
because of Agnes' "natural" unity of body and identity that
Ottokar has to resort to artfulness in order to take from Agnes the
outer trappings of her gender. Contrary to Ottokar's claim that he
is "the helpmate of nature" (l. 2486), who restores a primeval
state, Ottokar's "allmähliche Verfertigung des Geschlechts beim
Anziehen" leads to the greatest imaginable alienation from
nature. However, to conclude that Kleist posits the existence of
a "natural" femininity that is destroyed by man's interference
would be rash. Rather, any such interpretation must take into
account Kleist's tendency toward "ideological self-deconstruc-
tion" (Labhardt 162). Kleist's *The Family Schroffenstein* questions
not only the "naturalness" of nature and gender but also the
assumption that death is a privileged moment of truth.

Although Agnes is portrayed as a child of nature, her "natural" instincts are not always correct. Initially, Agnes is convinced
that the Rossitz relatives are her enemies and must be shunned.
Innocence, so it would appear, is not "naturally" conciliatory.
Moreover, one might claim it is not Agnes' body that is the foundation of trust between Ottokar and the young maiden, but the
lengthy conversation between the two lovers that succeeds in dis-
pelling all doubt. More importantly, given that Agnes and
Ottokar have deduced the facts correctly and could have com-
municated them to their families, their death is not the necessary
foundation of a better order but a meaningless sacrifice. In fact,

their dead bodies do not even tell the truth anymore. Interestingly, Kleist's stage directions for the last scene demand that Agnes be equipped with two sets of clothing. Thus, when Ottokar claims to remove the alien cover and restore original nature, he is merely taking off Agnes' coat (Überkleid). Consequently, it remains undecided whether Sylvius recognizes the true identity of the dead because he touches the actual bodies or because he touches the first set of clothing hidden underneath Ottokar's coat and Agnes' Überkleid. In the end, the hoped-for naturalness may be nothing but another cultural sign, enacting an infinite deferral in which the truth of the body will always remain hidden.

In the fifth act of The Family Schroffenstein, Kleist distances himself from the Christian tradition in which the body of the crucified stands in for the truth of his message. Agnes and Ottokar's deaths do not authenticate "the word turned flesh" (W. Kittler 64) nor do they function as foundation for a new and better order. Indeed, the joy of having deprived his readers of a clear-cut solution in spite of all appearances to the contrary might also explain why Kleist and his friends could not help but break out in laughter when reading the final scene. Although Kleist may have wished that personal identity, "that unspeakable being," could be spoken by the (dead) body, he also made fun of such a "stupid thought." Kleist was acutely aware that such an epistemological "emergency brake" must remain unsatisfactory because the authentication of truth is identical with the death of the testifying subject. In order to discover the truth about each other, humans need to rely on communication. The body in and of itself is an unreliable agent of truth. Kleist may have wished to send his heart in a package, but he knew very well that such a gift would never do.

If Kleist in his Familie Schroffenstein strives to introduce woman as "the medium of divine nature" (Labhardt 120–121), this attempt is undermined by his doubts as to whether moral laws could ever be naturally given. It is this doubtfulness that he has in common with his contemporary Karoline von Günderrode, whose texts Mora and Darthula According to Ossian are also haunted by the absence of a moral teleology.

KAROLINE VON GÜNDERRODE'S Mora AND Darthula According to Ossian

The reception of Karoline von Günderrode's works has long been impeded by a tendency to neglect her texts while focusing on the author's life as her real "oeuvre."[56] Repeatedly, Günderrode's literary achievements were interpreted in light of her spectacular suicide.[57] While Foldenauer's claim that some critics "even counted the daggers featured in her poems" (86) may be exaggerated, biographism has surely contributed to the marginalization of Günderrode's philosophically and aesthetically significant oeuvre.[58] Some critics, for example, looked down upon Günderrode's artistic accomplishments—"she was not an early genius" (Drewitz, "Günderode" 99)—but claimed that her life provided ample compensation for the alleged absence of momentous works. Others, even more problematically, celebrate the author's demise as the fulfillment of a work that was preoccupied with death. Heuschele, for example, proclaims in a sweeping statement that Günderrode's "sacrifice of self-chosen death, so unlike every weak and cowardly suicide, unites her life and poetry into a whole" (40).

Aware of the dangers of such biographism, the following analysis walks the tightrope. Though rejecting the substitution of life for oeuvre, it takes into account Günderrode's seemingly similar desire for a fusion of life and fiction. An analysis that chooses to ignore Günderrode's deliberate blurring of the boundaries between fiction and life deprives itself of the chance to understand one of the few strategies through which an eighteenth-century woman writer could cope with the constraints that her society imposed on her. In her epistolary novel Goethe's Correspondence with a Child [Goethes Briefwechsel mit einem Kinde], Bettina Brentano-von Arnim describes how the substitution of pleasurable fantasies for an unsatisfactory reality offered women a way out of the disappointments of their daily lives. In the fantasy world of the two young women, dream journeys made up for actual confinement:

> We planned a journey, we invented the paths and adventures, we wrote everything down, we imagined everything, our imagi-nation was so busy that we could not have experienced it more intensely in reality, often we read the diary of our invented journey and rejoiced in our favorite adventures that we had experienced, and the inventions turned into memories whose relations continued into the present. Of that which happened in real life we made no mention.[59]

Where reality is found wanting, happiness can only be achieved by blurring the boundary between reality and imagination. The recurrence of this motif in Günderrode's work certainly attests to the fact that, like her friend Brentano-von Arnim, she considered the transgression and obfuscation of boundaries a viable escape from the distortions of her life. Moreover, Günderrode attributed a transformative power to poetry itself, which, as she believed, was capable of transcending the boundary between matter and mind: "Poetry is the transformation of ideas into bodies, of ideals into reality, philosophy also transforms bodies into ideas, return of the real to the ideal" (qtd. in Hopp and Preitz 289).

Günderrode's fascination with Schelling's philosophy, docu-mented by the numerous excerpts from his work in her study book, must also be understood in this context. Rather than pro-viding syllogistic means to bridge the gap between individuality and universality, between matter and mind, between essence and form, Schelling's system convinced Günderrode of the theoreti-cal impossibility of such dualities:

> Our imaginations would be absolutely empty, mere forms if there were no corresponding things. Consequently, things without imaginations are not only unthinkable for us, and

imaginations of things without these things are nothing, empty
terms without essence, in order for things to have reality for
us, and in order for our imaginations to have reality, philosophy searches for their absolute unity, the identity of object and
subject, but she cannot choose any other way to this goal but
that of self-contemplation.[60]

Read carefully, this quote shows that the price Günderrode has to
pay for the desired unity of imagination and reality, of object and
subject, is very high. Such unity is only possible in self-contemplation, in the falling back of the subject upon itself. Thus, in a
circular motion, the remedy for the prohibition of agency imposed
on the woman writer by society is to be found in her self-deter-
mined rejection of all reality but that of the self.

Günderrode's efforts to break away from the dichotomy of traditional gender roles are caught in a similar, self-defeating motion.
For Günderrode, gender-bending and cross-dressing are not just
literary motifs but real-life projects outlined in her letters. Unlike
Kleist and Schiller who, in trying to solve their existential problems, never felt pressed to resort to cross-dressing in real life,
Günderrode toyed with the thought of actually putting on male
clothing to put an end to her female misery. It is likely that the
heightened relevance of cross-dressing for her life raised her awareness of its inherent dangers, thus contributing to her skeptical
stance towards cross-dressing as a solution to woman's plight.

Günderrode not only chose the male pseudonym Tian for the
publication of *Poems and Fantasies* [Gedichte und Phantasien,
1804] and of *Poetic Fragments* [Poetische Fragmente, 1805], she
also identified with a male persona in her letters. In her correspondence with Friedrich Carl von Savigny she often refers to
herself with the gender-neutral name "das G" or "das
Günderrödchen." At times she calls herself "der liebe Freund" and
expresses her wish to be Savigny's brother (*Zärtliches Pfand* 113).
Here, just like in her correspondence with Friedrich Creuzer,
assuming a male persona allows her to negotiate the follies of a
"ménage à trois." It eliminates Günderrode as a potential mistress

by reducing her to the role of a male friend. But while Savigny addresses her in the second person, her correspondence with Creuzer reduces her to the role of friend in the third person.[61] She refers to herself with the personal pronoun "he" in order to hide her gender from Creuzer's wife.[62] She also devises a plan that seeks to transform her grammatical masquerade into a lived experience of cross-dressing. Proposing to don the dress of a servant, Günderrode hopes to achieve the desired union with the beloved man via a gender detour: "The friend has told me that, if this war should threaten to endanger him and his wishes, then he would purposely put on clothing for you and escape and become your servant, you would not have it in you to chase him away and he would do such a good job of pretending that no one should recognize him."[63] Günderrode hoped to accompany Creuzer to Russia in men's clothing and live with him as a man among men.[64] Her cross-dressing, however, though it was meant to make her dreams come true, also prevented the fulfillment of her wishes by effacing her identity as a woman ("that no one should recognize him").

In addition to contributing to her personal suffering, Günderrode's gender effacement did not further her recognition as an author. On the contrary, in the literary arena her supposed lack of femininity was held against her, as evidenced in the following statement by Clemens Brentano: "The only thing evil with which one could reproach this collection would be that it vacillates between masculinity and femininity, and here and there does not resemble poetry but rather spiritual exercises or compositions that have been very successfully executed."[65] Clearly, Günderrode is caught in a nefarious double bind. In her personal life her "unfeminine" intellectual endeavors are taken as proof of her unsuitability for marriage. In the literary sphere, the femininity which her lovers denied her bars the way to publicity and publishing. Seen in this light, gender hybridity is not a romantic fantasy but rather the visible expression of Günderrode's inability to conform to traditional gender roles: "The specter of Günderrode's acting and appearing as a man is the embodiment

of her unnatural, that is, unfeminine, assertions of herself in the
public sphere" (Obermeier 18). In Günderrode's texts, heroism
manifests itself in a female shell, while men are depicted as effeminate. Günderrode's own experience of a male spirit trapped in a
female body may have informed the creation of texts in which
outward signs of gender bear no meaning.

However, Günderrode's correspondence with Bettina
Brentano-von Arnim suggests that fantasies of gender-bending
also serve more positive and productive ends. Brentano-von
Arnim also calls Günderrode her (male) friend ("Freund") and,
transforming her last name, addresses her as "dear Günther."
Moreover, she, too, relates a plan to travel in men's clothing:
"Listen!—and in spring we would take our canes and walk for we
would be hermits and would not tell that we are girls. You have
to make a false beard for yourself because you are tall for otherwise nobody will believe it but only a small one that suits you
well, and I because I am small will be your little brother but then
I will have to cut my hair."[66] By assuming a male gender identity,
the young women hoped to enter the desired state of freedom,
adventure, and heroism so commonly associated with the male
sphere. In their fantasies, masculinity is the magic word that offers
an escape from the hated boredom and immobility of woman's
everyday existence:

> Yesterday I read Ossian's Darthula, and it has such an agree-
> able effect on me; the old wish to die a heroic death, seized me
> with great fierceness; it was insufferable to me to be alive still,
> more insufferable to live a quiet and mediocre life. Often
> already I have felt the unfeminine desire to throw myself into
> the wild throngs of a battle in order to die. Why was I no man!
> I have no appreciation for feminine virtues, for woman's hap-
> piness. Only the wild, the great, the glittering pleases me.
> There is an ill-fated but incorrigible misproportion in my soul:
> and it will and must remain this way for I am a woman and
> have the desires of a man without male strength. That is why I
> am so changeable and so divided in myself.[67]

For Günderrode the androgynous ideal of early Romanticism, which defines perfection as the fusion of male and female qualities, does not signify harmony but disunity and suffering. Her longing for heroism is trimmed down to the yearning for a heroic death.[68] Günderrode's female militancy is not a strategy of empowerment, as it is for Huber or Unger, but rather underlines the helplessness of her female heroines.

The motif of the heroine whose power exhausts itself in death dominates Günderrode's Darthula According to Ossian [Darthula nach Ossian], a text that sprang from her enthusiasm for Ossian's works.[69] The plot of Günderrode's poem follows that of Macpherson's Darthula: A Poem. Caibar, the king of Erin, desires Darthula, the daughter of King Colla of Etha. Both Darthula's father and brother die trying to fend off Caibar's attack. Darthula, who has honed her combat skills during numerous hunting expeditions, decides to join the fight but is taken captive. Nathos, the son of Usnoth, liberates her and flees with her across the sea. But unfavorable winds hinder their escape and they must finally face Caibar. Nathos challenges Caibar, but Caibar refuses to fight with a common warrior. Nathos and his two brothers Ardan and Athos are felled by spears, while Darthula succumbs to wounds inflicted by an arrow. It is only in death that the lovers are united.

From the beginning, Günderrode's ballad is haunted by the somber presentiment of an inescapable destiny. Darthula's life is overshadowed by the memory of dead loved ones, of her friends, her brother, and her father. War, enmity, and the uproar of nature prevent the consummation of her love for Nathos. Darthula's heroic strength and determination are but empty gestures in the face of the existential impotence and hopelessness that pervade the ballad. Resignation and weakness characterize male and female figures alike.[70] After the death of his son, Darthula's father Colla returns home with "his sword lowered / his gaze fixed on the ground" (Sämtliche Werke I: 13). His hope rekindles as Darthula, in a reversal of traditional gender roles, resolves to join the fight. Unlike in Macpherson's Darthula, in Günderrode's text, the virile daughter protects her emasculated father. But not even her extraordinary courage can save him: "Oh! In vain covered by my shield / the father fell in the throngs of the battle / and my gaze was flooded by hot tears" (I: 14).[71] Darthula's bravery also inspires her lover who, in the first stanzas of the poem, is fleeing from Caibar. Again, Darthula's determination restores Nathos' fighting spirit:

> Nathos! Hand me the sword of the brave,
> Father! I want to be worthy of you,
> I will go to the encounter of steel
> Never will I see Caibar's dark halls
> No, you spirits of my love! No!
>
> Joy shone in Nathos at these words
> Spoken by the girl with the beautiful curls:
> Caibar, my strength returns!
> Come with thousands, ruler of Erin!
> Come to the fight! My strength is awake![72]

But Nathos' newly restored courage dwindles as soon as Caibar denounces him as an unworthy opponent and refuses to fight with him. Nathos, thus insulted, begins to cry while Caibar, the only man in *Darthula According to Ossian* who possesses no "feminine" tenderness and compassion, prevails.

Caibar's power feeds off his callous and unkind behavior. Determined to possess Darthula against her will, he rejoices in her defeat. Maliciously pursuing Nathos and Darthula, he destroys every hope of a peaceful life for the two lovers. But while Darthula's defeat is inevitable, it is not caused by her femininity. Nathos and his brothers also succumb to Caibar's superior might. In Günderrode's ballad, gender is dissociated from power, just like power is dissociated from morality. Consequently, assuming a male persona by cross-dressing will not boost a person's courage nor can it invigorate the fighter. Where gender itself is void of any permanent inscription, clothing cannot be anything but an arbitrary sign.

Günderrode does not construe men and women as polar oppo-sites.[73] Rather, effeminate men and heroic women are positioned against brutal warriors such as Caibar. Darthula's disguise, intended to conceal her identity from Caibar, is as unreliable as her shield: "Faithlessly the girl's bosom was revealed / to Caibar by my torn dress" (I: 14). Where masculinity itself does not pre-vent victimization, the donning of male clothing cannot invest its wearer with a power that remains reserved for the ruthless. Nor does Darthula's body tell the truth about her identity since her feminine features only serve to highlight her manly spirit. However, neither Darthula nor Nathos can evade their defeat at the hands of Caibar. In *Darthula According to Ossian*, Günderrode imagines a world in which the victory of the good is not an option. Between the slavery of a union with a hated man and death as ultimate escape, there is no third way.[74]

A similar constellation characterizes Günderrode's dramatic sketch *Mora*, published in 1804 in the collection *Poems and Fantasies*. Out of love for Frothal, the king of spears, Mora agrees to accompany him on a hunting trip in spite of her dark premo-nitions. While Frothal is sleeping, Karmor enters the scene. Previously rejected by Mora, Karmor now wants to gain by force what he could not gain by love. But Mora anticipates his design and dons the armor of the Scandinavian kings. Mistaking the cross-dressed Mora for his rival Frothal, Karmor kills the object of his desire in a duel.

Like *Darthula According to Ossian*, *Mora*, too, is weighed down by the sinister antagonism of irreconcilable forces. By beginning her dramatic sketch with an antiphonal song of two bards—first praising the caressing winds of spring, then evoking the horrors of night and storm—Günderrode highlights the theme of a bat-tle of light against darkness. The characters of her dramolette are assigned to the poles of this dichotomy, with Mora representing the forces of life and love while Frothal incarnates combativeness and desire for glory. But just like spring gives way to thunder and lightning in the song of the bards, so, too, must Mora's thirst for life give way to Frothal's necrophilic desires. Aspiring to the

immortality that fame and glory bestow, Frothal refuses to be
guided by Mora's premonitions of death:

> FROTHAL: I should avoid hunting! Never, girl, never will I
> avoid danger, for as I was given love and glory, my death is no
> death, what should I be afraid of, daughter of Torlat?
> MORA: If you will die with glory and love, Frothal, you will still
> be dead for me.[75]

Mora's warning, inspired by her insight that the cold abstractions
of glory and immortality cannot replace the joy of lived togeth-
erness, remains unheard. Her attempt to convince Karmor of the
irrationality of his desire is also doomed to failure. Karmor ignores
Mora's admonition that love cannot exist where consent is not
granted willingly. To Karmor a woman is a prized object that
belongs to the winner of the fight.

> KARMOR: He has taken from me the soul of my bosom, I loved
> the daughter of Torlat and she chose him.
> MORA: She chooses him and not you. What good is the fight?
> What good is the victory.[76]

Karmor, just like Frothal, will not be convinced, and attacks Mora,
who now takes up the fight with a jubilant cheer. The reader never
learns if Mora rejoices because she wishes to die in her lover's stead
or because she hopes that her death will put an end to all fighting.
But whatever her motivation may be, Mora does not achieve her
goal. Günderrode's cross-dressed heroine dies a meaningless death.
Failing to initiate her lover's catharsis, Mora's sacrifice is denied its
redemptive purpose. Frothal, still obsessed with his craving for
glory, immediately plots his revenge, thus perpetuating indefinitely
the circle of violence and counter-violence.[77]

Clearly, Mora's proclamation of "female" values is just as inef-
fectual as her imitation of "male" behavior. It is not Günderrode's
intent to offer positive solutions nor does she mean to suggest
alternatives to the reductive roles of male warrior and female

object of the war. Rather, the radical thrust of Günderrode's text consists in its refusal to celebrate female death and sacrifice by endowing them with redemptive powers. Death is refused an ennobling purpose as *Mora's* last lines state the irrevocability of loss: "Mora! Mora, the bloom of spring will not awaken you, nor the glitter of the morning, not the purple of the evening, not the call of love. It is beautiful to walk in the light of life, but the grave is narrow and dark, eternal the slumber, therefore mourn Mora for she will not return to the light."[78] While Brentano-von Arnim's discussion of the dream diary toys with the idea of substituting imagination for actual experience, Günderrode's drama rejects such replacements. In *Mora,* the telling of a heroic tale, while granting immortality and glory, cannot make up for the loss of life, nor can poetry transform death into a meaningful event. Tragically, Mora's words also hold true for Günderrode herself: While her works will immortalize her, they cannot make up for a life that ended too soon.

Schiller's, Kleist's, and Günderrode's works explore the connection between the body, gender, and truth. In Schiller's works, the dead female body bridges the gap between signifier and signified, between language and reality. For Kleist and Günderrode, the body per se is no vessel of truth. Kleist's texts reject any inherent connection between the gendered body and the moral order even as they enact a nostalgia for it. In the works of Günderrode, the death of the female cross-dresser remains an empty, meaningless gesture. It cannot restore moral order nor does it legitimize the traditional gender dichotomy.

While Schiller, Kleist, and Günderrode are concerned with the interrelation between gender, truth, and moral order, Goethe's texts center on the connection between gender and societal order. Moreover, both Goethe and his contemporary and friend Charlotte von Stein portray a new variant of the gender-bender. In addition to exploring a performative model of identity, Goethe and von Stein's cross-dressers signify a lack. They point to the absence of woman in the homosocial economy of eighteenth-century society.

Chapter 4

CLASSIC AMAZONS:
Performing Gender in Goethe's Weimar
ॐ

In the late eighteenth century, a rather unlikely location was the home of Germany's cultural elite. Tourists to Weimar usually found the city a dismal sight. They were struck by its smallness and poverty, by its shabby houses with roofs of straw and shingles, by the absence of street lights, and by the sheep, pigs, and cows that moved about freely all over town. The city—with roughly 6,000 inhabitants (6,120 in 1785, Eberhardt 4) and located far off the major trade routes—was characterized by a stark contrast between its squalid streets and its dominating palace. Herder speaks of an "unfortunate midpoint between residence and village"[1] and Madame de Stael flatly declares: "Weimar is not a little town, but a great palace."[2]

Echoing the dichotomy between material lack and intellectual splendor, between village and castle, is the contrast between the eminent reputation of Weimar's male writers and thinkers and the relative obscurity of their female contemporaries. I believe that this obscurity of the cultural products of the female sex has led to a lopsided reception of German Classicism. In order fully to understand the gender concepts inherent in Weimar Classicism, we must read canonical works alongside marginalized texts by women writers of the time. This chapter expands upon recent efforts to de-center and de-mythologize Weimar by comparing Goethe to Charlotte von Stein. It conceives of the lonely Olympian as only one agent in the complex discursive re-negotiation of gender that took shape in this eighteenth-century hotbed of cultural creation. We will approach the struggle to redefine the relation between body and identity, and between gender and social order, through one of its central metaphors: the figure of the cross-dresser as it presented itself at the

Weimar "redoubts," on the Weimar stage, and in texts by Goethe and Charlotte von Stein.

In Weimar, cross-dressing was by no means limited to the realm of literary imagination. A court so rich in festivities and thespian revels provided manifold occasions for sartorial experimentation. Masked balls or "Redouten," as they were called, took place every week or fortnight in Anton Hauptmann's "Redoutenhaus," which also served as a temporary home for theatrical performances after the old theater in the ducal palace "Wilhelmsburg" was destroyed by fire in 1774. Due to the enormous popularity of the balls (attended by 200 to 400 participants), however, this estate soon proved too small. In 1779, Karl August commissioned Hauptmann to construct a new "Redouten- und Komödienhaus," whose inaugural festivities took place on January 7, 1780. Both the increasing number of balls (up to 15 per winter) and their financial profitability attest to the continued fascination with the redoubt and its concomitant freedom from sumptuary laws. Aside from balls, there were masked processions with as many as 100 participants, some of them cross-dressed. We know, for example, that one such procession, with the theme of a Venetian Carnival, featured the wedding of a peasant couple portrayed by military officers who disguised themselves as bridesmaids, bride, and mother of the bride (Lyncker 126).

That Goethe shared his century's predilection for masks and masquerades is evident in his life and writing.[3] He frequented the Weimar redoubts and, in his function as maître des plaisirs, organized elaborate masked processions. At times, his delight in masks crossed over into the realm of the quotidian. On their excursions through the countryside, Duke Karl August and Goethe were wont to don costumes. Goethe's knack for traveling incognito, which often took the form of dressing down, is another example of the willful play with social identities. We might read his involvement with masquerades as an indication of his interest in the performative nature of a person's social identity, and his fascination with the cross-dresser as expressing his recognition of the performativity of gender.

The masquerades were, of course, not the only kind of entertainment available in Weimar. At least equally important was the
theater, with its long tradition of cross-dressed casting.[4] Until the
time of Duke Johann Wilhelm (1554–73), all female roles were
performed by men. Johannes Veltheim (1640–93) is known as the
first principal to engage female actors (Schrickel 14), but cross-
gendered performances were still to be found after his time. We
know of men who portrayed women and of women who portrayed
men. Typically, the cross-dressed man played a wicked and/or old
woman, whereas the female-to-male cross-dresser played an adolescent boy. Examples of the first variety include Siegmund von
Seckendorf, whose portrayal of the wicked landlady Fullmer in
Cumberland's *The West Indian* (1771) [Der Westindier, translated
by Johann Joachim Christoph Bode] was generally admired (see
Lyncker 63), and Bode, who played the title role in *The Governess*
[Die Gouvernante, adapted by Bode from the play *La
Gouvernante*, attributed to Nivelle de la Chaussee, 1774] on July
31, 1779. In Friedrich Schiller's adaptation of *Macbeth*, the witches
were played by men. Clearly, the limited scope of characters available for male-to-female gender-benders indicates that in these
instances the detachment of a woman's social gender from her
biological body does not constitute a subversive act. Rather, the
male witch or governess, far from undermining gender stereotypes, has a cautionary effect. A female spectator might infer that
a character who lacks traditional female attributes such as beauty,
virtue, and compassion jeopardizes her femininity to the point of
renouncing her gender altogether.

The dynamic of female-to-male performances was different.
Rather than middle-aged men playing old witches, attractive young
women played boys. In part, this was due to casting difficulties.
Many popular plays of the time demanded an almost entirely male
cast. Consequently, a young female actress would portray either a
peasant boy or page in plays such as Goethe's *Großkophta* (the
actress Malcolmi as the boy Jäck), Goethe's *Götz von Berlichingen*
(Sophie Teller as a gypsy boy), or Goethe's *Stella* (Louise Becker as
Karl).[5] Some of these female-to-male performances were remem-

Stahlstich v. A. Weger in Leipzig.

Christiane Am. Louise Becker.
(Goethes Euphrosyne.)

CHRISTIANE BECKER-NEUMANN, Weimar actress known for her breeches parts.
Steel engraving by August Weger, Goethe-Museum, Düsseldorf

bered as outstanding. Karoline Jagemann (1777–1848), Weimar's
leading actress during Goethe's tenure as director of the Weimar
theater, won one of her greatest successes as Oberon, the male god
of elves, in Paul Wranitzky's opera *Oberon* (1797). Jagemann's
biographer reports that her Oberon was enthusiastically received
by the press wherever she performed (Bamberg 195). But whereas
Jagemann only occasionally starred in breeches roles (other examples are her portrayal of Gustel in *The Alchemist* [Der Alchemist]
and of Sextus in Mozart's *Titus*), Christiane Neumann came to be
identified with them. The Weimar actor Genast speaks to this special talent when he writes that Neumann "played breeches roles
with such perfection that she could deceive the whole audience
about her gender."[6] Neumann acted the roles of Jakob in *Old and
New Time* [Alte und neue Zeit]; Walter Tell in Friedrich Schiller's
Wilhelm Tell; a boy in Schiller's *Don Carlos*; the title character in
J. Engel's *The Noble Boy* [Der Edelknabe] on February 2, 1787; and
Prince Arthur in William Shakespeare's *Life and Death of King John*,
on November 20, 1791.

Goethe himself shared the general admiration that Neumann's
performances aroused, and commented on the miraculous impact
of her play (Schrickel 90). Genast reports that, while Goethe's
suggestions at rehearsals were normally limited to general
remarks, Christiane Neumann was the only person to receive his
special attention (48). One might well claim that Goethe's attraction to the young actress was due largely to her association with
breeches roles. Even the poem *Euphrosyne* (1789), which Goethe
wrote after her untimely death, includes a reference to this fact:
"a boy seemed I, a sweet child, you called me Arthur."[7] But why
this fascination with the male impersonator? At the time of these
performances, Christiane Neumann was an adolescent girl who is
generally described as very slim. It is unlikely that her breeches
accentuated her "feminine" features, thus accounting for the popularity of her performance. One might therefore speculate that
the contemporary fascination with Christiane Neumann is
founded in a dynamic of homoerotic desire, where the guise of
the actor on stage allows for the disguise of the spectator's desire

because "love for—or cathexis onto—a 'boy' turns out to be love for or cathexis onto a woman, after all" (Garber 175).[8]

While all statements concerning the spectators' desires must remain speculation, an analysis of the economy of power is more clear-cut. Interestingly, all of the examples of male impersonation from this period are not merely portrayals of boys—that is, of adolescents on the threshold to full masculinity—but of boys of lower-class status: peasants, gypsies, servants. One might wonder whether actresses were restricted to the portrayal of powerless male adolescents in order to circumvent an otherwise possible female assumption of male power on stage. After all, the eighteenth century believed in the theater as an educational tool which could effect a transformation of its audience, as exemplified in Kant's words: "For when people play roles, the virtues, whose semblance they assume for a considerable time, may little by little be aroused in reality, and become part of their way of thinking."[9] It seems that this otherwise desirable transformation of appearance into reality was a rather frightening possibility if applied to gender roles. It is therefore not surprising that the casting decisions were designed to render impossible the potential deconstruction of masculinity on stage. Consequently, women who wanted to assume the prerogatives of men could not do so in the theater but were relegated to the realm of fiction. It was left to the imaginative devices of the female author Charlotte von Stein to depict powerful female agents in male guise.

CHARLOTTE VON STEIN'S A New System of Freedom, or the Conspiracies Against Love AND The Two Emilies

Charlotte von Stein (1742–1827) was a member of the cultural and social élite of Weimar. The daughter of Duke Konstantin's majordomo von Schardt, she became a lady-in-waiting at Anna Amalia's court in 1757 and married Duke Karl August's equerry Josias von Stein in 1764. She participated in the activities of the court and entertained a close friendship with Duchess Luise throughout her life. But even though von Stein enjoyed the privileges of nobility, she was keenly aware of the discrimination from which women suffered. In her letters she expresses indignation about the fact that, even though many of the "thousand little chores" of women's daily life require more strength of mind than the work of the genius, it is the latter who reaps all honor and reward while women's work counts for nothing.[10] She also draws a connection between women's domestic chores and the lack of women artists. Because few women find the time to write at all, and because, even among men, it takes countless authors to produce a few good ones, only an increase in the number of women writers could result in more female talents.[11] But even though von Stein was committed to the arts, she refused to set aesthetics above ethical concerns. She believed that greatness of mind as such does not deserve our admiration; it is only when it is put in the service of worthy goals that we owe deference to it. One cannot but detect hidden reproof directed at her ingenious friend Goethe when von Stein insists that talent does not relieve one from the moral obligation towards other human beings and society as a whole. Certainly, von Stein did not shrink from criticizing her famous friends as is evidenced by her frequent comments on the gender bias implied in Schiller's and Goethe's works.[12] Her drama *Dido* (1794), for example, has recently been read as a rejection of Goethe's concept of the Eternally Feminine as expressed in *Iphigenie auf Tauris* (Bohm 46; Lange, "Epische/Dramatische" 343–345).[13]

While Charlotte von Stein's situation was contradictory in that she was marginalized as a woman and yet privileged as a member of the aristocracy, the reception history of her work adds yet another paradox. Susanne Kord points out that, in spite of numerous biographies and articles about von Stein as Goethe's lover, Goethe's friend, Goethe's muse, and so on, practically no information about her work as a writer is available (Kord, "Image" 53–55; Kord, *Namen* 147–150).[14] The focus on Goethe has gone to such extremes that those dramas which cannot be construed as allusions to him were not handed down at all. Charlotte von Stein's prose comedy *A New System of Freedom or the Conspiracies Against Love* [Ein neues

Freiheitssystem oder Verschwörungen gegen die Liebe], which she wrote in 1798, first appeared in print in 1867.[15] It was edited by von Stein's great-grandson Freiherr Felix von Stein, who revised the play significantly (see Kord, "Image" 59).[16] Although Felix von Stein's changes are extensive, Charlotte von Stein's sparkling wit and her keen awareness of the double standard applied to women's actions are still clearly visible.

The title of the play refers to the extravagant philosophical tenets of Daval, one of the protagonists. Daval, lord of the manor in Buchdorf, devotes his life to waging war on love—which, for him, is equivalent to tyranny. Inspired by this philosophy, Daval prevents the marriage of his friend Avelos and his own sister Menonda by forging letters. When the play begins, Daval has engaged Avelos to kidnap two actresses whom he needs for his private theater in Buchdorf. His friend Avelos, however, kidnaps the wrong ladies: Theodora, the niece of a major from Warsaw, and her cousin Menonda, his own lost lover. But the intended victims, the actresses Luitgarde and Florine, are also on their way to Daval's estate. Finally, all are united at the castle—including young sergeant Montrose, who came to rescue the abducted ladies—and the stage is set for a happy ending. Menonda and Avelos are reunited, Theodora and the young officer Montrose confess their love for each other, and even Daval is teamed up with Luitgarde.

Disguises and intrigues are ever-present in this play. But all intrigues go wrong, and all logical deductions that bring them about are flawed. While the characters Orgon, Dodus, and Aratus in von Stein's *Dido* are examples of an intellect in the service of the wrong cause, *A New System of Freedom* demonstrates how eloquent argumentation can prove the most absurd points.[17] The most striking illustration of reason gone awry is Daval himself. In forcing others to do what he thinks is good for them, he becomes a living refutation of his own professed advocacy of freedom. In fact, Daval's philosophy wreaks havoc wherever it is applied. Even his horse succumbs to his "new philosophical method of riding" ("neuen philosophischen Reitmethode," 14) and suffers from colic. In von Stein's play, the powers of the male mind cannot be trusted. The more educated a man is, and the higher his social position, the more absurd and confused is his reasoning. In contrast, the socially inferior servants in the play are characterized by their firm hold on reality and common sense. Repeatedly, the servant Peter points out to his master Avelos that he kidnapped the wrong ladies, but Avelos does not listen to him. Another servant, Conrad, is the only one who knows where the abducted ladies are hidden, while Daval's coachman understands perfectly well why his master's horse is sick. But whenever one of these servants tries to impart his knowledge, his voice remains unheard.

This is not the case with their female counterparts. Whenever the maid Susette or the actress Luitgarde try to intervene, they do so successfully. While the socially respected Menonda and Theodora resign themselves to their fate, the maid Susette and the actress Luitgarde foil the men's scheme (Kord, "Image" 61). Thus, when the young officer Montrose, upon learning about the abduction, threatens to kill the perpetrator, Susette immediately takes action in order to prevent a disaster. She dons Montrose's clothes and gives the real Montrose wrong directions to the castle. She then goes to the castle herself and claims to be Montrose. With great ease, she succeeds in imitating the young officer's martial behavior and flowery language with his "parrot-like references to Greek mythology" (Kord, "Image" 61). Evidently, the uniform suffices to transform her into an officer, just as Montrose himself, whose features are very feminine, relies on the uniform for his manhood.[18] That Susette, the copy, is more convincing than the original is proven when Montrose—who finally finds the castle—cannot persuade Daval's servant Friedrich that he truly is himself.[19] Friedrich flatly refuses to let him enter. All that is left to Montrose is to make do with the vacant part, so that he, as the major says, is promoted to the position of maid ("zur Kammerjungfer avanciert," 29).

Meanwhile, Susette, who—still in her disguise—has gone to her mistresses' room, is also not admitted at first because the ladies think that she is really Montrose pretending to be Susette. Susette, however, manages to establish her true identity:

THEODORA. First the password that you really are Susette.
Which saint hangs above my desk at home?
SUSETTE. I've completely forgotten. There you see that I am
Susette, who forgets everything, even the saints.
MENONDA. This is unmistakable proof.[20]

Obviously, the maid Susette changes her roles easily. She possesses great flexibility in the game of ever-changing identities. But her superiority is only temporary. The obligatory happy ending that the genre of comedy demands enforces the reinstitution of the original order, and Susette must return the uniform to its rightful owner. In spite of that, I want to argue that her victory was not a superficial one. Not only did Susette prove that a woman can hold her own ("ihren Mann stehen"), her actions also question the numerous marriages at the end of the play.[21] When Susette returns Montrose's uniform unwillingly, the major comments that "women are always crazy about uniforms" ("die Frauenzimmer doch immer des Teufels auf eine Uniform sind," 29). Suddenly, the common heterosexual interpretation of this statement, according to which women always want to marry a man in uniform, becomes questionable. Actually, it seems more likely that they want for themselves the power and privileges connected with having such a uniform.

Moreover, Susette is not the only one to master the game of uniforms and gender identities. Luitgarde and Florine, who as actresses have perfected the donning of other clothes and characters, change roles several times. They come to Daval's castle in male disguise, as Harlekin and Scapin, and explain their cross-dressing as a necessary precaution for women who travel alone. Daval, however, doubts their virtuousness because he had in the past occupied a room in an inn that bordered on the actresses' room and had heard male voices in the neighboring chamber. But Luitgarde and Florine convince him that these were not the voices of visiting lovers but rather that they themselves played the parts of lovers. Unlike Daval, the reader is not fooled, having already learnt that Daval had indeed witnessed a secret assignation. Thus, in a remarkable coup, Luitgarde manages to convince Daval of her moral purity by pretending that she pretended to be an officer. By substituting a supposed performance for an authentic body, she succeeds in erasing the presence of a real man in her room. She creates the appearance of innocence and eventually achieves financial security by marrying Daval; and she does so by convincing him that his philosophy of the tyranny of love is of innermost concern to her, too. Clearly, Daval's metaphysics is no match for Luitgarde's wit and performative skills. If von Stein's tragedies can be said to portray deception and cunning as male qualities, as Goodman claims ("Sign" 82), her comedies can be read as the victory over this deception through parody and role-play.

In von Stein's comedy, mimicry proves to be a superior strategic weapon for women (Kord, "Image" 61). By imitating men, women salvage a situation that was created (and wrecked) by male reasoning, which is itself shown to be inherently flawed. Consequently, Susette becomes Montrose in order to prevent violent acts that the latter might perpetrate, and Luitgarde pretends to correspond to Daval's ideal so as to undermine his philosophy clandestinely. The deception succeeds, as neither body, nor voice, nor handwriting guarantee authenticity. Montrose's own face looks like that of a girl. Susette and Luitgarde's voices are taken for men's voices, and Daval can easily forge the handwriting of his sister. All these examples of cross-dressing and mimicry demonstrate that in von Stein's play a person's identity is not a derivative of the body but the result of a complex interplay between individual and society. In insisting that gender identity is not established through one's body, but constructed through "performative acts" (Butler, *Bodies* viii), von Stein refutes a model that institutes biology as the foundation of social order. In her play, power is not an innate quality but a product of specific ideological formations. Indeed, von Stein's comedy must be credited with undoing the work of ideology by exposing that "something seemingly natural, universal and eternal" is "in fact political, partial and open to change" (During 6).

Its de-essentializing thrust is not the only reason for the fasci-

nation that von Stein's play holds for modern readers. Another
is predicated on *how* von Stein achieves this effect. The fact that
mimicry plays such an important role, that is, that women outwit
men by imitating them, points to a strategy that Judith Butler has
described as "subversive repetition": "a repetition of the law
which is not its consolidation but its displacement" (*Gender* 30).
In depicting women who parody men, von Stein encourages her
readers to regard men themselves as parodies of masculinity, thus
questioning the concepts of masculinity and femininity altogether. The fact that this is not frightening but entertaining is due
to genre conventions. The threat that is latent if identity is conceived of as "a normative ideal rather than a descriptive feature
of experience" (Butler, *Gender* 16) is defused by the genre of comedy and its seemingly harmonious resolution of a happy ending.
Instead of ending with a dreaded loss of self, the play depicts the
joyous triumph of the weak.

Disguise and intrigue also play an important role in von Stein's
drama *The Two Emilies* [Die Zwey Emilien, 1803]. *The Two Emilies*
is the only one of von Stein's works which was published during
her lifetime,[22] and the only one that is based on another literary
text, namely on Sophia Lee's novel of the same name.[23] Von Stein
retained the English names of the original but chose Italy as the
setting for the rather Byzantine action of her play. Emilie Arden,
the daughter of Sir Eduard Arden, is betrothed to her cousin, the
Marquis of Lenox. But the happiness of the young couple is overshadowed by an ominous past. Emilie Fitzallen, a foundling and
the companion of Emilie Arden's youth, believes that the latter
swindled her out of her inheritance and seeks to take revenge. She
disguises herself as the painter Hypolith and befriends the Marquis
of Lenox fully aware that he is her cousin's suitor. She follows him
to Italy where she pretends to be Emilie Arden, thus tricking
Lenox into marrying her. Immediately after their wedding, they
are separated by an earthquake. Lenox, believing his wife to be
dead, now wants to marry the right Emilie. But Fitzallen appears
ghost-like at the altar and begins to blackmail him. Sir Eduard,
enraged about his nephew's previous marriage, wounds him in a

duel before he is informed about Fitzallen's malicious trickery and Lenox's innocence. In the end, Fitzallen turns out to be the illegitimate daughter of the Duke of Aberdeen, who is also the Marquis of Lenox's father and married to Sir Eduard's sister. Fitzallen had been removed from her father's house because Sir Eduard felt that his sister's marriage to the licentious Aberdeen was threatened by the presence of a mistress and an illegitimate daughter. Both mother and daughter were thought to have died in a shipwreck. The discovery of Fitzallen's relation also clears the way for Lenox's marriage. Because he and Fitzallen are now known to be siblings, their marriage is annulled, and all ends well.

Von Stein's text fascinates its readers with its multifaceted blurring of boundaries. Otherwise incompatible poles of a dichotomy, such as right and wrong, man and woman, fantasy and reality, blend into one another with amazing ease. Because of Fitzallen's sudden disappearances and even more sudden returns, even life and death appear to be interchangeable states. Twice presumed dead, Fitzallen survives both earthquake and shipwreck. Lenox too is only seemingly dead after the duel. It is hardly surprising that this confusing presence-in-absence infects the characters' memories and thoughts. Even though convinced of Lenox's demise, Emilie Arden insists that her beloved is still near her:

> Alas! Is there truly such an unsurpassable chasm from the deceased friend of my heart? O! If he had torn the tender ties faithlessly? Then there would be! But no! It is no deception, I feel I am still near him [. . .] I feel a terrible delight to call my beloved Lenox forth from the grave—I converse with him, I press him to my heart! Can you, supernatural friend, hear my words? Give me a sign that you are near me if my mortal eye can no longer hold your heavenly image.[24]

In Emilie's mind the lost beloved is embodied. But while the dead husband is resurrected as a mental image, Lenox's subsequent appearance in the flesh is interpreted as fantasy. Clearly, the status and meaning of the body are matters of interpretation. In light of such precariousness of bodily reality, one might even wonder whether in von Stein's drama the mind is more "real" than the body, or, rather, whether there are any bodies independent of the power of the mind. Certainly, the ever savvy Fitzallen knows how to employ the conflation of material and mental presence for her own purposes when she refashions herself as a ghost. During her very real and material appearance at Lenox's second wedding ceremony, she, in the manner of all true ghosts, is visible only to him ("Nobody but I has noticed this figure," 197). Even Lenox himself is led to believe that the person he has seen was nothing but "a phantom of his imagination" (197). His memories of Fitzallen melt away "like a bad dream" (196). Again, mental representations erase physical presence. In *The Two Emilies*, it is the mind that accords the body its meaning and even its reality. Indeed, according to Terry Castle, the "ghostliness" that adheres to von Stein's characters is typical of late eighteenth century culture as a whole:

> A crucial feature of the new sensibility of the late eighteenth century was, quite literally, a growing sense of the ghostliness of other people. In the moment of romantic self-absorption, the other was indeed a phantom—a purely mental effect, or image, as it were, on the screen of consciousness itself. The corporeality of the other—his or her actual life in the world— became strangely insubstantial and indistinct: what mattered was the mental picture, the ghost, the haunting image.
> (*Thermometer* 125)

Castle claims that all rational explanations of such ghostliness— inevitably proffered by these texts—cannot efface its uncanny effect but rather displace it. Thus, readers, who learn that Lenox was not killed in a duel and that Fitzallen did not die during the earthquake, may be relieved that there were no ghosts after all. But this reassurance does not obliterate the disturbing knowledge that a soul can be haunted by images and memories that are far more uncanny than ghosts, nor can it change the even more frightening realization that there are no bodies without "ghosts."

The ghost that torments Lenox is that of Hypolith as the now cross-dressed Fitzallen calls herself. Unsurprisingly, the figure of the cross-dresser, whose presence is always already marked by absence, is ideally suited to embody the uneasy amalgam of the body and the imaginary that characterizes von Stein's text. The gender-bender, who always already signifies the missing (wo)man, replicates not only the interlacing of different modes of reality but also the simultaneity of differing interpretations of the body. However, one might even take this one step further. I would like to propose that, in *The Two Emilies,* the cross-dresser expresses not only the imaginary dimension of the body but functions as an agent that reveals the underlying homosocial structure of von Stein's fictional society.[25]

Fitzallen's juggling of different identities is carried to the extreme when she pretends to be her own cousin Emilie Arden. The reader who was previously informed that Lenox had gone to Italy with the distinct objective of avoiding marriage to said cousin, is puzzled by the fact that such a determined bachelor now consents to marry a cross-dresser who not only pretends to be an already rejected lover but clings to her male apparel even at her own wedding. But while Lenox's devotion to Hypolith may or may not be inspired by homoerotic desire, theirs is certainly a relationship in which traditional gender roles have lost their validity. Whereas Fitzallen is said to possess the soul of a man, Lenox's behavior and character are feminized. While Fitzallen surpasses her later lover Montalto in bodily strength (165), Lenox has "nerves as tender as those of a woman" (151). If Fitzallen is guided by her mind, not her emotions, Lenox is governed by his melancholy moods. When Fitzallen/Hypolith pursues Lenox, he swoons. One rather wonders whether the natural disaster that follows immediately upon their marriage was inserted to cut short an "unnatural" union. Indeed, if we follow Freud's definition of the uncanny ["unheimlich"] as that which is most familiar ["heimlich"] and which, though banished into the unconscious, has reemerged into the open, then Hypolith's phantom-like reappearance, and Lenox's emotional uproar in the wake of this "ghost," might be interpreted as the return of his repressed homoerotic desire. Significantly, Fitzallen is again wearing men's clothing when she surfaces at Lenox's wedding to Emilie. Unsurprisingly, it is this visitation that instigates Lenox's alienation from Emilie.

While Lenox is enthralled by Fitzallen's male persona, the latter's courting of Lenox seems strangely directed at Emilie Arden. Fitzallen appears to be interested in Lenox only insofar as he is useful for her plot of revenge against Emilie (148). She uses Emilie's identity to seduce Lenox, apparently in order to hurt Emilie. At first glance, Lenox is nothing but a pawn in the struggle between two women, a struggle that concerns money, power, and social privilege. Ironically, Fitzallen's relationship with Lenox inverts traditional patterns of homosociality to the point of creating a gyno-social structure. But the reader is soon informed that Fitzallen's wrath is misdirected, as it was not Emilie Arden who took Fitzallen's inheritance from her. Fitzallen lost her rightful possessions and title because of the illegitimacy of her birth. Thus, her first expropriation must be laid at her father's door while the second injustice, her expulsion from the family home, was ordered by Emilie Arden's father. Interestingly, Fitzallen herself is very aware of the gender-specific origin and nature of the unfair treatment that was inflicted on her:

> My betrayal was just revenge.—Yes, it remains true and certain. Never have women stood at their due place, neither according to the law of nature, nor according to the contract of societal institutions. That in which one woman succeeds, pushes the other down. Excellent qualities often hurt them, their mistakes are often useful for them and elevate them from an unknown sphere into a higher part. One time we are everything and soon after nothing—But I have the soul of a man and I will not be chained in any way.[26]

Fitzallen's speech exhibits an amazing solidarity with her own sex and a perceptive awareness of the workings of a homosocial society. Indeed, Eduard Arden is now revealed to be the true target

of Fitzallen's revenge. As Emilie Arden (now Lenox) is reunited
with Lenox, Sir Eduard is overcome by the recognition of his own
guilt. The zero-sum game in which the success of one woman
inevitably leads to the defeat of another, is ended. The guilt is
redirected to its male originators. Both Fitzallen and Emilie
Arden emerge as winners. While Sophia Lee's original novel
depicts Fitzallen as a dying and remorseful sinner, von Stein's
Fitzallen triumphs in the end (Kord, "Image" 64). Her revenge
is not the malicious behavior of a madwoman but is justified as
an understandable endeavor necessary to heal the wounds of a
previous injustice. Her method originates from her profound
understanding of the workings of patriarchal society. The last
scene shows a Fitzallen who, rejecting the retreat to a monastery
that Aberdeen suggests, exits as a "true amazon" (223). Von
Stein's drama turns the fight among women into a fight against
patriarchy, a fight, however, which can only succeed if it has
recourse to the mimicry of the cross-dresser.

Both *A New System of Freedom* and *The Two Emilies* depict
women who imitate men in order to outwit them and thus secure
their own happiness. In von Stein's texts the flexibility and adaptability of the gender-bender is the only remedy against a social
order whose odds are stacked against the weaker sex. But while
in von Stein's comedy the figure of the cross-dresser mimics masculinity, in *The Two Emilies* s/he indicates a void. Through his/her
presence-in-absence the cross-dresser points to the empty space
that is the place of woman in patriarchal society. Von Stein's
cross-dresser not only capitalizes on woman's non-existence in
patriarchy but also exploits the fact that man's desire is directed
toward his own sex only. The phantom of the cross-dresser haunts
the text until the injustice inflicted upon Fitzallen is uncovered.
Once Emilie Fitzallen's two-fold erasure through her father and
uncle's agency is made visible, the ghost of the missing woman
disappears.

In the following, I will compare von Stein's portrayal of cross-
dressed characters with Goethe's depiction of gender-benders.
Surprisingly, some of Goethe's texts also lay bare the arbitrariness

of the body-gender connection and introduce a performative concept of identity. But unlike von Stein, who delights in the playful dissolution of gender roles, Goethe is troubled by the social
anarchy that comes in its wake and ultimately moves to contain
the gender-bender's disturbing potential.

Goethe's "Women's Parts Played by Men in the Roman Theater," Roman Carnival, AND Wilhelm Meister's Apprenticeship

Although the theme of cross-dressing features prominently in
several of Goethe's texts—both Wilhelm Meister's Apprenticeship
and The Italian Journey, for example, contain portrayals of cross-
dressed characters—his "Women's Parts Played by Men in the
Roman Theater" [Frauenrollen auf dem Römischen Theater
durch Männer gespielt, 1788, in Gedenkausgabe] is the only text
that engages in a theoretical discussion of cross-dressing. The following reading of this intriguing essay focuses on the concatenation between the author's concept of art, his epistemology, and
his ideas on gender. Paradoxically, it is precisely Goethe's attempt
to define the essence of femininity that opens up an abyss between
his ideal of gender and the reality of the women of the Goethezeit.
The Eternal Feminine vanishes as Goethe tries to capture the
truth about gender.

"Women's Parts Played by Men in the Roman Theater," published anonymously in 1788 in the German Mercury [Teutscher
Merkur, 1773–89], was inspired by a visit to the theater in Rome
on January 3, 1788, to see a performance of La Locandiera. Due
to the papal ban on women on the stage, Goldoni's play was presented by an exclusively male cast. Goethe, who had produced
this work in Weimar in 1777, enjoyed the performance exceed-
ingly. But as the pleasure ("Vergnügen" and "Reiz") that he took
in it seemed to disturb him somewhat, he set about explaining its
origin.[27] Whereas in von Stein's play all cross-dressers are taken
for real, the spectator Goethe stresses in his account that he is

never deceived but always aware that he is watching cross-dressed men, not women. He goes on to explain that it is precisely this awareness that accounts for the pleasure of the spectator, in that it reminds him of the self-reflectivity of art. The fact that one sees the imitation of a woman, not a real woman, demonstrates that art itself is concerned with imitation. In watching cross-dressers, one becomes conscious of, not absorbed in, the theatrical illusion.

Surprisingly, thus far Goethe and Marjorie Garber would seem to agree. Garber also claims that the transvestite contains the essence of theatricality, which consists of the substitution of one signifier for another (40). But unlike Garber, of course, Goethe assumes that there is a "thing" to which the signifier refers, that is, that art does imitate nature. However, as he himself admits, the term "imitation" is slippery, and the relationship between signifier and signified is complicated. According to Goethe art does not just imitate nature as it is, but intends to capture its true essence ("wahres Wesen"). It is this concern with essence that explains why a young male actor can portray a woman much better than a female actor can: "The young man has studied the characteristics of the female sex in its essence and bearing [. . .] he does not portray himself but a third nature actually foreign to him. We come to know this nature even better because someone else has observed it, reflected on it, and presents us not with the thing itself but with the result of the thing" (tr. by Ferris 49).[28] Clearly, true femininity is best presented by a man. But what is true femininity? In order to penetrate to the essence of nature, to its idea, one must abstract from the empirical object. Goethe describes this process in the context of his philosophical reflections on science. He assumes that a scientist proceeds from the "empirical phenomenon," the object as it is observed, to the scientific phenomenon, which is approached through a process of abstraction based on a multitude of comparable objects. Finally, he arrives at the "pure phenomenon," which contains in itself the result of all experiences and is void of all accidental traits (see Günzler 136). Consequently, and because this pure phenomenon cannot exist empirically, an aporia presents itself. In order to cope with the

overwhelming mass of empirical phenomena, the scientist needs
to rely on a concept of the pure phenomenon, of the type. But
while individual cases cannot be analyzed without a pre-formed
concept, such a concept cannot be found without a prior analysis of all individual cases (see Kleinschnieder 182). Due to this
dilemma, all knowledge must necessarily contain a subjective
component; however, because of this subjective component, the
pure phenomenon may not be a truthful representation of the
empirical phenomena after all. In fact, not even the causal connection between the pure phenomenon and the empirical objects
that it represents can be ascertained beyond doubt, as Goethe
explains in a letter to Sömmering: "An idea about the objects of
experience is like an organ which I use in order to capture them,
in order to appropriate them. The idea can be very handy for me,
I can demonstrate to others that it will be handy for them as well:
but it is, in my opinion, only with great difficulties, or maybe not
at all, possible to prove that it really corresponds to objects and
necessarily converges with them."[29] If one applies this logic to the
phenomenon of gender, one arrives at a surprising conclusion. If
one accepts that the true phenomenon expresses the essence of a
thing, void of all accidental traits, one must indeed concede that
a male actor can represent true femininity. But, according to the
same theory, one must also concede that "true femininity" may
have little to do with the empirical phenomenon of real women.
Thus, an intriguing ambiguity adheres to Goethe's ideas on cross-
dressing. By severing femininity from the body of woman and
transposing it onto a male actor, Goethe introduces a performative concept of gender.[30] But while such performativity implicitly
contradicts the theorem of a body-gender connection and thus
serves to deconstruct gender stereotypes, the theatrical representation of "true femininity" by male actors—and according to the
script of male writers—may be employed to reinforce conservative notions of femininity. It is of note that Goethe does not allow
for the representation of "true masculinity" by female actors.
Clearly, Goethe himself was aware of the fact that the Eternally
Feminine represents a normative ideal rather than a natural

entity, as is evidenced in a conversation with Eckermann: "My idea of women is not abstracted from the appearances of reality but is rather innate, or it developed within me God knows how! My female characters therefore all come off well; they are all better than one would find them in reality."[31] It is because Goethe knew of the non-representational nature of his era's notions of womanhood that he felt compelled to admonish Charlotte von Stein that "a woman should not want to shed her femininity" ("Ein Weib soll ihre Weiblichkeit nicht ausziehen wollen," letter to von Stein, September 21, 1785, *Gedenkausgabe* XVIII: 874). Keeping this in mind, one might read Goethe's own works as an attempt to prevent women from wanting to strip themselves of their femininity, or rather to teach them how to perform their gender "correctly."[32] However, the oxymoronic structure of Goethe's imperative "you should not want to" ("nicht wollen sollen") already points to the precarious nature of his endeavor. Moreover, it would be wrong to assume that Goethe's gender philosophy is driven by a deep-seated misogyny. The following analysis of Goethe's depiction of the Roman Carnival will demonstrate that the anxiety caused by a possible dissolution of the gender dichotomy is closely connected to the fear of social anarchy in general.

During his journey to Italy, Goethe experienced the Roman Carnival on two different occasions. Interestingly, the account of his first acquaintance with the popular spectacle is predominantly negative. In a letter to Herder, Goethe gives voice to his dismay: "I am sick of Carnival! It is, especially during the last beautiful days, an incredible noise but no heart-felt joy. The great ones are economical and reserved, the average citizen is without means, and the people are lame."[33] This account of Goethe's disappointment is clearly different from the fascinating description of the Roman festival that dates from the author's second stay in Rome. Published as a separate edition in 1789, this revised and more enthusiastic version later formed part of the narrative of his second visit to Rome, which appeared in 1829. Unfortunately, the manuscript which records Goethe's original impressions and which was the basis of his later reconstruction of the journey was burnt by the author himself. The extent and manner of the editing process can thus no longer be ascertained.[34]

In the edited version, Goethe's feelings of alienation—so vivid in his letter to Herder—are much more subdued, though they have not vanished completely. Goethe begins his narrative with the rhetorical objection that a written report cannot do justice to an event of this nature (XI: 533)—an assessment he had voiced before, when he first witnessed the Roman Carnival.[35] He continues with a description of the discomfort that this festival incites in strangers: "We must confess that the Roman Carnival leaves neither a complete nor a pleasing impression on a foreign spectator who sees it for the first time and can and wants to watch only."[36] In the following text, Goethe emphasizes repeatedly that his "narrative seems to transcend the limits of credibility" (XI: 548) to such an extent that the festival appears more like a dream than lived reality (XI: 566). Though Goethe's status as a foreigner may account for some of these feelings, it is hardly sufficient to explain the magnitude of his unease. By the time of the Roman Carnival Goethe had already spent a year and a half in Italy. He was also no stranger to the idea of a Carnival, since masked balls were a very popular form of entertainment at his native court of Weimar. One might therefore wonder just what it was about the Roman Carnival that gave rise to Goethe's intense feelings of alienation and discomfort.

One of the striking features of the Roman festival, which Goethe singles out in his account, is the suspension of traditional class boundaries. Even though the mingling of different social classes also characterized the masked balls in Weimar, the Weimar celebrations, unlike the Roman festival, did not include the lower classes. While the regulations for the balls in Weimar expressly prohibited the servant class from wearing masks, the servants and coachmen at the Roman Carnival, as Goethe emphasizes, disguise themselves just like everybody else (XI: 546).[37] Moreover, in addition to extending the privilege of disguise to all classes, sartorial markers of a person's professional affiliation or social rank are themselves turned into masks (XI: 543). Some Romans dress up as beggars, others disguise themselves as stable boys or fishermen.[38]

The practice of social masquerade is both enticing and disconcerting. For if clothes make the man, that is, if one's social standing is derived from external attributes which can be put on and off at one's discretion, then the social order itself is not a God-given hierarchy but an arbitrary institution. Thus, the freedom of the Carnival questions the supposed naturalness of the societal order, as Bakhtin has claimed: "The moment of laughter, the carnivalistic attitude toward the world [. . .] destroys the narrow seriousness as well as every claim to a timeless meaning and immutability of the ideas of necessity. They liberate human consciousness, the thoughts and imagination of human beings for new possibilities" (28). It would appear that it is the destabilizing effect of the Carnival that is at the root of Goethe's discomfort—especially since he was convinced that the Carnival exercised considerable influence on everyday Roman life. In fact, according to Goethe, the Roman Carnival is "nothing new, nothing foreign, nothing unique, but follows naturally from the Roman way of life [. . .] It appears to be Carnival all year long" (XI: 536).

Goethe himself, however, is determined to stem the tide. Intent on maintaining his distance, he insists that, as a stranger, he occupies a place outside of the exotic world of classless masquerades. But in the carnivalesque world, the figure of the stranger is as fragile as every other social position: it too can become a mask (XI: 544). In spite of his objective stance, the narrator himself cannot escape the whirlpool of destabilization that the Carnival sets in motion. Thus, disgust gives way to fascination, and discomfort melts away as pleasure takes its place.

In order to fend off the corroding influence of the Roman Carnival, Goethe takes recourse to rhetoric. He denies that there is any reality to these social games at all. They are but surface phenomena without any basis in real life: "The difference between high and low *seems* abolished for a moment" (XI: 534). The Carnival passes "like a dream, like a fairytale, and perhaps less remains behind in the souls of the participants than in our readers" (XI: 566). However, even though Goethe proclaims to be convinced of the fleeting nature of this topsy-turvy world, the proliferation of signifiers of social anarchy in his description indicates that the author's growing anxiety persists. Indeed, the flame of fear finds new nourishment as Goethe notices that the dissolution of class boundaries is complemented by a lack of differentiation between public and private. In the course of the festival, inside and outside merge into one as the Roman streets and places take on the characteristics of an interior space: "The street seems more and more habitable. In leaving one's house, one believes to be not outside and among strangers, but in a room with acquaintances" (XI: 539). However, if it is no longer possible to tell the difference between the public and private spheres, it becomes impossible to maintain any form of civic order, whether it be an absolutistic or an enlightened one.[39] As the order of the state itself is based on the dichotomy of public and private, anarchy ensues where this differentiation is no longer valid.[40] Appropriately enough, "sia ammazzato," which translates as "murder him," becomes the greeting of choice in this arena of public disorder (XI: 564). The general inversion is completed as the light of a thousand candles turns the night into day.

By sweeping away the hierarchy of social classes and the boundaries of private and public, the Roman Carnival brings an end to all forms of civic order. Closely associated with this anarchy is the dissolution of the gender dichotomy. In fact, the abolition of the gender order is both an expression of and a possible reason for the disintegration of Goethe's Southern society.[41] Rome is teeming with cross-dressers since "women are just as inclined to show themselves in men's clothing as men are to let themselves be seen in women's clothing" (XI: 541). Apparently, both genders take great pleasure in their disguise. Goethe observes a female officer who "displays her epaulettes to the people with great contentment" (XI: 537). She seems to be delighted with the new rank and power that her uniform bestows on her. Men too enjoy their transformation. A male-to-female cross-dresser, "with exposed breast and cheeky self-sufficiency" basks in the erotic possibilities inherent in his costume. Goethe himself admits to being fascinated with gender-benders: "One must confess that they succeed in being highly attractive in their hybrid shape" (XI: 541). But while he too is attracted by them, he is also committed to re-erecting the proper boundaries amidst the chaos. Even though cross-dressers are omnipresent in Goethe's text, the author does not succumb to the temptation to play with his readers and keep them in limbo as to which gender they are dealing with. Rather, he is eager to emphasize that it is always the woman underneath the clothes who is the true focus of his attention. Thus, before he begins to describe an attractive officer, Goethe is sure to introduce this ambiguous character as a woman ("*eine* Schöne," XI: 536). Before he describes the costumes of the Pulcinelli, Goethe designates them as "Freundinnen" in order to establish their gender identity beyond any doubt. In another passage, he assures his readers that the characters in question are men. Only then does he proceed to give details about their costumes (XI: 540 and 547): "Young men, made up in the Sunday dresses of women of the lower classes" (XI: 540). But patrolling the border is never easy. As Goethe describes how the cute little feet and high heels of the Pulcinelli, who sit high up in a coach, flutter around the heads of the passersby (XI: 547), and as he delights in the sweetness of a female officer, the adjective "cute" (niedlich) clandestinely makes its way from the description of women in men's clothing to that of men in women's clothing so that, all of a sudden, the cross-dressed coachmen are portrayed as "charming" [reizend, XI: 546]. The attempt to rein in desire to keep it from straying into forbidden realms is only partially successful. And how could it be otherwise since it is precisely the unreadability of the cross-dresser that emerges as the origin of his/her erotic appeal? The longer the party goes on, the more the author's intent to delineate clear boundaries must falter. Thus, the German visitor moves through discomfort to pleasure, and from pleasure to discomfort, and here the circle ends. It is because Goethe loved nothing better than to dress down (to engage in social drag so to speak), because he was fascinated with the dissolution of gender dichotomies that he produced a narrative that explicates the dangers of transgressive cross-dressing even as it evokes the pleasure connected with it.

In Goethe's account of the Roman Carnival, the instability of dichotomous categories such as inside and outside, high and low, male and female reveals them to be social constructs rather than natural facts. In order to keep from falling into a state of anarchy, a society must reconstitute these boundaries in an unceasing process of performance.[42] The threat of anarchy and revolution haunts the gaiety of the Roman Carnival, which, unlike its Weimar counterpart, lacks the ordered hand of a master of revels. It is this threat that turns the allure of the cross-dresser into a dangerous temptation. Thus, it is hardly surprising that Goethe's fictional treatment of cross-dressing in his novel *Wilhelm Meister* is designed to contain the destabilizing effect of the gender-bender. But although *Wilhelm Meister* re-anchors gender in the body, the cross-dresser once again elides and points to a crucial void: the missing woman whose cross-dressed presence unwittingly uncovers the underlying homosocial structure of Goethe's fictional society.

Of all texts discussed in this book, *Wilhelm Meister's Apprenticeship* [Wilhelm Meisters Lehrjahre, 1796–97] features the largest number of cross-dressers.[43] Indeed, the sheer quantity of cross-dressed characters serves as evidence of Goethe's strong interest in the relation between body, gender, and identity. Almost all female protagonists wear men's clothing, some only once, some repeatedly. The figure of the gender-bender makes its first appearance in the character of Chlorinde, the heroine of Torquato Tasso's *Jerusalem Delivered*. The child Wilhelm is fascinated with this heathen warrior who is killed by her lover Tankred because the latter fails to recognize her in men's clothing (VII: 28). Later on, Wilhelm himself casts cross-dressed characters in his function as founder and director of a children's theater.[44] Theatrical cross-dressing is also practiced by Serlo's company, in which Elmire, the daughter of the Polterer, acts the part of Rosenkranz. But the most memorable theatrical cross-dresser is the actress Mariane, who delights her audience in the charming outfit of an officer. In fact, Mariane herself is so pleased with her attire that she refuses to take it off after the performance. The androgyny of the child Mignon is different from that of Mariane, who is always identifiable as a woman.

When Wilhelm first meets Mignon, he is disturbed by his inability to decipher her gender. Furthermore, while Mariane's cross-dressing is justified and rationalized by its theatrical context, Mignon refuses to participate in dramatic performances and insists on wearing her sailor's pants in everyday life. Another cross-dresser, the baroness, whom Wilhelm meets during the course of his adventures and who loves to don the clothing of a page or hunter, is also not affiliated with any theater but enacts her gender masquerade at court. Even the practical Therese is fond of her hunting outfit, and Natalie, the beautiful amazon, wears the jacket of her uncle when she first happens upon Wilhelm. Given this abundance of women in men's clothing, it is surprising that all the amazons are portrayed as truly "feminine" characters. Though *Wilhelm Meister* embraces and celebrates the erotic allure of the cross-dresser, it does not present cross-dressing as a transgression against conventional gender roles. On the contrary, the novel conjures up the specter of the masculinized woman only to affirm that such masculinization did not take place.

The first cross-dresser who finds herself reduced to a state of helplessness is the actress Mariane. Like the cross-dressers in *Roman Carnival*, Mariane too wears a uniform whose foremost effect consists of heightening her erotic appeal. In fact, the appeal of her outfit outshines that of the actress herself. Thus, Wilhelm's passionate embrace of his beloved is portrayed as a sartorial encounter: "With what delight did he embrace the red uniform, did he press the white vest of atlas to his breast" (VII: 11). In this description, the synecdoche of clothing obliterates the bodily presence of the actress. Initially, however, it seemed as though Mariane's new clothes were rather more than an aphrodisiac. Her uniform appeared to endow the actress with courage and determination. Clothed in her martial garment, Mariane had refused to do the will of the pander Barbara, who wanted to set her up

MIGNON ASPIRANT AU CIEL (1838). Almost all depictions of Mignon emphasize her femininity. *Illustration by Ary Scheffer. Beinecke Rare Book and Manuscript Library, Yale University*

with the rich Norberg. Confronted with Mariane's insubordination, Barbara thinks that her dress is the reason for her unruliness: "I will have to make sure, she exclaimed, that she will again wear long dresses soon if I want to be sure of my life. Away, undress yourself! I hope the girl will apologize for the pain that the fickle squire inflicted on me; down with the jacket and always so forth down everything! It is an uncomfortable costume, and dangerous for you, as I notice. The shoulder-straps excite you."[45] Even though at first glance it might seem as though Mariane was strengthened by her costume's aura, her short-lived self-confidence does not constitute a "deliberate rejection of the trappings of femininity" (MacLeod, "Pedagogy" 397). Not only is Mariane's insurgence motivated by the romantic desire to surrender herself to Wilhelm instead of Norberg but it is also completely ineffective. Though Barbara responds to the moods of her "mistress" by making small concessions, her manipulative skills always carry the day. A closer look reveals that Barbara's speech about the power of Mariane's uniform is delivered in the spirit of ridicule and preceded by the loud laughter of the old crone (VII: 10). Rather than assuming the authority that her uniform represents, Mariane is diminished by her costume. She becomes a little officer ["Offizierchen"]. In the end, Mariane's cross-dressing only serves to highlight her helplessness.

Goethe's novel not only portrays Mariane's fall but also gives reasons for it. Barbara prevails because Mariane is "used to certain wants" (VII: 513), and these material needs make her vulnerable to seduction. Mariane's innate "feminine" weakness, which is equated with her inability to transcend material needs— more an unwillingness to starve than a craving for luxury items— is stronger than her momentary bravery, which remains as alien to her nature as her outfit is to her body. However, one might also claim that the real reason for Mariane's tragic end is to be found in the moral parameters of the bourgeois novel which preclude a union between the hero and a fallen woman even, or especially, if she fell because of him. Interestingly, Goethe's original outline for his novel, entitled *Wilhelm Meister's Theatrical Mission*

[Wilhelm Meister's Theatralische Sendung], was supposed to end with a reconciliation between Mariane and Wilhelm. One might speculate whether Goethe's inability to finish this early project indicates an inner resistance to the strictures of the bourgeois novel which would not permit an embarrassing marriage between the hero and his former mistress. Traces of this ambiguity are still visible in *Wilhelm Meister* in that Goethe's novel excuses Mariane's sexual promiscuity with a reference to the exigency of her financial situation, but then punishes her for straying from the path of virtue as though this connection did not exist. In the end, Mariane can be reintegrated into Goethe's narrative family only as a dead body.

In contrast to Mariane, whose masculinity is but a surface phenomenon, Therese is introduced as a "true amazon," different from those others who are "mere well-behaved hermaphrodites" (VII: 473). Indeed, Therese takes on many jobs that are traditionally assigned to men. She is knowledgeable in finance and economy and occupies herself with agriculture, forestry, and orcharding. In carrying out her administrative duties, Therese rides through the country in men's clothing. She is respected by all for the punctilious fulfillment of all tasks. One might be tempted to assume that, for Therese, men's clothing is the true expression of her inner "masculine" being. However, a closer inspection of Therese's responsibilities reveals that Goethe does not propose a role reversal but rather expands the realm of female activity to encompass not only the kitchen and pantry but the "entire household." Therese, who is in charge of maintaining cleanliness and order, never loses sight of woman's true goal.[46] All her knowledge and work are subordinated to one overriding purpose, "that one take care in every way of the happiness of men and the household" (VII: 493). It is only when Lothario expresses his conviction that overseeing a household is the most honorable occupation for a woman that Therese recognizes in him her soul mate. But if she might more justly be called a true housewife rather than a true amazon, why then her masculine clothing? And why does Schiller predict that Therese will find but few admirers?

Is she, who concentrates all her ambition on the domestic realm and is willing to forgive all infidelities of her husband (VII: 496), not the perfect embodiment of the ideal bourgeois mate?

One possible reason for Schiller's antipathy is Therese's complete lack of appreciation for all things aesthetic. In fact, Therese's competence in practical matters seems directly proportional to her ignorance of literature and art. Her miniscule library, as she herself admits, consists not of books that she keeps but of those that she does not toss out. In addition to her bibliophobia, her alienation from the artistic realm is also evident in the disdain she shows for the amateur theater of her mother:

> I cannot tell you how ridiculous it seemed to me when human beings, all of whom I knew very well, had disguised themselves, stood up there and wanted to be taken for something else than what they were. I always saw nothing but my mother and Lydia, this baron and that secretary, whether they appeared as dukes or counts or farmers, and I could not understand how they expected me to believe that they felt good or ill, that they were in love or did not care, were stingy or generous, even though I was mostly well aware of the opposite. Because of this I very rarely remained among the spectators.[47]

Obviously, the world of beautiful appearances holds no attraction for Therese. Indeed, one might wonder if the numerous mentions of the smallness and narrowness of Therese's house are symbols of her aesthetic narrowmindedness, and, moreover, if Lothario's sudden offer of marriage was not so much inspired by love as by the necessity of salvaging an estate burdened with the debts of his American campaign. But even so, given Therese's housewifely nature and her outspoken disapproval of all masks and role-play, her decision to appear in the guise of a man in order to attract Lothario's attention presents a riddle: "For the first time in my life it occurred to me to seem or, so as not to put myself in the wrong, to be regarded as that which I am in the eyes of the excellent man. I put on my men's clothing, took the rifle on my back and went outside with our hunter."[48] Why would Therese, so "feminine" in her willingness to subject herself unconditionally, choose to appear as a man in order to be recognized as an ideal partner by Lothario? And how can one account for the fact that Lothario, whose love life so far was a succession of partners, is now willing to commit to a lasting union?

I believe that, in order to answer these questions, one must address an even more general puzzle: why is it that all male protagonists in Goethe's novel fall for women who at first wear men's clothing? Whether it be Jarno's passion for the baronesse in her hunting outfit, Lothario's interest in the cross-dressed Therese, or Wilhelm's love for three gender-benders—the little officer Mariane, Nathalie in her uncle's overcoat, and Therese, who wears the clothing of a hunter when Wilhelm first meets her— the relationship with a woman always originates in the desire for the cross-dresser. And yet, Goethe's female cross-dressers are portrayed as truly feminine creatures in spite of their dashing masculine exterior. Clearly, their cross-dressing does not destabilize the gender dichotomy; rather, it is a sympton that speaks of the underlying homosocial structure of Goethe's male alliance.

The case of Natalie best exemplifies this dynamic. Even though Natalie wears a man's overcoat when she first meets Wilhelm, she is introduced as a woman and characterized with pronouncedly feminine attributes such as softness and compassion. Natalie has devoted her life to promoting the welfare of others. Her desire to cater to the needs of her fellow humans and to alleviate all suffering and lack is so strong that Dick sees in her the "idealization of instrumental servitude" (13), a "self-sacrificing, female eunuch who has neither a will nor any wishes of her own" (123). For Schlaffer, Natalie is the "embodiment of rolelessness" (88). One might add that she is also the epitome of shapelessness and facelessness, as evidenced in Wilhelm's vision, where she dissolves into nothingness as soon as she takes off her uncle's overcoat: "He saw the enveloping dress fall from her shoulders, her face, her shape disappear in splendor" (VII: 252).[49] Wilhelm himself emphasizes that his experience with Natalie would be indistinguishable from a dream if it were not for the overcoat which testifies to the reality of her being. Indeed, the passing on of her uncle's overcoat, which inspires in Wilhelm "the most lively desire to clothe himself in it" (VII: 252), appears to be Natalie's true mission. Through the gift of the coat Natalie establishes a bond between Wilhelm and her uncle. Significantly, this uncle is the very same person who acquired the art collection of Wilhelm's grandfather. Through his union with Natalie, who is now the mistress of this collection, Wilhelm is reinstated into his inheritance. Paradoxically, Natalie—who herself has no appreciation for art and who is excluded from all symbolic systems to such an extent that she does not even participate in monetary circulation but distributes natural produce to do good—functions as a mediary who reintegrates Wilhelm into the male family alliance.[50] It is Natalie who, in Wilhelm's dream, leads Felix to his father, and it is also through Natalie that Wilhelm is connected to her brother Lothario and thus, ultimately, to the Tower Society. Given these relationships, one might claim that in *Wilhelm Meister* heterosexuality is "nothing but an alibi for the frictionless relationship of man with himself, for the relationships among men" (Irigaray 179).[51]

Even though Irigaray's definition of homosociality pertains to the entirety of Goethe's fictional society, the relationship among men that is considered most important in *Wilhelm Meister* is that of father and son.[52] Whether Natalie establishes a connection between Wilhelm and his father or Wilhelm and his son, the issue of fatherhood is clearly at the heart of the novel. It is present in Wilhelm's nagging doubts about whether Felix is truly his child, in his dependence on the assurances of the Tower Society that he is, as well as in Friedrich's mischievous comment that "fatherhood [. . .] is based on a conviction; I am convinced, and therefore I am a father" (VII: 600). One might even suggest that the novel's heightened concern with patrilinearity is responsible for its tendency to eliminate biological mothers. Does *Wilhelm Meister* do away with Mariane in order to establish Wilhelm as sole progenitor? Why is it that Wilhelm's own mother vanishes from the text without any further ado? Gradually, Natalie fills the void left by the disappearance of the biological mothers. She can do so because her own emptiness is ideally suited to guarantee the functioning of the male genealogy as well as of the symbolic order as such:[53]

> The women, animals capable of language like men, have the chance to guarantee the usage and circulation of the symbolic without taking part in it. The non-accessibility, for them, of the symbolic establishes the societal order. They can only real- ize their function to relate men to each other, to set up a con- nection between them, by renouncing their own right to speaking, and, beyond that, to their animality. (Irigaray 196)

Natalie's facelessness and her asexuality are essential for the func- tion that she fulfills within Goethe's novel.[54] Consequently, in *Wilhelm Meister's Journeyman Years* [Wilhelm Meister's Wanderjahre, 1829], where Wilhelm's integration into the male alliance is already established, Natalie is reduced to a "correspon- dence bride" (MacLeod, "Pedagogy" 423). Far from transgressing against traditional gender roles, the cross-dresser Natalie marks a void. It is her emptiness that upholds the symbolic system.

The assumption that heterosexual relationships provide a smokescreen for an underlying homosocial structure is further sup- ported by an analysis of the figure Mignon. Unlike Natalie, the child-woman Mignon is a true hybrid. The grammatical confusion which adheres to this androgynous being attests to the impossibil- ity of identifying her/him with one pole of the gender dichotomy. Mignon is often referred to as "creature" or "figure" ("Gestalt" 91). At times, the text even resorts to masculine pronouns when speak- ing about Mignon (VII: 616).[55] When Wilhelm first perceives Mignon, he is unsure whether he is dealing with a boy or a girl. Both the surgeon and the harper are convinced that Mignon is a boy. Mignon herself identifies with the male gender ("I am a boy, I don't want to be a girl," VII: 222) and refuses to wear women's clothing.[56] The consequences of Mignon's gender ambiguity are severe. They might be summarized as the inability to gain "Bildung." In spite of her efforts, Mignon never learns to read or

write. Her ability to express herself in German is extremely limited.[57] Like Natalie, Mignon, too, is excluded from the symbolic
systems of culture. Her true homeland is the pre-cultural realm of
feeling.[58] It is only through her death that Mignon, now an
enbalmed object, can be integrated into the sphere of Bildung.[59]

   While this explanation of Mignon as a symbol for a realm or a
concept of art that precedes Bildung is important, I would like to
suggest that there is another level of meaning that is obfuscated
by a discussion of Mignon's inability to gain Bildung. In his study
of the Mignon figure, Eugen Wolff has drawn attention to several
similarities between Goethe's gender-bender and the Berlin singer
Elisabeth Schmeling-Mara. Wolff is convinced that Mignon is the
result of a conflation of two different people and even two different genders: "While the model of Elisabeth Mara had a deter-
mining influence on Goethe's Mignon-figure in a number of characteristic traits, it is reasonable to suspect that Goethe adopted
the name Mignon from her companion, yes, that both characters
met in his fantasy" (Wolff 110). Wolff further points out that
Schmeling's husband, the violoncellist Mara, used to be the
"mignon," that is, lover of Prince Heinrich. If we assume with
Wolff that Goethe was familiar with the situation at the Berlin
court, one might conclude that the unspeakable realm of feelings
which Mignon embodies is that of homoerotic desire.[60] Within
this context Mignon's death might be understood as a form of
exorcism. However, the fact that her enbalmed body is then
placed in the hall of the past, the core of the Tower Society,
reveals that, though dead, she is still the center of this male
alliance. If one accepts this premise, then Goethe's claim that
Mignon—who in a diary entry of September 1786, is still referred
to with a masculine pronoun ("dem Mignon")—is the reason why
the entire work was written acquires a different meaning.[61] The
desire for a "mignon" that can neither be acknowledged nor abandoned informs the entire structure of Wilhelm Meister and helps
to explain the proliferation of cross-dressed characters. One might
speculate that it is precisely because Mignon holds an irresistible
attraction for Wilhelm (VII: 105) that the desire for her must give

way to a different form of relationship in which homoeroticism "prevalent everywhere, but prohibited as a practice [. . .] is played out via the bodies of women" (Irigaray 179). Seen in this light, homosociality is a sublimated form of homosexuality in which the desire for other men is symbolically mediated through the female body, as exemplified in the male characters' relationships with Therese and Natalie. Significantly, Mignon dies as Wilhelm embraces Therese (VII: 583). Moreover, reading Mignon as a symbol of homoerotic desire begs the question whether the incest motif is indeed, as Wolff claims (156), a later addition intended to displace and obfuscate the original theme of homosexuality which could not be addressed directly. By introducing the theme of incest, the homogeneity of same-sex desire could be transposed onto the pathology of intra-familial sameness. Thus, the madness of an improper relationship ("Wahnsinn eines Mißverhältnisses," HA VIII: 616), that Goethe attributes to Mignon's birth, might conceal a "Mißverhältnis" of a different kind, namely that between Mignon and Wilhelm.

Although Goethe's *Wilhelm Meister* can truly be classified as a novel of Bildung, the Bildung that it strives to achieve does not stop at the expulsion of androgyny[62] but aims for the sublimation of homosexual desire. However, homosexual desire, though banished from the surface of the text, is reinstated as the foundation of the homosocial community of men, who are welded together through the figure of the female cross-dresser. Moreover, though Goethe ostensibly condemns such "improper relationships," Mignon's transsubstantiation into an angel, that is, a genderless, transfigured being, might be read as the glorification of a desire sacrificed at the scene of her death.

Just like the social practices of the masked ball and the theater, Goethe's and von Stein's texts formed an integral part of the contemporary re-negotiation of the meaning of gender. At the Weimar theater, the use of cross-dressed actors, ostensibly well suited to undo stable definitions of gender, did not question traditional gender stereotypes, but rather reinforced them by means of casting decisions. It was left to Charlotte von Stein to challenge the model of "Geschlechtscharakter" that references the body to legitimize the disenfranchisement of women. But due to her own precarious position as a woman writer, von Stein's texts were largely ignored by her contemporaries as well as by literary scholars. Rediscovering her works not only adds a new voice, it also alters our understanding of already familiar texts. Reading Goethe against von Stein allows us to detect the inconsistencies and blind spots in Goethe's conceptualizations of gender.

In von Stein's texts, male clothing enables women to overcome the powerlessness of their female existence. In A New System of Freedom, the hollowness of male bravery and seeming superiority is unmasked through the cross-dresser's playful performance of masculinity. In von Stein's comedy, biology does not determine destiny. The power of a character is dependent on socially coded signs, on a repertoire of predictable phrases and gestures. Interestingly, just like A New System of Freedom, Women's Parts Played by Men also presents femininity as a quality that can be severed from the female body. Goethe believed that male actors were ideally qualified to represent the essence of femininity. However, the fact that Goethe fails to attribute similar talents to female actors is not accidental. While a male actor may represent true womanhood, a woman should never attempt to strip herself of her femininity and aspire to pass as a man. Goethe's Roman Carnival provides ample evidence that to him the dissolution of the gender dichotomy is not a site of pleasure, as in von Stein's comedy, but a signifier of social disorder and anarchy.

While Goethe's essay and travelogue are concerned with the performativity of a person's identity, his Wilhelm Meister relocates gender in the body. Paradoxically, cross-dressing makes Goethe's female characters more feminine, because their innate feminine nature proves to be stronger than the deception effected by their clothing. But even as it heightens a character's femininity, cross-dressing also signifies the absence of woman. It marks the empty space where the woman should be and thus ends up betraying what it was meant to hide: the homosocial structure of male society in Wilhelm Meister. Like Goethe's novel, von Stein's The Two

Emilies, is also concerned with the homosocial structure of society. Here too, the cross-dresser signifies the missing woman. But unlike Goethe's gender-benders, von Stein's cross-dresser enacts her own disappearance in order to reclaim her place in the male genealogy. By staging her own death, Fitzallen regains her rightful inheritance.

As different as Goethe's and von Stein's texts are, they both conceive of the dissolution of the gender order as a trading of places. In usurping male power, von Stein's cross-dressers may occupy the other pole of the gender dichotomy, but they never inhabit a space in between. It was left to the Romantic writers Dorothea Schlegel and Bettina Brentano-von Arnim to forge a new poetology out of indeterminacy and unresolved ambiguities.

Chapter 5

FEMALE FANTASIES:
Poetology and Androgyny

ℛ

Women in men's clothing and men in women's clothing are common motifs in the literature of German Romanticism. The phenomenon of gender-bending could not but fascinate a generation that considered the transgression of polarities—including those of art and life, philosophy and poetry, nature and culture—the core of its program of "progressive Universalpoesie." Cross-dressers figure prominently in many works by both male and female romanticists. In Joseph von Eichendorff's *From the Life of a Good-For-Nothing* [Aus dem Leben eines Taugenichts, 1826], the painter Guido turns out to be a young lady, and the Taugenichts himself is mistaken for a cross-dressed woman. In Achim von Arnim's "Isabella of Egypt: Emperor Karl the Fifth's First Love" [Isabella von Ägypten: Kaiser Karl des Fünften erste Jugendliebe, 1812], a mandrake hides his identity under women's clothing, and Bella, the female protagonist, disguises herself as a boy. In Clemens Brentano's *Godwi* (1801), the reader meets an amazon on horseback. Cross-dressed characters also appear in Eichendorff's *Premonition and Present* [Ahnung und Gegenwart, 1815] and *Poets and Their Companions* [Dichter und ihre Gesellen, 1834]; in E. T. A. Hofmann's *Artus' Court* [Artushof, 1817]; and in Tieck's *Franz Sternbald's Migrations* [Franz Sternbalds Wanderungen, 1798].[1]

The romanticist fascination with gender-benders stems from the same artistic longing that celebrates androgyny as an ideal of human wholeness, a longing that found expression in the works of romantic writers and philosophers such as Friedrich Schlegel, Friedrich Ernst Daniel Schleiermacher, Novalis, Franz von Baader, and Georg Friedrich Creuzer (see Friedrichsmeyer).

Feminist scholarship has pointed out that such androgynous perfection, symbolized by the union of woman and man in heterosexual love, is one-dimensional. It was man's progression towards
an androgynous ideal that these male writers had in mind.
Woman was only a "step in the journey towards *Bildung* of the
male soul which yearned for a fusion with the feminine in order
to achieve a higher state of humanity" (Becker-Cantarino,
"Priesterin" 122).[2] Man is defined as an individual in search of
perfection, whereas woman represents the desired Other of nature
and emotion that is to complement male reason (cf. Becker-
Cantarino, "Priesterin"; Weigel; MacLeod, *Embodying*).

The portrayal of cross-dressing in Dorothea Schlegel's novel
Florentin is informed by an acute awareness that the striving for
androgynous wholeness was not meant for the female gender. The
female cross-dresser in *Florentin* is not liberated by her new clothing. On the contrary, her male disguise renders her especially vulnerable to abuse. This is not to say that Schlegel's novel advocates a return to, or expresses nostalgia for, the clarity of
dichotomous structures. Rather, the refusal to conform to binary
categories constitutes the motivating force of Schlegel's writing.

Just as Dorothea Schlegel's novel can be read as a response to
her husband Friedrich Schlegel's celebration of androgyny in
Lucinde (1799), so can Bettina Brentano-von Arnim's gender philosophy be understood as a refutation of her brother Clemens
Brentano's idealization and subsequent demonization of the
French amazon Louise de Gachet. Brentano-von Arnim's novels,
though written around 1840, are based on correspondence from
around 1800. Because of this historical duality, they interlace the
late-eighteenth-century reconfiguration of gender with mid-nine-
teenth-century discourses, thus providing a fitting conclusion to
my investigation of the changing concepts of gender and the body.

Brentano-von Arnim's epistolary novels deconstruct the ideology of the "gendered character" by dissociating masculinity
from male bodies. Her heroines lay claim to male privileges along
with men's clothing. Moreover, Brentano-von Arnim was courageous enough to live the transgressions that she describes in her

BETTINA BRENTANO-VON ARNIM. Several contemporaries describe Brentano-von Arnim's appearance as androgynous. *Portrait by Achim von Arnim-Baewalde, the grandson of the writer. Photo: AKG London*

work. She undertook several journeys in men's clothing, thus joining a long tradition of cross-dressed travelers ranging from the famous Englishwoman Lady Mary Montague and the German poetess Sidonia Hedwig Zäunemann (see Ohnesorg 161–168), to Ulrike von Kleist (see Ohnesorg 172–176) and the daughters of

Wilhelm von Humboldt. Annegret Pelz has pointed out that the freedom born of their gender masquerade was based on a paradox: "the presence of female absence in the public sphere" (84). Unlike women passengers in a coach—another variation of the presence of female absence—the cross-dressed traveler represented "the horrifying and fascinating spectacle of a femininity which can no longer be manipulated but which independently and autonomously stands on its own feet" (84).

It is the paradoxical nature of cross-dressing—the presence of female absence—that will be at the center of the following analyses. One must look to the unresolved ambiguity of the cross-dresser to capture the recalcitrant energy of Schlegel's and Brentano-von Arnim's writing. By insisting on paradox and internal contradiction, by refusing to provide closure while staging a capricious play with polar categories, Bettina Brentano-von Arnim and Dorothea Schlegel were able to cope with the constraints that threatened to stifle women writers of the eighteenth and nineteenth centuries.

Dorothea Schlegel's *Florentin*

Like Bettina Brentano-von Arnim, Caroline Schlegel-Schelling, Sophie Mereau, and Karoline von Günderrode, Dorothea Schlegel wrote and lived in the context of German Romanticism.[3] But while Brentano-von Arnim has received much critical attention, there is little secondary literature addressing Schlegel's artistic achievements.[4] Literary histories, if they mention her at all, focus on her supportive role as servile wife and secretary of Friedrich Schlegel. Far from receiving praise for her housewifely drudgery, Dorothea Schlegel's labor of love has been denounced as zealous and obsequious devotion to her husband. Ricarda Huch, for example, called her Friedrich's "evil demon" (28) and claimed that her "blind submissiveness" and doting love were responsible for the "ever more obtuse harem-like stoutness" of her husband (28). While Huch's attack on Dorothea Schlegel's character focuses on her later years,[5]

Schlegel's contemporaries found fault with her early libertinage. After all, the unconventional behavior of Dorothea Veit, who left her husband and children for a partner who was seven years her junior and whom she did not marry until several years later, inspired the scandalous title character Lucinde in Friedrich Schlegel's eponymous novel of 1799.[6] The practice of free love—along with its literary glorification in *Lucinde*—led to Dorothea Schlegel's social marginalization, which left her unprotected in the face of vicious invectives against her character in numerous contemporary publications. Often the condemnation of her alleged immorality was interspersed with thinly veiled anti-Semitic slander.

Dorothea Schlegel's novel *Florentin* was written during this turbulent phase of her life.[7] Schlegel had just moved to Jena, where she shared a house with her lover Friedrich, Friedrich's brother August Wilhelm, and the latter's wife Caroline. She began writing *Florentin*—originally entitled *Arthur*, then *Lorenzo*—in November 1799, and completed it after only 9 months.[8] Like all her other works, this one was published under her husband's name.[9] It was greeted with reviews by several well-known authors, among them Schiller, who, in disdainful condescension, considered it new proof of "how much this dilettantism can accomplish at least with respect to the mechanics and the hollow form [of art]" (letter to Goethe, March 16, 1801, XXXI: 19).

Schlegel's only novel has often been read as a female response to *Lucinde*.[10] Several scholars have emphasized *Florentin's* kinship with Friedrich Schlegel's scandalous novel as well as with other novels of Bildung such as *Wilhelm Meister's Apprenticeship* (1795–96) and *Franz Sternbald's Migrations* (1798). The affinity of Dorothea Schlegel's work to these famous predecessors has wrongly been interpreted as a lack of creativity on her part.[11] Even though *Florentin* bears superficial similarities to the aforementioned texts, these common motifs do not diminish the singularity of Schlegel's artistic accomplishment.[12] In fact, the abrupt ending of Schlegel's novel refuses its readers the genre-typical closure qua genealogy, and suggests that *Florentin* might more justly be described as an "anti-Bildungsroman" (Helfer 150).[13]

Initially, Dorothea Schlegel planned to write a sequel, but she did not carry out her intention.[14] All we have of this projected second part are some fragments, among them a segment of a novel entitled *Camilla*. Stuebben Thornton suggests that Schlegel's unwillingness to finish the project might have been motivated by a change of heart with respect to the Catholic Church, which, in keeping with enlightenment tradition, is portrayed rather negatively in *Florentin*. I wish instead to propose that, while such ideological incompatibilities may have contributed to Schlegel's hesitation, the fragmentary state of *Florentin* and its sequel might also be attributed to Schlegel's poetological vision at the time.

Schlegel claimed that she consented to the publication of her novel because of financial constraints and expressed doubts about its quality. Her self-criticism grew more pronounced as the years progressed.[15] She calls her novel "childish" and "clumsy"[16] and agreed with Novalis, who felt that it was a work with much "Bildung" but without an overriding plan (cf. *Briefwechsel* I: 255). Modern readers might concur with this evaluation as they notice that the novel delights in detailing narrative strands, which it then abandons silently, and in alluding to mysterious secrets whose significance is never revealed.

It is indicative of this playful confusion that Florentin, the protagonist of the novel, is first introduced as a traveler who has lost his way. Trying to find his bearings, he happens upon Count Schwarzenberg, whom he saves from an attack by a wild boar. The count invites him to his country estate where Florentin meets Schwarzenberg's wife, Eleonore, his daughter, Juliane, and Juliane's fiancé, Eduard. The text hints at a ménage à trois in which Florentin's affection for Juliane is counterbalanced by his homoerotically tinged friendship with Eduard. The tension of conflicting desires reaches a climax as the two friends and the cross-dressed Juliane embark on an outing into the countryside, during which Florentin narrates the story of his childhood and youth.[17] When a thunderstorm surprises the three, they take refuge in a mill. On the next day Juliane and Eduard's wedding is supposed to take place. Clandestinely, Florentin leaves his friends and visits

Juliane's aunt Clementina. He gets involved in a conflict between Betty, a protegé of Clementina's, and her fiancé, Walter. Upon beholding Florentin, Clementina faints. The novel ends with the laconic remark: "Florentin was nowhere to be found."

The abrupt ending of Schlegel's novel leaves its readers puzzled. The tensions that threaten to destroy the relationships between Betty and Walter and Juliane and Eduard are not resolved. The secret of Florentin's ancestry remains hidden. Indeed, the reader's attempts to reconstruct the genealogy of the characters are as futile as Florentin's endeavors to find a purpose in his life. Schlegel's novel teases its readers by first invoking genealogy and teleology only to reject them later. Such presence-in-absence suggests that Schlegel's writing revolves around the conscious display of indeterminacy, of which the motif of the cross-dresser is yet another manifestation.

Florentin devotes a considerable share of its narrative energy to the motif of cross-dressing.[18] It contains a detailed account of Juliane's disguise, of her behavior when cross-dressed, and of the discovery of her "true" gender in the mill. However, the narrative weight of this episode is inversely proportional to its empowering potential. Far from expanding her realm of agency, Juliane is intimidated by the potential dangers of her sartorial adventure. Paradoxically, the experimental reversal of gender roles intensifies her experience of dependency and victimization (Schmitz 106). Such a failure of the adoption of masculinity is even more astonishing if we compare Juliane's humiliation in the mill with her previous, far more successful ventures of male impersonation: "As Juliane was a good rider and often rode in men's clothing, she was not unaccustomed to it, and walked in such an easy and unconstrained manner as though she had never worn any other clothing, and, she looked equally beautiful as a boy."[19] The contrast between these two episodes demonstrates that Schlegel is aware of the liberatory potential of cross-dressing. Why then does the excursion to the mill result in such a painfully humbling experience?

In order to account for the failure of Juliane's masculine venture, we must consider its prelude. Juliane's initial exhilaration is curtailed by her parents' resolute prohibition. Even though her parents finally give in to her persistent entreaties, their warnings accompany her preparations and stifle her joy until Juliane is firmly resolved "not to transgress against anything and never to desire such permission again" (*Florentin* 37). But it is not just her parents' intimidating admonitions that make it impossible for her to enjoy the excursion. In spite of her disguise, Juliane cannot cross over into the realm of male potency. Cross-dressing in *Florentin* does not reclaim male privilege for women but induces a dissolution of established gender roles that leaves the disguised woman unprotected and helpless. Schlegel seems to suggest that the traditional gender roles, though restrictive, also function as safeguards against male license and the social stigmatization of the female victim that follows in its wake.

Schlegel portrays the forest to which the three betake themselves as uncharted territory that renders societal conventions and norms invalid: "The wish of the moment was their law" (*Florentin* 37). Gender categories, social classifications, and commonly accepted standards of behavior do not extend into this sphere. This freedom, however, is not liberating. On the contrary, the breakdown of established societal codes in the forest accounts for the fact that Eduard abandons his usual reserve towards his fiancé: "He pressed Juliane to his breast with fervor; forgetting the presence of the friend he checked himself no longer, his lips were firmly pressed to hers, his embrace grew more daring, he was beside himself. Juliane was frightened."[20] Here, the suspension of traditional norms and conventions does not liberate woman but makes her an easy prey to male obtrusiveness.[21] Institutionalized codes of interaction are safety mechanisms that protect the "weaker" sex. Seen in this light, Juliane's new role is highly ambiguous: while the pre-social realm of the forest is marked by the absence of restrictive gender roles, it also lacks social conventions that prevent trespasses.

Juliane's helplessness is highlighted further when she and her companions seek refuge from a thunderstorm. Juliane, whose disguise has stripped her of the privileges of her social class, is subjected to the impertinent remarks of the miller's wife: "Soon she [the miller's wife] became so insolent that she took the liberty of making some obscene jokes about Juliane, whose social standing she was far from guessing."[22] One cannot help but be reminded of the scorn and contempt that had been directed toward Dorothea Schlegel after her separation from Veit. Clearly, Schlegel was aware of the humiliating insults that awaited a woman who dared to overstep the narrow confines of female propriety. Just like her heroine, Schlegel broke free from societal conventions and was ostracized because of her courageous decision. But unlike her heroine, Schlegel employed fiction to convey experiences and insights whose undisguised expression is silenced by the prohibitions of bourgeois society: "Because it is against the bourgeois order such as it is, and it is absolutely not permitted to introduce romantic poetry into life, one had better insert one's life into romantic poetry; no police and no educational institution can object to that."[23] Even though she chose to cloak her own illicit experiences in a fictional guise, and even though her novel highlights the motif of a woman in male dress, Schlegel herself remained deeply ambivalent about such false fronts. Indeed, the ubiquity and necessity of masks and disguises form the centerpiece of Schlegel's social critique. In her diary, she compares the bourgeois order to a masquerade that prevents individuals from expressing their true selves: "Not to deny one's individuality, to live according to one's own disposition and conscience is indecent and arrogant, as though one wanted to appear at a masquerade without one's mask."[24] To Schlegel, wearing a mask is a highly ambivalent trope. She thoroughly loathed masks insofar as they are synonymous with the denial of one's individuality.[25] Schlegel believed in the existence of a true self which, though it may be hidden, can never be obliterated completely. It was her declared goal to live in accordance with her inner self. But in spite of this, she also delighted in the kind of role play and disguise that is the essence of all literary imagination. Comparing the characters of her fiction with naked bodies that are clothed by the author, Schlegel likens writing itself to putting on a costume:[26]

I would have liked for you to see the manuscript [*Florentin*] first [. . .] I could send you the first brouillon but, in addition to the cost of the postage, there is also red ink everywhere [. . .] for the devil always rules precisely where dative and accusative should rule, and you should not first see it in this form, I will not do this to the humorous good-for-nothing. Have patience until he gets dressed and wears his gala uniform, then he will present himself beautifully.[27]

Here, perfecting her text stylistically is compared to putting on a gala uniform. In "Dedication to the Editor" [Zueignung an den Herausgeber (Schlegel, *Florentin*, 156–159)], Schlegel again associates the act of dressing with the writing of a story:

I am never entirely content if the poet leaves no room for me to add or dream. Thus, I can occupy myself with one single story for a rather long time and delight in giving it now this now that ending. In this, I feel like the little girls who would rather play with a naked puppet, which they can dress differently every hour and to which they can give an entirely different form, than with the most splendid and perfectly dressed puppet to which the pieces of clothing and thus its accomplished purpose have been sewn forever.[28]

Preferring the variety of ever-new clothing to the splendor of one uniform puppet, Dorothea Schlegel refuses to be limited to only one "dress." She is afraid that fixating her thoughts in writing will reduce the initial plethora of meaning to only one dimension and purpose. For Schlegel, the ideal novel is like an empty sheet of paper. It delays closure and allows for a multitude of possible interpretations. Thus, the fragmentary state of *Florentin* might be seen as a direct result of Schlegel's poetology of openness: "Alas, in reality, in certainty, that is where all my wistfulness and all my dissatisfaction start. My reality and my satisfaction lies in longing and in anticipation."[29] Martha Helfer has pointed out that *Florentin* is marked by an "ironic aesthetic of absence." She claims

that this absence—we might also call it openness—"performs a
critique of gender by constantly deferring the production of closure" (157). In refusing definitive choices and decisive endings,
Schlegel eludes the pitfalls of binary systems in which traditional
gender roles are housed. Although Schlegel affirms the protective
dimension of societal conventions, the aesthetic structure of her
novel dissolves cultural systems of order in a radical way.
Suspending all traditional categories in midair, Schlegel's enactment of an aesthetics of longing realizes a utopian state.
Paradoxically, fulfillment, as Dorothea Schlegel defines it, is
found in the perpetuation of non-fulfillment. Since every form of
fulfillment necessarily brings an end to the desired state of longing, it is only the infinite deferral of satisfaction that keeps desire
alive. In this respect, Dorothea Schlegel's concept of desire
resembles that of Jacques Lacan, summarized by Marjory Garber:

> Desire is neither the appetite for satisfaction, nor the demand
> for love, but the difference that results from the subtraction of
> the first from the second, the phenomenon of their splitting
> (Spaltung). Thus desire is by definition that which cannot be
> satisfied: it is what is left of absolute demand when all possible
> satisfaction has been subtracted from it. (75)

Interestingly, Garber then claims that transvestites are privileged
signifiers of this kind of desire since in them the presence of masculine clothing is marked by the absence of masculinity. Seen in
this light, Schlegel's poetology and its celebration of ambiguity
are in perfect tune with the prominent presence of a cross-dresser
in her text. Moreover, Schlegel's preference for openness also
explains why her gender-bender exercises such a magical spell.
The yearning for that which Juliane's cross-dressed appearance
promises must remain unfulfilled. In this, the cross-dresser incarnates the impossibility of closure that Schlegel valued so highly.
But, like masks, cross-dressers are ambivalent tropes. In addition
to embodying Schlegel's aesthetics of openness, cross-dressing
also symbolizes the painful distance between signifier and signi-

fied that Schlegel laments in her "Dedication to the Editor": "I was always under the impression that I wrote down what I had just thought, but it was a delusion" (157).

Just as the cross-dresser is defined by the dissociation of body and dress, so is Schlegel's writing afflicted by the non-identity of word and meaning. Schlegel's literary imagination is haunted by the loss of an unquestioned confidence that language is capable of expressing one's inner thoughts and feelings. This awareness of dissociation might be said to derive from the constitutional inadequacy of language as such. But in Schlegel's case, it was also intimately tied to her experience of social marginalization:

> Often they laugh at me and feel rather superior if I seem to lack the proper words, the fashionable expressions with which they designate everything so easily [. . .] Alas, I know these words very well, they are words! But I am afraid to use them. They might signify something entirely different as of today, rather the opposite, and nobody would be astonished about it at all. That which one cannot name is always that which is most dear and the best and really that which one means.[30]

On one level, Schlegel acknowledges that the meaning of words is the result of societal conventions and negotiations. But she also suggests that there is a true meaning which conventional language cannot express. Again, there appears to be a conflation of two predicaments. One pertains to the existential difference between world and word. The other describes the impossibility of repossessing a language that is deformed by "fashionable expressions." In the second scenario, Schlegel's painful inability to express her inner self might be related to the untenability of a female subject position in a language that is propelled by the laws of a patriarchal society. Schlegel's answer to these societal strictures is her refusal to submit to the meaning of others. However, self-expression of this kind can only be purchased at the expense of communication. Schlegel herself is acutely aware that meaning, where it is not embedded in a social context, ceases to exist altogether. In *Florentin*, the protagonist himself finds "his very own meaning" but fails to share it:

> Now it appears as though he associated the words with a differ-
> ent meaning from the one that they are supposed to have;
> then he looks indifferent to the most flattering things that are
> being said to him, rather as though it could not be any differ-
> ent; then, against all odds, he is happy about an unintentional
> word that is spoken by chance; he always finds his very own
> meaning, I don't know, whether he brings it to it or takes it
> from it.[31]

For Florentin, words have lost their conventional meaning. His empty word shells lack an inner core just like the cross-dresser lacks an inside that corresponds to his outside. This lack questions the very possibility of communication, but it is also the precondition for an openness that spawns a variety of diverging and even conflicting interpretations.

Unsurprisingly, Schlegel's novel extends its commitment to openness to include the concept of identity itself. *Florentin* not only rejects rigid interpretations of words, it also does away with the notion of an immutable personal essence. By conceiving of identity as continually changing and internally heterogeneous, Schlegel's text facilitates shifting identifications.[32] One of the first and most attentive readers of *Florentin*, Schlegel's friend Friedrich Schleiermacher, recognized this. He was delighted that "the story of *Florentin* so neatly plays a trick on psychological readers where they are looking for perfect clues regarding the development of his character" (Schleiermacher to Dorothea Schlegel, December 6, 1800, *Briefwechsel* I: 65). Refusing to construct a consistent, psycho-logical hero, Schlegel devises many-faceted characters who draw out the hidden desires of their readers:

> The knowledge of human nature is so deep, so manifold and so
> inevitable in them that there cannot be any lack: every human
> being who is educated or striving to educate himself must dis-

cover the infinitely deep and refined psychology of his own innermost being somewhere in one of these portrayals and can contemplate himself perfectly like in a mirror without having to pay for this self-knowledge with his own experience.[33]

In *Florentin*, every reader is represented somewhere, but no single individual is represented entirely. Schlegel vehemently rejected the assumption that *Florentin* is a roman à clef and disapproved of all attempts to uncover its living models.[34] She emphasized the idea of personal discontinuity and non-identity by creating character collages that tease readers with their resemblance to particular individuals but do not add up to actual representations of these models. Furthermore, Schlegel highlights the fact that people change over time. Non-identity with one's own previous self is portrayed as an essential trait of personal identity itself. To illustrate this idea, Schlegel utilizes visual representations since they capture only one moment in time. Thus, a portrait of the youthful Clementina bears nothing but a faint resemblance to the now aged woman (28). In the remaining fragments of the projected sequel, insistence on the ever-changing nature of identity is also evidenced by Schlegel's continual renaming of her characters. Hilario becomes Jeronimo and then Laurentius, Rosalie is renamed Jucunda, and Camilla is turned into Veronica and then Aloysia.

Schlegel refuses to effect closure not only by withholding the ending but also by denying her characters consistent identities. She undermines causal concatenations and psycho-logical explanations by introducing seemingly potent motifs which are then forgotten, and by alluding to promising possibilities which remain unexplored. Schlegel goads readers by hinting at a secret genealogy but never reveals the mystery of Florentin's birth, nor does she portray how her protagonist founds a family of his own. Even though *Florentin* is framed as a Bildungsroman, any development of its hero is conspicuously absent. Schlegel's text is implicated in a discourse of teleology but obstructs its readers' attempts to decipher its purpose. In *Florentin*, Schlegel imagines a language whose meaning is open, and a form of desire whose fulfillment is deferred into infinity. Appropriately, the figure of the cross-dresser, whose existence is based on the refusal to commit to only one of two options, functions as a central metaphor for her aesthetics of openness. It is by embracing paradox itself that Schlegel negotiates the paradox of being a woman writer around 1800.

Bettina Brentano-von Arnim's *Clemens Brentano's Spring Wreath*, *The Günderode*, and *Goethe's Correspondence With a Child*

Bettina Brentano-von Arnim's[35] epistolary novel *Clemens Brentano's Spring Wreath* [Clemens Brentanos Frühlingskranz], published in 1844, was based on her correspondence with her brother Clemens from 1801 to 1803.[36] However, though it is rooted in reality, Brentano-von Arnim's text is not intended to provide an authentic account of her experiences.[37] In *Spring Wreath*, as in all of Brentano-von Arnim's epistolary novels, facts and fiction blend into an indivisible whole. Confused by this innovative procedure, previous research has often attempted to sift the chaff from the wheat (cf. Oehlke).[38] Only recently have scholars begun to conceive of Brentano-von Arnim's mythologization of her life as a technique used deliberately to break down the hierarchy between author and text, subject and object, self and other (Frederiksen and Shafi 54; Liebertz-Grün 18f.; Simpson 247). The following interpretation is indebted to this later research in that it does not reconstruct the author's life from her fiction but analyzes Brentano-von Arnim's conceptualization of gender as it was developed in *Clemens Brentano's Spring Wreath*.

Brentano-von Arnim's epistolary novels span two different time periods.[39] They depict the author's adolescence—the time when the original correspondence, on which the novels are based, was written—but they also bear traces of her mature years when the novels were conceived and published. Even though the extent of her revisions cannot always be determined, as the manuscripts are not always extant, it is certain that Brentano-von Arnim changed the original letters considerably in order to make them more conducive to her purpose (Weißenborn 154, 228; Burwick, "Bettina" 63). Indeed, all of her novels were designed not to cherish memories of the past but to influence the political situation of the present (Mander 132; Ockenfuß, *Bettine* 40).

In the case of her third epistolary novel, *Clemens Brentano's Spring Wreath* (1844), Brentano-von Arnim's wish to support a liberal agenda led to the choice of Egbert Bauer as publisher, which ultimately caused the prohibition of the novel. It is against this political background that one must interpret the mature Brentano-von Arnim's description of the societal strictures that threatened to stifle her adolescent spirit as well as her resistance to them. But it is also against this background that the *Spring Wreath* calls for political change. It is characteristic of Brentano-von Arnim's oeuvre that the change that she wants to effect not only pertains to the re-definition of traditional gender roles, but is played out in her poetological technique.

It is not accidental that Brentano-von Arnim chooses to convey her message through the portrayal of the French amazon Louise de Gachet. De Gachet casts a magical spell on the fictional heroine Bettine because in her person three momentous motifs melt into one: the chaos of war, the freedom of travel, and the category-defying power of the cross-dresser. It is possible that Brentano-von Arnim's interest in gender-benders was stimulated not only by her own desire for freedom and travel but also by the fact that she herself was often perceived as "androgynous" by her contemporaries. Caroline Bauer, for example, called her "boyish" (qtd. in Wolf 540), and Amalie von Helvig thought that Bettina was feminine in essentials but not in her outward appearance (qtd. in Drewitz 104). Caroline Schlegel-Schelling describes her as "neither like a man nor a woman" ("weder wie ein Männlein noch wie ein Fräulein," *Caroline und Dorothea Schlegel in Briefen*, 260) and Heinrich Grunholzer characterizes her as "coarse, clear, manly firm" (diary entry, February 26, 1843, qtd. in Hirsch 145).[40] Brentano-von Arnim herself contributed to this confusion by referring to herself with the gender-neutral term "child." Her practice inspired others to numerous androgynous epithets such as "elemental being" ("Elementarwesen"), "goblin," "mignon," or "pysche" (cf. Perels 285; Goozé, "Reception" 381). It appears that the young Bettina's alleged lack of a feminine physique corresponded to her boyishly unrestrained behavior and her concomitant refusal to submit to familial and societal constraints.[41] In *Clemens Brentano's Spring Wreath*, Brentano-von Arnim describes her character's revolt against such constraints as well as her ultimate triumph over recurrent attempts to instill proper femininity in her.

It is well-nigh impossible to give a plot summary of the *Spring Wreath*. The novel consists of fleeting moments, bits of everyday life, impressions of the world and thoughts about the people that Bettine encounters. Its unifying thread is a passionate endeavor to grow up female and free—against the resistance of philistine conventions and even against the resistance of a loving brother.

At the beginning of the novel, the young Bettine is already an orphan. In this respect, the biography of the fictional heroine mirrors that of her author.[42] After the death of her mother, Bettina Brentano spent four years at the Ursulinen convent in Fritzlar near Kassel.[43] When her father died in 1797, she went to live with her grandmother Sophie La Roche in Offenbach. Even though life with the famous author of *History of Lady Sophia Sternheim* [Das Fräulein von Sternheim, 1776] must have provided considerable intellectual stimulation for the young girl, Brentano-von Arnim depicts a heroine who experiences intellectual deprivation caused by a gender-specific socialization. From the outset, Bettine questions gender stereotypes and offers resistance to what she calls the "very special police . . . that persecutes young girls" ("ganz eigne Polizei . . . womit man die jungen Mädchen verfolgt," *Frühlingskranz* 102). In one of her first letters to Clemens, she expresses her discontent with the advice that education traditionally has in store for girls: "Yes, I would have to talk about my astonishment about everything that I see and hear in the world! About the advice which those people give me who want to bring me up to be an agreeable and lovely girl. But what other people call well-mannered and educated, I do not find that agreeable at all but rather horrific."[44] Bettine's dissatisfaction with the destiny prescribed for women is rooted in her longing to change the world, to be active, to travel, to live free and heroically. Brentano-von Arnim had already given expression to these desires in her previous epistolary novel *The Günderode* (1840), based on her correspondence from 1804 to 1806 with her friend and fellow writer Karoline von Günderrode. In this novel the protagonist's melancholy springs from a hunger for action which remains unrealized.[45] The life of an adolescent girl is compared to a river made of bricks ("ein backsteinerner Fluß"), where the oarsmen attempt in vain to stir up waves.[46] In *Spring Wreath* as well, the young Bettine's frustration is caused by the fact that the world that surrounds her cannot provide an outlet for her energy, her strength, and her courage:

> To be and to become are two different things, I know it very well, and to become is to feel strength for the real life and to apply it and not just dream of becoming a hero. And this is what often makes me afraid of myself, that I have chosen for myself such a splendid role in the land of fantasy, which I play without danger, but which does not touch reality.—What can I do to be delivered from this exile from reality.[47]

In *Spring Wreath*, the possibility of overcoming this painful "exile from reality" appears in the form of a cross-dresser. Just like in Brentano's previous novel *Günderode*, the wish to lead a different life is entangled with the wish for a different body. In *Günderode*, an existence as a man or boy is presented as a means to escape from an unheroic world: "If I should make out your character," Günderode writes to Bettine, "I would prophesy that, if you were a boy, you would become a hero."[48] Again and again, Brentano-von Arnim designs male roles for her fictional alter ego Bettine and her friend. She describes Günderode as dominant master and Bettine as goblin (*Günderode* 70). Bettine is the (male) student,

SELF-PORTRAIT BY BETTINA VON ARNIM. *Photo: Stiftung Weimarer Klassik,*
Goethe- und Schiller-Archiv

her friend the (male) preceptor. Due to a "male" mind Günderode thinks masculine thoughts: "And flames will soar, inspired by the law of your breath, from your soul and ignite in the hearts of youthful generations, who, thinking themselves boyish manly, will never guess that the youth's breath which lights their breast, never came from the mind of man."[49]

In *Spring Wreath* the dreamed-for possibility of changing one's gender becomes tangible when the French cross-dresser enters center stage. Louise de Gachet, who is said to be the model for Goethe's *Natural Daughter* [Natürliche Tochter, 1799–1803], had been a military leader of the royalist resistance in the Vendée. She was also a physicist and had come to Germany to pursue her studies. Even though Sophie von La Roche housed many French emigrants, de Gachet stood out among the stream of guests. Unsurprisingly, Brentano-von Arnim's fictional account stresses the excitement stirred up by the arrival of the French amazon in the small German town of Offenbach. The commotion surrounding her arrival is borne out by her subsequent importance for Bettine's development.

The encounter with the French cross-dresser and warrior woman deeply influenced Bettine's definition of her own gender identity, which she developed in reaction (and contrast) to her brother's perception of the amazon. In the beginning Clemens' perspective dominates. Clemens, who had met de Gachet on a journey to Mainz, announces her visit to his family. He starts his epistolary introduction of the woman from the Vendée with an enthusiastic eulogy. De Gachet performs miracles, Clemens tells us. Not only is she intrepid like a woman from the Nibelungs ("ein Weib aus den Nibelungen")—riding on wild horses—and knowledgeable in science but she is also exceptionally beautiful. Clemens' second letter on the subject is equally ardent. In fact, his hymns of praise for the celebrated amazon rather surpass the ones expressed in his first letter:

> You don't know how happy I am that I can tell you this through
> the most lovely woman who due to her destiny surpasses the

ordinary circle of men, but even more due to her independence,
due to her firm earnest will, with which she fought against this
destiny and suffered heroically, walking calmly and alone
amongst the terrors of the bloody regime. She often rode on
wild horses through the Vendée in order to meet with the great
heroes there whom she often preceded on nightly dangerous
walks, quite a few of these poor peasants (Chouans) she saved
by risking her own life, but her whole family was devoured by
the guillotine.[50]

Clemens, as Brentano-von Arnim portrays him, is sexually
attracted to de Gachet's Valkyrian qualities. He displays a
masochistic desire for a woman involved in the horrors of war. He
celebrates her as an invulnerable goddess who—calmly strolling
among the terrors of blood and destruction—saves ordinary mor-
tals from distress. In his description, de Gachet is transformed into
a superwoman, an almost Nietzschean "Übermensch." But the
text provides ample evidence that his admiration is contingent
on de Gachet's relegation to a mystical realm, that is, on her
removal from everyday societal and familial contexts. By isolat-
ing her from the realm of normality (the "gewöhnlichen Kreis"),
Clemens makes a miraculous being out of de Gachet. We may
well suspect that his recommendation of de Gachet as a model
for his sister would be unthinkable had the former not been safely
located in this surreal-mythical sphere. Indeed, in the following
letter, Clemens has second thoughts about his glowing report
when he realizes that the Valkyrie is about to be a guest in his
own sweet home. In his third letter to Bettine, he qualifies his former recommendation: "Also, you should love her like the most
ingenious person, but only her mind and heart; but the scars
which her experience and destiny inflicted upon her, the manly
wildness of her being and intellect, you should overlook, and in
general not give yourself up to her, remain mine and God's."[51]
Suddenly, Clemens' admiration for the heroic independence of
this extraordinary individual comes into conflict with his ideas
about what he considers "true" femininity. He remembers his self-

imposed obligation to educate his sister to be a proper woman, which, in his view, is incommensurably different from being a proper man ("ein vortreffliches Weib etwas ganz anderes ist als ein braver Mann," *Frühlingskranz* 158). He resolves this dilemma by admonishing his sister to love everything human about de Gachet and to overlook all that is manly and wild. But as all of de Gachet's admirable qualities are coded as masculine, Clemens must ultimately withdraw his recommendation completely. He is tormented by sleeplessness until he finally writes his fourth letter: "And again about this de Gachet, but God knows, it chases me out of my bed again [. . .] I regret it very much and it was too hasty that I gave her my letter to you."[52] We do not know to what extent Brentano-von Arnim changed her brother's original letters. But it seems likely that even for a romantic outsider like Clemens Brentano, there was an abyss between his fascination with the exotic amazon on her wild horse and his demands on his sister—whom he entrusts with the knitting of his stockings (*Frühlingskranz* 113), and whom he advises to stay away from dangerous amazons.

Luckily, Bettine did not fall for this ideology, nor was she inclined to follow her brother's advice to stay away from amazons. Despite all of Clemens' warnings, Bettine experiences the arrival of the superwoman as an event that turns her little world upside-down:

> From one day to the next the world here in Offenbach has turned in a somersault [. . .] Behold, there came rushing in a storm a cabriolet like a darted arrow to our doorstep, down jumps the driver, a youthfully strong, beautiful man-youth with jingling spurs, two riders, who accompanied him, enter with him, I was, I don't know how, not why, seized by fright, so that I forgot to talk, and didn't think to call my grandmother, who was in the garden. The duke asked who it was, I intimated to the stranger that he was blind, and said: "C'est un jeune cavalier, Monseigneur, avec deux messieurs." "Au contraire c'est une femme," said the youth and came closer.[53]

De Gachet's arrival is like a whirlwind that takes Bettine away from her familiar environment (for example, she forgets to call her grandmother). But she soon overcomes her initial shock and speechlessness and feels exhilarating joy: "I have to shout out of joy about an indefinite something. What can it be?" ("ich muß jauchzen vor Vergnügen über ein unbestimmtes Etwas. Was mag es sein," *Frühlingskranz* 50, 51). Unlike her brother, Bettine is not attracted by de Gachet's violence but by her ability to defy dichotomous categories. She is fascinated by the "Mannjüngling," a mixture of man and boy, before she realizes that de Gachet is really a combination of man and woman, a "Mannweib." Even after de Gachet's explanation that she is "une femme," Bettine continues to call her "Jüngling." She, too, is erotically attracted to de Gachet's appearance, wounded by love's arrow, as well as enraptured by the promise of freedom and heroic action that the Frenchwoman symbolizes for her. But just as de Gachet's nature is mixed, so are Bettine's feelings. She wants to travel with the amazon, who invites her to come along. Bettine need only mount her horse and leave her narrow little world behind. But her longing is marred by her anxiety about being overpowered by an older, more experienced personality, and she declines de Gachet's invitation to travel with her. To her, de Gachet is a devil of a woman, but so is she. Thus, she knows that she has to stay away from de Gachet if she wants to be independent. Even though her close relationship to her brother, which also betrays an erotic component, may have played a part in her decision (Bettine declares her loyalty to him, and promises not to surrender to the stranger ["sich nicht hingeben," *Frühlingskranz* 52]), her refusal to join the amazon is not driven by anxiety but by the wish to stay true to herself. She lives according to her insight that to be oneself is to be a hero (*Frühlingskranz* 87). Even though she regrets the missed opportunity and comments on de Gachet's departure with "it's over with flowers" (*Frühlingskranz* 60), she knows that it is not yet time for her to leave. And even though she distances herself from the amazon, the encounter changes her relationship with Clemens. Encouraged by de Gachet's example, Bettine refuses to adopt her brother's ideal of a "proper" woman.[54] She receives all of Clemens' often bestowed misogynistic statements with silence or with rejection,[55] as she starts to dissolve the rigid dichotomies that he imposes on her. She tells him that his ideas are illusions which are bouncing up and down in his texts like grasshoppers:

> The most leathery grasshopper is the one where you absolutely want to point out the big difference between an excellent woman and a good man. May these two meet each other on some lucky star, only this one thing I ask of you, that you do not inform me of it; and once and for all I want to be excluded completely from this sanctuary!—And secondly—your warning against all male company! The Günderode tells me she does not know any male company but mine. I, too, dear Clemens, do not know any male company but the hop-poles which the milkmaid bought for me for the coming spring; they are the most coarse amongst my acquaintance [. . .] The *nice ingrata*, who even though she is your university friend, and who, after you had paid the graduation meal for her, ran off with your best clothes, has a beard and perhaps wants to be taken for a man; but she looks into the mirror and sings *nice bella*, and who has any doubts that she is a *nice*.[56]

Bettine's playful irony deconstructs Clemens' gender ideology. She invents a scale of masculinity on which she herself figures prominently right along with the hop-pole and much higher than Clemens' university friend, the "nice ingrata." According to this scale, masculinity is a quality that can be detached from the male body. In Brentano-von Arnim's text, masculinity and femininity are not derivatives of a prior physical state but the consequence of a person's behavior. This definition of gender is astonishingly close to what Judith Butler calls gender performance when she asks: "Does being female constitute a 'natural fact' or a cultural performance, or is 'naturalness' constituted through discursively constrained performative acts that produce the body through and within the categories of sex?" (*Gender* viii). In Butler's theory as

well as in Brentano-von Arnim's text, gender identities become
free-floating entities.[57] It has been noted that in her letters to her
family and friends, Brentano-von Arnim often chooses to use pronouns that do not match the gender of the person to whom she is
referring or writing (Waldstein 70). This phenomenon is also visible in the *Spring Wreath*. Her grandmother's friend Ebel, whom
Bettine calls a "naturforschender Mistfinke," is endowed with the
female name "Empusa." Bettine judges that he is no longer a man
but has to pass as female ("Er wird auch nicht mehr maskuliniert,
sondern muß weiblich passieren," 138). Bettine herself declares
that from now on Jeanne d'Arc will be her model. She turns away
from Clemens as Karoline von Günderrode becomes her new most
intimate friend. She begins to identify with male characters and
proves her newly gained masculinity by preventing the execution
of an androgynous chicken, the "Männewei" (Mannweibchen).
But Bettine's, and one might add Bettina Brentano-von Arnim's,
new concept of gender identities leads to more daring actions than
saving a chicken.

In Brentano-von Arnim's epistolary novel *Goethe's Correspondence with a Child* [Goethes Briefwechsel mit einem Kinde,
1835],[58] the author's fictional alter ego Bettine takes a journey in
male attire;[59] again, a war offers an excuse for her gender-trans-
gression. Bettine's fictional account is based on an actual journey
taken by the author. In 1807 Bettina Brentano, her sister Lulu and
her sister's husband, Jordis, were on their way to Weimar.[60] Both
women wore men's clothing; Bettina was attired in a yellow vest,
gray pants, a brown jacket, and a black cap. The disguise was meant
to protect them against the French occupational army.[61] However,
in Brentano-von Arnim's novel, Bettine's enthusiasm about her
pants exceeds such pragmatic considerations:

> A pair of pants? Yes—Cheer—now come different times—and
> a jacket too, and an overcoat. Tomorrow everything will be
> tried, it will fit, for I have ordered everything comfortable and
> wide, and then I will jump into a chaise and travel night and
> day express through all armies between enemy and friend; all

fortresses will open before me . . . Just think, Weimar always seemed so far away, as though it were in a different part of the world, and now it's right in front of my doorstep.[62]

Obviously, Bettine's new trousers are more than just another piece of garment. They function as a symbol of strength and endow their wearer with magical power (Ockenfuß, *Bettine* 75). They open up new worlds and enable Bettine to brave all enemies. Most of all, they take her straight to Weimar, the home of Germany's cultural élite. Finally, Bettine's thirst for action (and writing) does not exhaust itself in fantasies anymore. When the coach loses its way, Bettine climbs up on a tree and directs her party back to the right path. She sits on the coachman's bench, helps to hitch up the horses, and even brandishes a gun: "Lulu was very afraid in the coach, but I under the open sky, with cocked gun, saber buckled on, countless glittering stars above me [. . .] all that made me courageous on my noble seat" (35). Clearly, her male disguise not only expands her realm of action but also endows her with (phallic) strength. Once again, the influence of the costume penetrates to the soul of the wearer.[63] By appropriating male clothing, Bettine appropriates qualities that are commonly attributed to men. Like Huber, von Stein, and Unger, Brentano-von Arnim demonstrates that power does not emanate from the body. Her power comes from pants, but it may take a war to show it. It seems that gender identities are easily accepted as natural entities in times of peace. But the turmoil of a war destabilizes many presumed certainties, and unmasks the cultural constructedness of gender itself. It is therefore no surprise that Brentano-von Arnim's actual cross-dressing, as well as her fantasies about it, are often linked to wartime experiences. Consequently, in *Goethe's Correspondence with a Child*, Bettine argues that it is only the lack of pants that keeps her from fighting for Tyrolese independence: "Oh, if only I had a jacket, pants, and a hat, I would run to the straight-nosed, straight-hearted Tyrolese right away" ("Ach, hätt ich ein Wämslein, Hosen und Hut, ich lief hinüber zu den gradnasigen, gradherzigen Tirolern," *Briefwechsel* 280).

In recent publications much attention has been given to Bettina Brentano-von Arnim as political activist. Studies have noted her concern for the poor, especially during the cholera epidemic of 1831; her defense of the Göttinger Sieben and of Tschech, the former mayor of Storkow, who attempted to assassinate the king in 1844; her support for the Tyrolese, Hungarian, and Polish struggle for independence; her opposition to capital punishment; and her advocacy of prison reform (French; Frühwald; Waldstein; Wyss 5–15; Meyer-Hepner).[64] Hahn even suggested that no political event escaped her notice (*Bettina* 20). But in spite of such active engagement in the affairs of her time, one lacuna is often noted, namely Brentano-von Arnim's "distance from any of the initial stirrings of feminist activity" (Goodman, "Lens" 116; cf. Dischner). However, as Goodman points out, the absence of direct comments on the emancipation of women cannot be equated with silence on gender issues. If Brentano-von Arnim's epistolary novels about the past are indeed interventions in the political situation of the present, the *Spring Wreath* must be seen as an expression of her concern with the restrictive gender roles of the 1840s. To effect a change in the conceptualization of gender, Brentano-von Arnim relies on the motif of cross-dressing and on her poetologically innovative technique.

In the *Spring Wreath*, cross-dressing is not the only site where dichotomies break down. Brentano-von Arnim's style, in which fact and fiction intermingle inseparably, also dissolves rigid categories. It is well known that she used only segments of the original letters. She combined passages from several letters into one and even changed the recipient (Oehlke 181–182; Ockenfuß, *Bettine* 29). In short, she fictionalized her authentic material (A. Kuhn, "Failure" 14) and thereby undermined a clear distinction between life and art.[65] While the figure of the cross-dresser draws attention to the split between signifier and signified by virtue of his/her clothing, Brentano-von Arnim's writing achieves a similar effect by describing the same event several times, with each portrayal differing from the others. But if Brentano-von Arnim dissociates signifier and signified, body and gender on one level, she reconnects them on another. Wherever the assumption of a male exterior brings about male comportment and power, appearance and reality become newly interwoven.

Such melting of polarities into oneness forms the center of Brentano-von Arnim's "Schwebereligion," ("floating religion") in which spirit and flesh, life and death, reality and fantasy, art and life are but two sides of one coin. They represent different states of aggregation which not only imply each other but also spring from the same source. According to Brentano-von Arnim, all things sensual and natural are symbols of the spirit, and all matter is to become spiritual again. Art itself is the sensual revelation and expression of the spirit of the poetess. Furthermore, this spirit of truth that finds its body in the artist will gradually become incorporated in the future world: "The future must cross over into that which the spirit has already for so long founded in poetry; for what would the poet be if he did not clear the way for the spirit of truth, which has long become flesh and blood in him, and now through him becomes the sensual body of the future."[66] Clearly, Brentano-von Arnim's amazons aspire to far more than just men's clothing. In the character Bettine, the physical combativeness of the French cross-dresser is transformed into spiritual resistance against the restrictions of traditionally defined gender roles. In turn, the spirit of resistance that the book expresses is meant to become flesh again. With the *Spring Wreath*, Bettina Brentano-von Arnim hoped to encourage her female contemporaries of the 1840's to become the amazons of the future and appropriate a world that was rightfully theirs.

Both Dorothea Schlegel and Bettina Brentano-von Arnim refuse to subject their thoughts and experiences to binary categorization. They insist on contradiction, openness, and transgression. But while Brentano-von Arnim's *Spring Wreath* is explicit in its rejection of traditional gender roles, Schlegel's *Florentin* merely refutes them implicitly. This is not to say that Brentano-von Arnim's enactment of the cultural constructedness of gender is simple and straightforward. Paradoxically, Brentano-von Arnim

employs a discourse on nature in order to justify her own deviation
from it. She claims that her inner being is naturally opposed to that
which society calls proper femininity, that it was nature herself that
made her this way, and that that which is natural cannot be bad.
While this argumentation may not be consistent, it certainly provides an ironic example of how the discourse on nature can be
turned against itself.

The difference between Brentano-von Arnim's strategies and
those of Dorothea Schlegel is also due to a difference in historical context. Schlegel's interpretation of cross-dressing is influenced by the gender-experiments of early Romanticism as represented in Friedrich Schlegel's *Lucinde*. To Schlegel, androgyny
evokes an experience of dependency, while Brentano-von Arnim
associates cross-dressing with freedom. Even though Schlegel and
Brentano-von Arnim differ radically in their evaluation of the
practical results of gender-bending, both are enamored with the
figure of the cross-dresser insofar as s/he symbolizes openness and
internal contradiction. The paradoxical principle of presence-in-
absence becomes part of the structure of their writing allowing
them to express the experiences of a gender that had no language
of its own.

CONCLUSION

୧୬

Stories about cross-dressing are stories about bodies in history, bodies in culture. They depict and re-negotiate the uneasy relationship between body and gender, body and identity, and body and truth.

This renegotiation, visible in texts from around 1800, is still with us. In our own culture the status and meaning of the body is hotly contested. We are faced with backlash movements that seek desperately to reinstate the predominance of biology, whether they lash out against Title IX of the Education Amendment of 1972 that prohibits discrimination based on sex in education programs or activities which receive federal financial assistance or, as Randy Thornhill and Craig T. Palmer have done, claim to lay bare the genetic and evolutionary foundations of the "natural" male drive to inseminate and even to rape. But we are also inhabitants of the brave new world of the internet in which the physical body recedes behind the primacy of words and images that is the hallmark of virtual reality or is surgically retrofit to conform to the demands of a gender identity that is considered primary. All too often we are poised between two extremes: a "female" version of identity construction that reduces us to nothing but bodies and a "male" version that dissociates personhood from bodily existence altogether. It is in this sense that the late-eighteenth- and early-nineteenth-century texts that I have analyzed constitute the genealogy of our own predicaments.

The end of the eighteenth century witnessed the emergence of a new gender ideology based on the assumption that woman's moral character was a consequence of her physical constitution. Thus, the exclusion of women from the public sphere was justified with a reference to the female body. Both Huber's and Motte-Fouqué's novels are attempts to work against or around the postulated incompatibility of the female body and the body politic. Cross-dressing is introduced as a strategy that allows the female gender-bender access to the male arena of politics and warfare.

However, as much as cross-dressing is the cure for social inequality, it is also a symptom that speaks of the irrecoverable Otherness of the female body. In Fouqué's novel, unease with the female body is documented in the ineluctable narrative pull towards its destruction. In Huber's text, the privileging of adoptive motherhood over biological motherhood combined with the physical isolation of the protagonist bears testimony to the problematic status of the heroine's female body. Although both novels contain captivating portrayals of female agency, the knowledge that female physiology is the root cause of woman's inferior status remains inscribed into their subcutaneous layers.

Like Huber and Fouqué, Unger and Paulus relied on the liberatory potential of cross-dressing in order to relieve themselves of the weight of the female body. Unlike Huber and Fouqué, they added nationality to the equation, thus creating an economy of projection and displacement that turned gendered bodies into national bodies and made femininity and agency newly compatible. By splitting the female heroine into a foreign cross-dresser and a German maiden, Unger and Paulus were able to portray transgressive acts without having to pay the price of the renunciation of the female body and its sexuality. The gender dichotomy is overlaid with a contrast between foreign depravity and German virtue so that the scapegoating of the national Other saves the German heroine from a position of alterity. It is this foreign Other that lacks an inner core and thus contrasts with German authenticity. Gender and class may rest on performative acts, but nationality is made to speak the truth. Often, this model rests on a Faustian bargain. In order to tear down the gender hierarchy, the authors hide behind the ramparts of newly erected national stereotypes.

While Unger and Paulus clear a space for female agency by offering nationality as a proxy, Schiller's, Kleist's, and Günderrode's texts are centered on the interrelation between the body, gender, and truth. Their dramas are conceived as experiments that probe whether the body might provide an anchor in a world that is perceived as epistemologically unstable and morally dubious. To Schiller, the woman in men's clothing embodies the split between signifier and signified, between language and reality. Unlike Unger and Paulus' gender-benders who personify flexibility and adaptability, Schiller's cross-dresser is employed to put a halt to the arbitrary play of signs. The dead female body becomes the foundation for the stabilization of the symbolic order. In contrast, both Kleist and Günderrode face the void without a safety net. Kleist ironizes and deconstructs his longing for a truth that inheres in the gendered body, and Günderrode rejects it out of hand. In her texts, the category of gender is void of any permanent inscriptions, and the dead female body possesses no redemptive powers.

While Schiller sets out to safeguard the moral integrity of language and art, Goethe is concerned with social stability. Although Goethe's texts evince an awareness of the rift between gender and the body, they are dedicated to policing the gender order. Indeed, the knowledge that femininity is not a natural given is read as a call to arms. Since nature cannot guarantee the social order, society itself is called upon to fortify its cultural systems of signification and stratification. However, one might wonder whether Goethe's reluctance to rely on biology is motivated by his perceptive recognition of a double bind inherent in the concept of gendered character. The new emphasis on women's bodies as anchors of woman's social position threatened to draw attention to men's bodies and to the inadequacy of male biology as a guarantor of paternity and patrilinearity. Goethe realized that the truism of "pater semper incertus est" cannot be remedied within a purely biological framework. It seems to me that further investigation of the gender dynamics in late-eighteenth- and nineteenth-century

texts might benefit from an analysis of issues of paternity and patrilinearity. Such an analysis might also shed some light on how contemporary forms of genetic testing designed to determine the
paternity of a child affect the social distribution of power between
the genders.

In *Wilhelm Meister*, paternity rests on a chain of signifiers that
is held in place by homosocial bonding. In von Stein's *The Two
Emilies*, homosocial bonding is interrupted by the female gender-
bender. The cross-dresser of *The Two Emilies* is a haunting apparition that embodies the presence-in-absence that characterizes
woman's status in a patriarchal society. In *A New System of
Freedom*, the cross-dressers are playful tricksters who personify
inspiring fantasies of female power. Von Stein's use of role-play,
parody, and mimicry is evocative of the postmodern concepts of
pastiche, irony, and fluidity. Her humorous subversion of male
power is wholly antithetical to the image of von Stein as the ethe-
real, moralistic, and quite possibly frigid companion so dominant
in traditional Goethe scholarship.

While von Stein's texts rely on mimicry and parody, Brentano-
von Arnim's and Dorothea Schlegel's novels enact ambiguity and
openness. In Schlegel's *Florentin*, male clothing no longer con-
notes power and freedom, nor does cross-dressing strike a blow
against the gender order. Rather, it is the celebration of indeterminacy, the refusal to effect closure that allows Schlegel to clear
a space for female agency and for literature by women. Schlegel
critiques the gender hierarchy through the subversion of binary
structures per se. Similarly, the heroine of Brentano-von Arnim's
Spring Wreath is attracted by the French cross-dresser's ability to
defy dichotomous categories. Through the creative obfuscation of
fact and fiction, the rejection of binary categories, and the crafting of a poetology of openness, Schlegel and Brentano-von Arnim
gained a measure of freedom from the strictures of late-eighteenth-
and early-nineteenth-century gender roles.

My reading of all these texts started with the assumption that
female writers responded differently from male writers to the new
conceptualization of the relation between body and identity. But

do the results of this study truly justify such a division along gender lines? For example, is not Kleist more progressive than Motte-
Fouqué? Does not Kleist refuse to locate gender in the body
whereas Motte-Fouqué insists on the naturalness of femininity?
Or are we simply asking the wrong question? I believe that the
difference is not one of ideology but of positionality. Women writers are acutely aware that a woman's identity is inseparably linked
with her bodily existence. Their writing sets out from this position even as it strives to discard or circumvent it. In contrast, male
writers are unburdened by the weight of a gendered biology. Their
identities are not wholly circumscribed by the body. They are thus
free to seek out the body as anchor and safeguard and to indulge
in their nostalgia for the truth of the soma even if they choose to
reject it in the end. The result of this difference in points of departure is that, in texts by women writers, the trope of cross-dressing
is intimately connected with questions of female agency. To
Kleist, Schiller, and Goethe, on the other hand, questions of
female agency are secondary at best. In their texts, gender often
functions as a metaphor for questions of epistemological, moral,
and social import.

Given the eighteenth-century conceptualization of the female
body, it is hardly surprising that many female writers embraced a
model of identity that emphasized performativity and interactiv-
ity. However, by creating characters whose identity no longer
emanates from an inner core but reconstitutes itself continually
in a never-ending performance, female writers became unwitting
advocates of the emerging capitalist economy and its endless need
for mobility, flexibility, and adaptability. It is of interest to note
that this ideological affinity was accompanied by the success of
women writers on the literary market place. Frequently, books by
women writers outsold the more prestigious works of their male
contemporaries. On the other hand, the tenuous market position
of many male writers was complemented by their rejection of a
performative model of identity. Male authors tended to favor
authenticity over performativity, and stability over fluidity. In
doing so, they also upheld the distance between the feudal and

the bourgeois model of identity construction. In insisting that the meaning of the body overrides that of its clothing, they rejected a model of society in which one's position is defined not by inner worth, but by the outer trappings of status. Moreover, by promoting a notion of identity that emanates from the inside out, they occupied a space equally removed from the theatricality of the feudal past and from the "exchangeability of parts" of the capitalist future.

Clearly, the texts by male and female writers are marked by their different positionalities. At times, however, the lessons to be derived from them are remarkably alike. Thus, both Kleist and Motte-Fouqué, although in very different ways, make us aware of the enormous cost inherent in any attempt to legitimize social or political orders with a reference to the body. Any endeavor to use our bodies for "a fiction-generating, or construct substantiating process" (Scarry 140), that is, to postulate an analogy between bodies and mental constructs in which the ultimate material substrate of the body is employed to confer reality and authority on these constructs, is liable to create what it purports to confirm. Though our bodies carry much, they cannot support the burden of our social order. Where bodies are the pillars of cultural constructs, they are often crushed by their overbearing weight. Although body and gender, body and identity, and body and truth are connected in a myriad of ways, these connections are neither stable nor straightforward.

Texts from around 1800 should make us wary of any endeavor to overextend the authority of the body. They also call for a cautious examination of the danger inherent in the problematic proximity of the performative model of identity and early capitalism. This connection may prove to be of particular urgency since the fluidity that around 1800 manifested itself as the textual malleability of a character's identity has been extended now to include the technological alterability of the physical body. From plastic surgery to genetic design, the body itself has become a site of self-invention. It is left to us to decide whether this new pliability represents the ultimate liberation or the ultimate commodification of the body.

Eighteenth-century authors portrayed a surprisingly large number of female-to-male cross-dressers. In the late twentieth and early twenty-first centuries male-to-female transvestites outnumber their female-to-male counterparts by far. While the eighteenth-century gender-bender represents a strategic move against the limitations placed on female agency, the twentieth-century TV is often read as a rejection of the pressures that are now associated with traditional masculinity. Certainly, the emphasis placed on fashion and chic, evidenced by the wide-spread marketing of transvestite clothing and accessories, speaks to this shift from agency to style. But modern transvestism may also originate in the belief that women possess a competitive advantage in today's image culture with its focus on glamour and appearance. However, even though modern male-to-female transvestism presents an inversion of eighteenth-century female-to-male cross-dressing, both are expressions of the two-sex model in which the two genders are conceived of as discrete, but complementary. Both are in danger of recreating the same economy of binaries from which they are trying to escape. Transsexualism and its medical manifestation in the form of sex-reassignment surgery, on the other hand, might be understood as the postmodern, surgical reenactment of the one-sex model. Paradoxically, sex-reassignment surgery is both a rejection and a reaffirmation of the belief in the identity-generating power of the body.

Even a cursory survey of contemporary gender-bending practices reveals that our culture is stuck, not in the same predicaments, but in the same dichotomies that plagued the eighteenth century. We too insist that gender and identity be either a direct expression of the body or that they be completely divorced from the body. What we often fail to conceptualize is the murky area in between these alternate philosophies: the idea that while personhood is never wholly independent from the body, it is also never wholly determined by the body. Tragically, our inability to come to terms with such mixtures carries in its wake the loss of "the ability to authentically represent the complexities and ambiguities of lived experience" (Stone 351). If we could learn from Dorothea Schlegel and Bettina Brentano-von Arnim how to be at home with ambiguity, indeterminacy, and contradiction, we might be a step closer to the freedom to which these courageous women writers aspired.

Notes

Introduction

1. For an account of Lincken's life see F. C. Müller. See also Kord, "Eternal Love," which contains a brief discussion of Lincken's case (229–230).
2. Cf. Entwistle, who points out that it is through dress that "bodies are made social and given meaning and identity" (7).
3. But we have also witnessed a backlash in the form of renewed attempts to biologize gender, such as the recent study by Randy Thornhill and Craig T. Palmer that claimed that men are genetically predisposed to rape.
4. One need only think of Carlyle ("Close thy Byron, open thy Goethe") and Margaret Fuller, who was influenced by the works of Goethe and Bettina Brentano-von Arnim to name but two examples.
5. Unless otherwise indicated, all translations from the German are my own.
6. Insightful research projects of this type have been carried out by Barbara Becker-Cantarino, "Die wärmste Liebe;" Sigrid Lange, *Spiegelgeschichten;* and Kord, "Performing Genders," to name just a few.
7. Laqueur's exemplary study displays theoretical awareness of this fact but does not elaborate on it.
8. That female organs were not differentiated from male ones is also manifest in the absence of the pertinent terminology. Laqueur points out that there was no word for "vagina" before 1700.
9. Interestingly, this paradigm shift is mirrored in the prevalent style of dress. Wilson claims that "until the seventeenth or even the eighteenth century, sexual difference in dress was not strongly marked" (E. Wilson 117).
10. Honegger's and Laqueur's work is further confirmed by Barbara Duden's analysis of case histories of numerous female patients recorded by Johannes Pelargius Storch, a physician in the eighteenth-century town of Eisenach. Duden claims that "the historical conditions that shaped our modern body perception did not emerge until the second half of the eighteenth century" (1).
11. In her study on hermaphrodites, Domurat Dreger provides evidence that scientists and doctors of the late nineteenth century were convinced "that females were actually underdeveloped males" (35). Fausto-Sterling reports

that in the 1970s American researchers suggested the concept of "female lack and male presence" (202). According to this model the female developmental pathway is referred to as the "default pathway" (204) because all embryos start as female and "the male is derived from the female" (204).

12. Cf. MacKenzie: "Everyday we do gender" (1).

13. "A repetition of the law which is not its consolidation, but its displacement" (Butler, *Gender* 30).

14. Fausto-Sterling names cortical reorganization in musicians and persons blind from birth as examples of how "material anatomical connections in the brain respond to external influences" (241) and suggests that there might be similar ways in which "gendered experience could become gendered soma" (240).

15. Barbara Duden makes a similar claim when she insists that "matter itself is historical" (7) and that it is necessary to "create a radically new historical dimension for the body" (8).

16. Barbara Duden also connects the emergence of a new perception of the body to economic developments of the time. Duden claims that toward the end of the eighteenth century, the body "acquired economic value" and became "the most elementary form of property" (13).

17. See also Annuß, who, relying on research by Jameson and Prodoehl, points out that Butler ignores the bourgeois compulsory law of competition (77).

18. It is of interest to note that Honegger perceives a connection between the rigidification of the concept of gendered character and the "development of a manly-healthy bourgeois culture set in opposition to an effeminate, feudal civilization" (7). As support for this line of argumentation, Honegger cites Christoph Meiners, a professor in Göttingen, whose *History of the Female Gender* (1788–1800) holds women's increase in power responsible for the decline of courtly civilization. The fact that gender stereotypes could be employed for the redistribution of class-specific privileges will have to be taken into consideration in the following analyses of literary texts.

19. McClintock assumes that "cross-dressers seldom seek the security of a perfect imitation; rather, they desire that delicious impersonation that belies complete disguise" (175). I believe that this emphasis on the display of ambiguity is itself a product of McClintock's focus on aesthetic portrayals of transvestism.

20. Cross-dressing "reveals the invented nature of social distinction" (McClintock 174).

21. Even Lehnert's more positive evaluations of cross-dressing are based on this assumption. At times, disguise is characterized as a "means to develop one's personality beyond social norms and constraints, beyond gender assignments" (59).

22. Wendy Doniger has captured the nature of this subversive potential when she claims that "masquerading as someone else begins by denying the otherness of the other, saying, "This other person is not different from me" (95).

23. Cf. Dekker and van de Pol's thesis that a positive evaluation of transvestites is directly proportional to the degree of their fictionalization (93).

24. Even though the English language makes it possible to circumvent this problem, a discussion of the pertinent German terminology is in order. Such a clarification is even more called for as the term "cross-dressing" can be translated into German only by resorting to clumsy and awkward paraphrases. Possible alternative expressions are fraught with unwelcome connotations and limitations. In eighteenth-century usage, the word "amazon," for example, frequently referred to a riding outfit, which consisted of a mixture of male and female clothing. The combination of a man's jacket with a skirt, however, does not correspond to the modern understanding of cross-dressing. Other terms, such as the word "Hosenrolle" ("breeches' part"), which designates cross-dressing in the theatrical realm only, are too narrow. If Germans want to avoid the ungainly Anglicism "cross-dresser," they need to rely on the word "Transvestit." This, however, represents an equally problematic choice, as the twentieth-century medico-psychological usage of this term has given rise to numerous negative connotations. I will use the term "cross-dresser" when discussing the eighteenth century while the term "transvestism" will be limited to twentieth-century cross-dressers.

25. The definition of transvestic fetishism reads "heterosexual males who have sexually arousing fantasies, urges, or behaviors involving cross-dressing" (http://allpsych.com/disorders/paraphilias/transvestite.html).

26. Even though the DSM-IV-R presents its definition of transvestism with the certainty of timeless validity, historical and intercultural comparisons demonstrate that it should be used with great caution. One cannot assume that the boundary between transsexuals and transvestites is as clear-cut as it is laid out in the manual. Docter, for example, points out that "transvestism typically has an early stage in which fetishism is predominant and a later stage in which a shift in gender identity is seen" (139). One should also not presuppose that all transvestites are heterosexual. Whitam's study of the populations of Java, Thailand, Guatemala, Peru, Brazil, and the Philippines, for example, demonstrates that in these cultures transvestites are mostly homosexual (Bullough and Bullough 302). It is also known that in the nineteenth century some male homosexuals resorted to cross-dressing in order to be able to live with their partners (Bullough and Bullough 189). Every definition of transvestism will have to take into account the fact that both the meaning and cultural evaluation of transvestism vary greatly in different places and different times.

While some cultures consider transvestism an illness (see, for example, the DSM-IV-R), others single it out as a hallmark of privileged connection to spiritual spheres and reward it with high prestige. Ackroyd, for example, points out that "in many shamanistic cultures, transvestites are regarded as sorcerers or visionaries who, because of their double nature as men dressed as women, are sources of divine authority within the community" (37). Ackroyd also points out that fertility goddesses are often portrayed as androgynous.

27. Cf. Docter: "Although women in our culture wear many articles of clothing which might be called 'men's clothing' their motive is not to imitate a man or take the social role of a male; such clothing is worn for the same reasons as any other clothing—for comfort, convenience, style, or protection" (39).

28. Sumptuary laws are generally associated with feudal societies in which a person's social rank is the result of her/his birth. Fashion, on the other hand, emerges within societies in which social mobility is possible (Entwistle 44). Some claim that the new bourgeois class adopted "fashion as a tool in the battle for social status" (Entwistle 59).

29. To these historical examples one might add their literary and mythological counterparts, such as Hercules, who wore female clothing at the court of Omphale, or Achilles, who disguised himself as a girl at the court of Lycomedes.

30. Cf. Ackroyd: "In the seventeenth and eighteenth centuries there are more recorded cases of women who dressed and 'passed' as men" (74).

31. These masquerades were even more scandalous as Elisabeth ordered every guest to appear without a mask (Kates 75). Elisabeth herself also preferred the riding outfit of the other sex (Ramet 16).

32. Castle draws attention to this connection when she points out that transvestism was suspected of encouraging female emancipation (*Masquerade* 164).

33. In 1662, Mary Frith published an autobiography entitled *The Life and Death of Mistress Mary Frith, commonly called Moll Cutpurse* (cf. Orgel 139f.; Crawford 358–367).

34. Hotchkiss counts 34 disguised holy women (14).

35. Cf. Torjesen: "by renouncing the body and sexuality and following the ascetic life, women seemed to transcend their femaleness" (83).

36. Some notable "professional" cross-dressers are Dr. James Barry, born in 1799, who worked as a doctor for the military (cf. Patricia's Duncker's recent novel *The Doctor*); Isabelle Gunn, alias John Fubister, who worked for the Hudson's Bay Company (Wheelwright 42); and, more recently, Jack Bee Garland (Babe Beans), who cross-dressed and worked as a reporter until her death in 1936.

37. For the eighteenth century, the documentation of English cases is better than that of other European countries. Some of the most often-mentioned names are the soldier Christina, alias Christian Davies (1667–1739); the sailor James Gray (formerly Hannah Snell, 1723–1792); Mary Anne Talbot, alias John Talbot (1778–1808); and Mary Lacey, who served in the Royal Navy (Wheelwright 42; Bullough and Bullough 124). In Russia, a certain Nadezha Durova (1783–1866) fought with the hussars of Alexander I against the French.

38. Cf. Wheelwright: "For many women their only liberation from the confines of domestic responsibilities was experienced during wartime" (13).

39. Wheelwright mentions Elizabeth Taylor, alias Happy Ned; Emma Edmonds, alias Franklin Thompson; and Loreta Janeta Velasquez, alias Harry T. Bruford.

40. Brulon retired in 1799 because of wounds received in combat.

41. The German Caroline of Hessia did not participate in any battles but posed for a portrait in the uniform of her father-in-law (Boehn, *Mode* 238).

42. Dekker and van de Pol point out that patriotically or romantically motivated cross-dressing was often admired whereas any association of transvestism and criminality led to much severer forms of punishment (75).

43. Romantically inspired cross-dressers included Elizabeth Southwell, a lady-in-waiting at the court of Queen Anne, who cross-dressed as a page in order to elope with her lover Sir Robert Dudley. Lady Arbella Stuart, a cousin of King James I, also used men's clothing in order to flee from the royally decreed house arrest and be united with William Seymour, to whom she had been secretly married (Orgel 112–115).

44. The actor Edward Kynaston was especially well known for his excellent portrayal of women (Bullough and Bullough 82).

45. Among the actresses who were known for their portrayal of men are Madame Vestris, Marie Wilton, Vesta Tilley (Bullough and Bullough 227), Mrs. Lefevre (Slide 53), Mrs. Julia Glover and Mrs. Powell (Holtmont 180). The actress and innkeeper Charlotte Charke (1713–1760) described her experiences in her autobiography.

46. It is to be assumed that for an eighteenth-century theater buff trousers parts were nothing out of the ordinary. In his remarks on Hogarth's *Strolling Actresses Dressing in a Barn*, Lichtenberg, for example, takes it as a matter of course that the represented men are really cross-dressed women (Möhrmann 124).

47. "Und vor allen andern, vier Bursche von den berühmtesten Sächsischen Academien, waren so unvergleichlich charakterisieret, daß ich mein Lebenlang nichts schöners gesehen habe [. . .] nemlich ein Schläger, ein Freund der morgenländischen Sprachen, ein Zäncker, und ein gallant

homme von einem viermal verkleideten Frauenzimmer so herrlich vorgestellt worden, daß ihnen nichts als eine männliche gröbere Stimme gefehlet" (Gottsched I: 350).

48. "Denn dadurch, daß Menschen diese Rolle spielen, werden zuletzt die Tugenden, deren Schein sie eine geraume Zeit hindurch nur gekünstelt haben, nach und nach wohl wirklich erweckt und gehen in die Gesinnung über" (Kant 151).

49. The motif of parents who cannot recognize their cross-dressed daughter is a recurrent element of these stories (cf. biographical accounts of Emma Edmonds and Catalina de Erauso).

50. Cf. Wheelwright: "But these women appear largely unconcerned about changing the society that produced the inequity which they felt most keenly in their own lives [. . .] They traded roles rather than forged new ones so their rebellion was never without a heavy price" (12).

51. Seen in this light, male-to-female transvestism is interpreted as a male presumption intent on demonstrating that men are better women than women themselves, or seen as a misogynistic denunciation of women that serves to confirm and ridicule gender-specific stereotypes (for example, reducing women to sexual beings, etc.).

52. One might also include numerous other texts, such as Johann Gottfried Schnabel's *Island Felsenburg* [Insel Felsenburg, 1731–1743]; Christoph Martin Wieland's *Story of Agathon* [Geschichte des Agathon, 1766–67], in which Psyche cross-dresses as a slave in order to flee from the unwelcome overtures of Narcissus; or Wieland's *Novella Without Title* [Novelle ohne Titel, 1803], in which the heroine's parents cross-dress their daughter in order to obtain an inheritance bestowed on a male heir only. One might also mention Clemens Brentano's *Godwi or the Stony Image of the Mother* [Godwi oder das steinerne Bild der Mutter, 1801], which features an amazon on horseback, or the dramas of Christian Felix Weiße, which are enlivened by a number of female cross-dressers.

　　Cross-dressers were especially popular with writers of so-called trivial literature. The daughter of a republican general fights in men's clothing in H. G. Schmieder's *The Heroine of the Vendée, a Female Abällino: Romantic Story from the French War* [Die Heldin der Vendée, ein weiblicher Abällino: Romantische Geschichte aus dem französischen Kriege, 1801]. In Karl Gottlob Cramer's *The Beautiful Fugitive: A Paroxysm of Love* [Der schöne Flüchtling: Ein Paroxysm der Liebe, 1803], a young lady follows the regiment of her beloved officer in the outfit of a hussar. A female pirate is the protagonist of Johann Ernst Daniel Bornschein's *Antonia della Roccini, the Pirate Queen: A Romantic Story from the Seventeenth Century* [Antonia della Roccini, die Seeräuberkönigin: Eine romantische Geschichte des 17. Jahrhunderts, 1801], and a female robber holds center stage in Bornschein's

The Miraculous Girl from Nordhaus, a Female Rinaldini: A Romantic Story [Das nordhäusische Wundermädchen, ein weiblicher Rinaldini: Eine romantische Geschichte, 1802].

Texts by women writers also abound with female-to-male cross-dressers. Gender-benders are portrayed in Meta Liebeskind's novel *Maria: A Story in Letters* [Maria: Eine Geschichte in Briefen, 1784] and in Christiane Benedikte Naubert's *Philippe of Geldern or the Story of Selim the Son of Amurat* [Philippe von Geldern oder Geschichte Selims des Sohnes Amurat, 1792]. Naubert's novel *Story of Countess Thekla of Thurn or Scenes from the 30-year War* [Geschichte der Gräfin Thekla von Thurn oder Szenen aus dem 30jährigen Kriege, 1788] features a cross-dressed heroine who fights in the army of Gustav Adolph. A Mignon-like character, named Bettina, makes an appearance as a cross-dressed musician in Caroline von Wolzogen's *Agnes of Lilien* [Agnes von Lilien, 1796–97]. Gender masquerades are also integrated into the plot of Wilhelmine von Gernsdorf's *The Twin Sisters or The Fickleness of Fortuna: A Family Portrait in Three Acts* [Die Zwillingsschwestern oder die Verschiedenheit des Glücks: Ein Familiengemälde in drei Aufzügen, 1797]. And there is a quasi-inflation of the motif of cross-dressing in German robinsonades with female heroines. Blackwell counted sixteen of these stranded transvestites in the period between 1720 and 1800 ("Island" 5).

CHAPTER 1

1. For more information on women and the Fronde insurrection see DeJean 21ff.; though cross-dressed soldiers abound, cross-dressing was more than an enabling device for martial Frenchwomen. During public festivals and carnivals, unruly women parodied important dignitaries, such as mayors, judges, and other powerful authority figures, by donning their clothing. Through their masquerade, these women both appropriated and rejected male authority.

2. Cf. Schmidt-Linsenhoff 471; in her speech of 1792 before the Société fraternelle des patriotes de l'un et de l'autre sexe, Méricourt also advocated the formation of a female battalion (cf. Levy et. al. 104).

3. For more information on these women see Levy and Applewhite 9.

4. For more information on Brulon see Gilbert 1–92.

5. "Yes, we lack weapons, and we want to ask for your permission to equip us with them [. . .] we want to be able to defend ourselves. You must not reject us, and society must not refuse a right which was given us by nature" (qtd. from Cerati 41).

6. It is not clear whether this troop ever existed (Opitz, "Bürger" 46).

7. In his *Letters from Paris*, Campe mentions a cross-dressed woman who claimed that she put on men's clothing in order to be able to support her indigent parents (195).

8. For more information on the role of women during the Vendée uprisings, see Yalom, *Blood Sisters*, 191–209.

9. "daß die Weiber in Paris und, wie es nach verschiedenen Vorfällen in den Provinzen das Ansehn hat, das ganze weibliche Geschlecht in Frankreich dem männlichen an Kultur, an Mäßigung und Sittlichkeit nachsteht, und, sooft es zu Gewalttätigkeiten kommt, sich fast immer durch Blutdurst und Grausamkeiten auszeichnet" (Campe 228). Note also "Thus, it was, for example, more these women than their husbands who stilled their lust for revenge through the corpses of the executed traitors of the people by dismembering them and by having their vulgar and barbarian fun with the separate parts for a while" [So waren es zum Beispiel mehr diese Weiber als ihre Männer, welche an den Leichnamen der hingerichteten Volksverbrecher ihre Rachlust sättigten, indem sie dieselben zerstückten und mit einzelnen Teilen noch eine Zeitlang ihren pöbelhaften und barbarischen Spaß trieben, 227].

10. The women who participated in barricade fighting in 1848 were met with distrust and exposed to denunciations. This is further evidence for the assumption that, although service for the fatherland justified a violation of gender roles in Germany, fighting for the republic did not.

11. "not a predilection for independence nor fancy but ardent love for the fatherland and the sublime mind, which awakened all over Germany so miraculously and to which it owes its freedom, has led them [these women] to the ranks of the defenders of the fatherland" (Tauentzien before the senate on January 22, 1815, qtd. from Noel 87).

12. "Welch tiefes Weh müssen diese einfachen, bescheidenen und stillen Frauenseelen über das vom Feinde mit Füßen getretene Vaterland empfunden haben, daß sie ihre häuslichen und Familienbeziehungen aufgaben, um für ihr Vaterland zu kämpfen" (Noel XIV).

13. "Ich müßte mich schämen, ein Mann zu heißen / Wenn ich nicht könnte führen das Eisen / Und wollte Weibern es gönnen / daß sie führen es können / Wer ist der Geselle, so fein und jung? / Doch führt er das Eisen mit gutem Schwung. / Wer steckt unter der Maske? / Eine Jungfrau, heißt Prochaska. / Wie merkten wir's nur nicht lange schon / Am glatten Kinn, am feineren Ton? / Doch unter den männlichen Taten / Wer konnte das Weib erraten? / Aber es hat sie getroffen ein Schuß! / Jetzt sagt sie's selber, weil sie muß. / Wundarzt, geh beileibe / Nicht unsanft um mit dem Weibe! / Zum Glück traf Dich die Kugel nicht ehr', / als bis Du dir hattest genügliche Ehr' / Erstritten in Mannesgebärden, / Jetzt kannst Du ein Weib wieder werden. / Doch ich müßte mich schämen ein Mann zu heißen,

Wenn ich nicht wollte können führen das Eisen, / Und wollte Weibern es gönnen, / daß sie es führen können" (Werke I: 107). Auguste Krüger alias August Lübeck, who received the Iron Cross, was also the subject of a poem by Rückert (46–47).

14. Therese Huber was born in Göttingen in 1764. She was the daughter of Professor Christian Gottlob Heyne. Huber had no systematic instruction but profited greatly from the intellectually stimulating atmosphere of her parental home. In 1785 she married Georg Forster, who had achieved early fame because of his journey around the world with James Cook. She followed Forster to Wilna in Poland, then to Mainz. Huber was very unhappy in her marriage and entered into a relationship with the writer Ludwig Ferdinand Huber. After her flight from Mainz, Huber and her children settled in Straßburg, then Neuchatel, and finally Bole in Switzerland. She married Ludwig Ferdinand Huber after Forster's death in 1794 and began to work as a translator and writer. Her works were published under her husband's name. In 1798 the family relocated to Stuttgart. When her second husband died in 1804, Huber decided to live with her daughter Claire in Stoffenried, then Günzburg. From 1816 to 1823, she was chief editor of Cotta's *Morgenblatt für gebildete Stände* in Stuttgart. Because her responsibilities were not well defined, Huber was engaged in frequent conflicts with Cotta, who interfered with her directions. Throughout her career, Huber, in order to protect her reputation, emphasized repeatedly that her true calling was that of needle and thread (letter to Viktor Aime Huber, January 9, 1817, *Freiheitsliebe* 167) and that unfortunate circumstances and duties forced her to assume more responsibility in the public sphere than is appropriate for her sex (letter to Henriette von Reden, June 15, 1818, *Freiheitsliebe* 170). Huber spent her last years in Augsburg, where she died in 1829.

15. *The Seldorf Family* appeared in May 1794 in Ludwig Ferdinand Huber's periodical *Flora* and was published in book format by Cotta in 1796–97. It was not until 1811 that Huber stopped publishing her works anonymously or under her husband's name.

16. Stephan points out that Huber's novel is revolutionary insofar as it depicts feudal depravity as responsible for the onset of the Revolution (188). Köpke calls Huber's critique of the aristocracy and the Ancien Régime radical and uncompromising ("Schatten" 123).

17. Roger's help for an impoverished peasant family is praised as exemplary because it does not remove the peasants from their social station ("um nichts aus seinem Kreis genommen, sondern mit praktischer Kenntniß dessen was ihm in seinem Stand am meisten nothtun mochte, ihm die Mittel verschaft, durch Fleiß und Thätigkeit sich wieder aufzuhelfen," I: 72).

18. "Eigennuz und Herrschsucht waren die Quelle deiner Wohlthaten: ich sollte dein Geschöpf seyn, und das Glük, das ich nicht aus deinen Händen nahm, wurde mir zum Verbrechen" (I: 256).

19. Cf. Kontje: "L**, Roger, and Seldorf each prove tyrannical in their love. Beneath the familiar tale of decadent aristocrats seducing innocent bourgeois girls lie several variants of a story about bourgeois husbands subjugating their wives" (26).

20. Cf. Köpke, who claims that Huber does not question the privileged position of the aristocratic-bourgeois upper class of educated individuals which she opposes to the "Volk" ("Schatten" 127). Certainly, Huber's novel contains no explicit criticism of the peasant-bourgeois power differential. But Huber's strong condemnation of all forms of mastery develops a dynamic of its own that extends to this relation as well.

21. Cf. Huyssen, who claims that the passivity and impotence of the bourgeoisie find expression in the depiction of female suffering (qtd. in Peitsch 265).

22. One might even suggest that Huber's model is more radical. Huber not only demonstrates that a woman's confinement to the private sphere has negative consequences for herself and her family, but also suggests that such an isolated existence is not possible. Her novel interlaces the private and public realm in manifold ways. Often political actions of the male protagonists are secretly driven by personal motivations, while the political sphere exercises its influence on the private sphere of the female characters (for example, the soldier who dies in Sara's apartment fleeing from a Parisian mob; or Martha, who becomes a victim of the guillotine because she happens to be near the site of an execution).

23. Becker-Cantarino rightfully points out that this constellation contains an implicit criticism of patriarchy ("Revolution" 245).

24. "Because we boys may help but cannot lament and comfort" (I: 5).

25. "Wenn du einst älter bist, wirst du lernen, daß es weibisch wäre, wenn Knaben und Männer liebten und trösteten, wie es deinem Geschlecht wohl ansteht, es zu thun" (I: 7).

26. At times, Huber expresses her critique openly (for example, her denunciation of Seldorf's gender-biased advice to his children, which is branded as unrealistic and harmful: "He did not consider how many bitter experiences in the real world he was preparing for two lonely, loving creatures whom he equipped with abstract concepts about beings who all represent some aspect of this portrait in thousands and thousands of variations but who will never be like it," I: 27).

27. Cf. Butler: "The forming, crafting, bearing, circulation, signification of that sexed body will not be a set of actions performed in compliance with the law; on the contrary, they will be a set of actions mobilized by the law, the

citational accumulation and dissimulation of the law that produces material effects, the lived necessity of those effects as well as the lived contestation of that necessity. Performativity is thus not a singular 'act', for it is always a reiteration of a norm or set of norms, and to the extent that it acquires an act-like status in the present, it conceals or dissimulates the conventions of which it is a repetition" (*Bodies* 12).

28. "Arme Wahnsinnige, rief er, einen Tropfen dieses Rachgefühls in dein kindlich Herz, und du wärest dem Bewußtsein wiedergegeben!" (II: 150).

29. One might agree with Becker-Cantarino, who claims that Sara's crossdressing demonstrates that it is impossible to live as a woman in a patriarchal society ("Revolution" 245). But one would also have to add that this impossibility is finally overcome in Huber's novel.

30. One might claim that this statement is merely a strategic move with which Huber justifies Sara's refusal of an offer of marriage by Roger.

31. Interestingly, this response is similar to that of eighteenth-century reviewers. The author of a review in the *Neue Allgemeine Deutsche Bibliothek*, for example, proclaimed that there was no reason why Sara should not fall in love with Roger (cf. Peitsch 266).

32. Sara and Roger's relationship is not destroyed by the political events, as Stephan suggests (171). With or without the Revolution, a marriage between these two is inconceivable.

33. Huber's novel illustrates that there is a price to be paid for freedom, as Stephan claims (181). But it is incorrect to state that Huber reproduces the traditional stereotype of woman as victim (183).

34. Caroline de la Motte-Fouqué was born in 1775 in Nennhausen in Havelland. She was a member of the old aristocratic von Briest family. She married the officer Rochus von Rochow in 1789 but left him after the birth of two sons and one daughter. The divorce was already on its way when Rochus shot himself, probably because of gambling debts. Very soon afterwards Caroline married the writer Friedrich de la Motte-Fouqué. This marriage is generally described as happy. Caroline died in 1831. For more detailed information about her life see Jean T. Wilde and Vera Prill.

35. To my knowledge, the only detailed analyses of *The Heroine from the Vendée* are to be found in Wagenbaur and Kontje.

36. Though planned, such a ball never took place.

37. *Memoirs of an Unnamed Person* features the cross-dressed daughter of a German duke who participates in the Spanish insurrection against Napoleon. In *The Blind Leader* the cross-dressed character Josephine fights in battles. In *Feodora*, which is based on an event in Russian history, a young woman disguises herself as an Austrian officer, and the Turkish character Ali turns out to be Feodora's sister.

38. *The Duchess of Montmorency* depicts the conflict between Protestants and

Catholics in sixteenth-century France. The heroine Marie cross-dresses as a page in order to facilitate the escape of her lover Guido, who then flees in her clothing. *Heinrich and Marie* is about two illegitimate children from the dynasty of the Stuarts, one of whom travels in the disguise of a boy. In *Edmund's Paths and Wanderings* the heroine Alinde attends a masked ball in the costume of a knight.

39. The Vendée insurrection lasted from March 1793 to May 1795, when the Vendée was obliged to recognize the Republic. For more information see Yalom 191–209.

40. The castle is lonely and dark, its surroundings deserted. The duke is ill, and there are many premonitions of death (I: 36, I: 187, I: 227, II: 189).

41. My analysis of Therese Huber's novel *The Seldorf Family* demonstrates that support for the goals of the Revolution also leads to internal contradictions because of the implicit identification of "human" and "male." The structure of the conflict, however, is different.

42. Even Elisabeth's decision to join the army is supervised by patriarchal authority. Kneeling in front of the crucifix and absorbed in ardent prayer, Elisabeth decides to don male attire and become a warrior for the fatherland (I: 77).

43. "So pries er die Frauen in ihrer reinen Selbstverleugnung, und wie dies Himmelsschild sich so stark und schirmend auf ihre Brust lege, daß sie der ernsten Lebensgefahr ohne sonderliche Anstrengung trotzen. Gewiß, setzte er gerührt hinzu, ihre Waffen sind nicht von dieser Welt" (Motte-Fouqué I: 137).

44. "Sich selber nicht bewußt, weder denkend noch wollend, hatte Elisabeth einem neben ihr Haltenden die weiße Fahne aus der Hand gerissen. Wie ein Blitz theilte sie die Reihen. Dorthin, wo der Federbusch des Prinzen im Gedränge hin und wieder wankte, zog es sie magnetisch. Ihre Hand zitterte nicht, sie konnte den Schaft, an welchem das Panier befestigt war, hoch in die Luft schwingen. Verlaßt Eure Fahne nicht, Vendéer, rief sie mit klarer Engelsstimme. Rettet die Ehre Frankreichs" (Motte-Fouqué I: 131).

45. After the death of the prince, Fouqué emphasizes that the distinct quality of gender is unmistakable ["des Geschlechts Eigentümlichkeit unverkennbar ist" (II: 54)], no masquerade can hide it (cf., for example, "Das bewegliche Minenspiel der Frauen ist stets ein Spiegel ihres Inneren. Nicht Kunst noch Wille mögen das hindern," 80). The discovery of Elisabeth's femininity is consistently associated with the absence or death of the prince. A first "hint of her gender" ("die Ahndung ihres Geschlechts," I: 241) is given when Elisabeth speaks in fever dreams after the prince has been taken prisoner. When in England, her mourning about the dead prince betrays her gender to her new ally Sombreuil (II: 54). More

and more, her femininity is an open secret and her male clothing an impotent disguise.

46. In the second part, Elisabeth challenges an insulting gallant to a duel. But her fatherly friend Sombreuil convinces her that he should fight in her stead.

47. There is a similar situation earlier on when Elisabeth tries to persuade the prince not to embark on a dangerous enterprise (I: 159). Her advice is ignored, the royalist army suffers a terrible defeat, and Elisabeth is taken prisoner.

48. Note also that the regiment of the heroic aristocrat Sombreuil received its training in Germany (Motte-Fouqué II: 60).

49. The parallel is even more obvious if one keeps in mind that Fouqué's second husband Friedrich belonged to the dynasty of the de la Motte-Fouqué, which formed part of the Vendée aristocracy.

50. "Wir sind hier oft bedroht worden und noch neuerlich war es nahe daran, daß die Mark verheert ward [. . .] Damals habe ich Stunden der Verzweiflung verlebt, von der ich niemand ein Bild machen kann," qtd. from Karl August Varnhagen von Ense, *Biographische Porträts* 145.

51. "Ha! Schrie sie, in den bewaffneten Haufen stürzend, ein Verräther! Bürger, ein Besoldeter des Conventes mitten unter Euch! Sie hielt Cornelius wild umschlungen und ihn gewaltsam hervorziehend, wiederholte sie: ein Verräther! Schlagt ihn tod, ein meineidiger Verräther. Im Augenblick ballten sich tausend Fäuste gegen Cornelius [. . .] und ehe er die geschmeidige Zunge rühren konnte, lag er [. . .] todt am Boden" (Motte-Fouqué II: 163–164).

CHAPTER 2

1. In the putting-out system, or Verlagssystem, work was allocated to individual sub-contractors who were subservient to a *Verleger*. The *Verleger* provided the raw material (for example, wool), coordinated the process of manufacture, and bought the finished product (for example, cloth). For more information see Kisch.

2. Black Aachen cloth, for example, was sold in the Middle East, in Spain, and in Russia (cf. Kisch 312).

3. This period of prosperity and growth ended as soon as English products were re-admitted (Schumacher 302–303).

4. Brüggelmann, the owner of the first spinning machine in Germany, had succeeded in importing a jenny but failed to get it to function properly. It was only with the help of an English mechanic that he finally succeeded (Mottek 100).

5. Mosse, for example, points out that masculinity, Germanness, and German respectability are closely intertwined (64).

6. Cf. McClintock who claims that often "the dangerous crossings of gender and class are negotiated by projecting onto them the rhetoric of race" (108).

7. A similar dynamic characterizes the life of Flora Sandes. Sandes, an Englishwoman, becomes a Serbian officer in 1915 and starts to wear men's clothing. However, for her Serbian companions her Britishness is of far greater importance than her gender. As an Englishwoman Sandes symbolizes the promise of allied assistance for the Serbian cause (Wheelwright 13).

8. Cf. Zantop's analysis of the works of Cornelius de Pauw. According to de Pauw, the degree of civilization of a particular tribe corresponds directly to the degree of difference between the men and women of this tribe (*Fantasies* 54).

9. For Germany, such distancing devices were analyzed by George Mosse in his excellent study *Nationalism and Sexuality*. Mosse postulates that the inhabitants of Protestant Northern Germany, captives of their own ideals of bourgeois respectability, projected their illicit sexual wishes onto other nations.

10. "Der Heldin dieses Romans gebührt insofern der Name einer schönen Seele, als ihre Tugenden aus ihrer Natur entspringen, und ihre Bildung aus ihrem Charakter hervorgeht. Wir hätten aber doch dieses Werk lieber Bekenntnisse einer Amazone überschrieben [. . .] Denn es zeigt sich uns wirklich hier eine Männin" (*Schriften zur Literatur 1*, Artemis XIV: 232).

11. "Die Hauptfrage, die das Buch behandelt, ist: wie kann ein Frauenzimmer seinen Charakter, seine Individualität gegen die Umstände, gegen die Umgebung retten?" (*Gedenkausgabe* XIV: 237).

12. While Lange's hypothesis is very convincing in the context of eighteenth-century women's literature in general, it seems to me that it is actually less so for *Bekenntnisse einer schönen Seele*. As Lange herself points out, there is a lesbian love story in Unger's Bildungsroman. Thus, the heroine Mirabella does not sacrifice her love for men, for it is inappropriate to speak of renunciation and chastity when one is simply disinterested.

13. Friederike Helene Unger (1741 or 1751–1811 or 1813) was married to the publisher Unger. She translated numerous works (among them Rousseau's *Confessions*) and wrote several essays and novels, for example *Karoline von Lichtfeld* (1787), *Countess Pauline* [Gräfin Pauline](1800), *Melanie or the Foundling* [Melanie oder das Findelkind] (1804), and *The French in Berlin* [Die Franzosen in Berlin](1809). She also managed the Unger publishing house after the death of her husband in 1804.

14. The image of the "madwoman in the attic" is taken from Sandra M. Gilbert and Susan Gubar's brilliant study *The Madwoman in the Attic*.

15. "Graf Silberbach konnte im Nachtkleide und dem Krankenanzug nicht

sonderlich imponieren [. . .] Das Nachtkleid demütigte ihn unbeschreiblich" (262).

16. It is of interest to note that it is the gender-bending Spaniard who possesses money and gold.

17. "In imitating gender, drag implicitly reveals the imitative structure of gender itself—as well as its contingency" (Butler, *Gender* 137).

18. "In seiner Galanterie und Gewandtheit war er jedem überlegen, und in der welt- und hofklugen Falschheit und Treulosigkeit suchte er seines Gleichen. Die Ingredienzien dieses empfehlenden Charakters hatte er mühsam und kostspielig aus allen Ländern und von allen Höfen zusammengeholt" (20).

19. Cf. Kammler, who claims that "women writers employ the numerous topoi of German morality and identity to discuss more than national character. For them these considerations provide an opportunity to introduce different models of femininity" (169).

20. It cannot be denied that the exceptional position of the heroine is bought at the price of denouncing all other female characters.

21. Albertine's uncle is decadent and weak, and Albertine loses her entire fortune because of his professional incompetence. In addition to being greedy and immoral, the poet Wassermann also lacks talent. Henriette Euler's unworthy fiancé refuses to marry her but squanders her money for presents for his mistresses.

22. Albert's "femaleness" is also suggested by the fact that he contracts a violent fever when Albertine rejects his first proposal of marriage (174).

23. In her discussion of novels by eighteenth-century British women writers, Craft-Fairchild has pointed out that "the woman's transgressiveness is usually contained and controlled at the end of the narrative through her confinement, exile, or death" (11).

24. "Adelaide nahm die Parthie ihres Geschlechts, und behauptete, es sei demselben nicht zu verargen, wenn seine Ansichten der Welt und ihrer Verhältnisse nicht die Kraft und Eindringlichkeit des männlichen Blicks habe. 'Bedenken Sie doch, Mademoiselle, in welchem Licht uns die Welt erscheinen muß, da unser Geist nur zu den infiniment petits gebildet wird, und wie jedes rechtliche Weib, das seinem Gatten oder seiner Familie nützlich werden will, sich zu den unedelsten Details des Hauswesens verstehen muß. Wer so sehen muß, der wird doch gewiß zuletzt ein moralischer Myops'" (255–256). Note also the following defense of her gender: "'Rarely, dear Albertine, do we deserve the reproach that we love too little,' said Adelaide comfortingly. 'Alas, we love much too much, we oblige men with much too much tiring love. We bear their bad behavior with much too much love. O, if they were not so excessively sure of us, the gender relations would be more tender and piquant even in marriage'" (308).

25. "Er bedachte nicht, daß es in der Natur der Dinge liegt, und daß es unbil-
    lig ist, vom Weibe zu fordern, was der seltne Mann nur vermag: allem zu
    genügen. Würde sich weibliches Talent im Wettstreite mit dem
    männlichen nicht ungehemmter entwickeln, müßte sich das Weib nicht
    zugleich hundert zeitversplitternden Arbeiten hingeben? Und die Hand
    auf's Herz, ihr Künstlerinnen, und schriftstellerischen Weiber, wenn ihr
    den Pinsel aus der Hand legt, wenn euch eben ein Reim oder lebhaftes
    Bild auf der Zunge schwebt, gehet ihr dann mit eben so lebhaftem Interesse
    in die Küche oder an den Wäschschrank, als ihr euch an euren
    Schreibtisch oder an die Staffelei setzet? Ich sage nein! Und der Mann, der
    es von euch fordert, daß die Geistesunterhaltung untergeordnet bleiben
    soll, ist ein unbilliger" (282–283).

26. See for example the comment that the transition from servile lover to
    despotic husband is inevitable (30).

27. Adelaide's statement is prompted by Laurette's reproach that she uses too
    much makeup.

28. "Einst kam ich von einem Spaziergange zu Hause; da hieß es: ein junger,
    schöner Knabe habe nach mir gefragt; er sei, um meiner zu warten, in die
    nahe Kirche eingetreten. Wer konnte hier nach mir fragen! Nach einer
    halben Stunde erschien wirklich ein sauber gekleideter Knabe in
    Bediententracht, in dem ich, beim ersten Anklang seiner Sprache,
    Adelaiden erkannte" (246–247).

29. The narrator comments on the brutalizing effect of war, which spoilt Louis
    for a quiet life in the country. Louis' reaction to Albertine's illness is also
    designed to alienate readers. He reproaches her and turns from her because
    a disfigured woman cannot satisfy his sexual cravings.

30. Karoline Paulus was born on September 14, 1767, in Schorndorf/
    Württemberg. She was the daughter of the district magistrate Paulus.
    Paulus married her cousin, the well-known professor of theology H. E. G.
    Paulus, and followed him to Jena, later to Heidelberg. She was acquainted
    with the Jena Romantic circle and was especially close to Dorothea
    Schlegel. In addition to *Wilhelm Dumont*, she wrote *Adolf and Virginia*
    (1811) and a collection of short stories (1823). Paulus also translated
    Voltaire's *Semiramis*. Her daughter Emilie Paulus was a writer as well.

31. The fact that Wilhelm's story is presented as an addendum to one of
    Adelaide's letters testifies to its lesser importance.

32. "Die Fesseln waren mir nun angelegt; [. . .] Ich spreche hier nicht von
    äußerer Freiheit; denn dieß ist bei weitem der kleinste Verlust bei der Ehe.
    Ich spreche von dem weit wichtigeren Verlust unserer moralischen
    Individualität. Eine Frau, welche die unsinnigen Gesetze, die unnatür-
    lichen Pflichten der Ehe erfüllen will, muß ihre schönsten Empfindungen,
    ihre edelsten Regungen, sie muß die ihr, wie jedem menschlichen Wesen,

von Gott verliehene Willensfreiheit auf dem Altar der Vorurtheile opfern. Sie muß ihrem Manne ähnlich zu werden suchen, er mag seyn wie er will; [. . .] Und wenn die bessere Natur der Frau sich dagegen empört, so muß sie wenigstens vor der Welt die Schwächen ihres Mannes zu vertheidigen, seine Fehler zu verstecken suchen. Sie muß also falsch werden" (85–87). Adelaide's critique of the institution of marriage is even more poignant if we take into account that she compares her former hopes for marital happiness to those of Clara, claiming that her own expectations of Eduard were as high as Clara's trust in her future husband is now (89).

33. "Wenn er mich nur heiter sah, so war er vergnügt, und seine eigenen Wünsche vergessend, lebte er nur in meinem scheinbaren Glück" (98).

34. Wilhelm's "feminine" nature is also indicated by the fact that he derives his last name from a woman, namely from his sister Margot. Interestingly, the reader never learns Eduard's last name. His appropriation of Adelaide must thus remain incomplete.

35. "Adelaide reist zu ruhig, sie zieht fast nur Erkundigungen ein, und läßt sich die gehofften Freunde mehr vom Schicksal und Zufall entgegenbringen, als daß sie solche durch Bemühung und Tätigkeit erreichte und erränge. Darzustellen wäre gewesen ein leidenschaftliches Bemühen" (*Gedenkausgabe* XIV: 240)

36. Paulus repeatedly attributes Rosalie's behavior to her nationality, not to her character: "It is essentially our national qualities that make us charming and that appear original" (238–239).

37. "eine braune Perücke, schwarz gemalte Augenbrauen und dergleichen werden das blonde Gesichtchen ziemlich unkenntlich machen; auch ist sie groß genug, um für einen ansehnlichen Herrn passieren zu können, und eine Französinn—weiß sich in jede Rolle zu schicken" (216).

38. When Eduard tries to persuade Adelaide to participate in an amateur production, Adelaide insists on a play that suits her character.

39. "Eine sucht, was sie nicht finden kann; die Andere sucht sich und Andern zu verbergen, daß sie gefunden hat, was sie unwillkührlich suchte; und die Dritte genießt, was sie hat, ohne sich dadurch abhalten zu lassen, noch mehr zu finden" (279).

40. Repeatedly, Adelaide compares the two nations and sets French love of life ("Lebenslust," 278) and cleverness ("Gewandtheit," 222) against German clumsiness ("Unbehülflichkeit," 223) and gloomy spirit ("trüber Geist," 278).

41. "Ihre neue Rolle kleidet sie sehr gut. Die geübteste mimische Künstlerin könnte die männlichen Bewegungen und Geberden nicht anmuthiger und getreuer nachahmen, als sie. Ich bin gewiß, diesen kecken, ungezwungenen, feurigen jungen Mann wird niemand für ein Mädchen halten. Sie täuscht mich sogar zuweilen" (224–225).

42. The negative impact of a father figure is also evident in Wilhelm Dumont's
    story. Wilhelm was conceived before his mother was married. But the
    prospective groom died before the wedding, and his grandfather refused to
    accept a bastard son into the family. Wilhelm's mother was forced to give
    the child to foster parents. When Wilhelm ran away from there, she lost
    touch. Like Adelaide, Wilhelm's mother roamed the countryside to find
    her missing son but died before she succeeded.

43. Interestingly, Wilhelm's life is marked by a similar family constellation (see
    note 42 above). Fatherly injustice is rectified through motherly interces-
    sion as Adelaide's mother, a friend of Wilhelm's mother, reinstates
    Wilhelm in his rightful inheritance (Wilhelm's mother had entrusted
    Adelaide's mother with the safekeeping of Wilhelm's inheritance).
    Furthermore, the relationship between Marie and her beloved brother,
    Jakob, is also threatened by a malevolent father.

44. The world of theater, masks, and appearance are consistently associated
    with Adelaide's father and with her husband, Eduard. It is Adelaide's father
    who instructs her about the value of appearance over essence ("kommt
    denn nicht alles auf das an, was man ist?—Nein, meine Tochter! Besonders
    bei einem Mädchen kommt oft mehr darauf an, was sie scheint," 38–39)
    and it is Eduard who persuades her to appear in an amateur production of
    Iffland's *Hagestolz*.

CHAPTER 3

1. For an extensive discussion of the Chevalier d'Eon see Gary Kates.

2. Garber questions the import of such final "truths" when she asks "what
   does it mean to say that 'he' was really 'she'? If a person lives his or her life
   consistently under a gender identity different from that revealed by
   anatomical inspection after death what is the force of the 'reality'" (204).

3. That such revelations are still possible today became evident in 1989,
   when the death of the jazz musician Billy Tipton led to the discovery that
   Tipton had been anatomically female.

4. Bullough and Bullough report that some female saints were able to hide
   their true gender until they died (51). Garber calls doctors and morticians
   the ultimate agents of discovery (203). See also Wheelwright 19 and
   Doniger 419.

5. Cf. Ariès, who assumes that, in the eighteenth century, the preoccupation
   with one's own death gradually replaced the fascination with the death of
   the other (la mort de toi), and that, accompanying this change, death
   became a privileged moment of truth (*Western* 55–82).

6. But it is by no means a matter of the past; cf. the brutal murder of Teena Brendan represented in the movie *Boys Don't Cry*.

7. Even in Joan of Arc's case, the accusation of cross-dressing was combined with that of heresy (Hotchkiss 51).

8. Cf. Dekker and van de Pol: "If the cross-dressing was instigated by patriotism or family feelings—praiseworthy sentiments in women—then she might be judged mildly. If, however, the fraud or disguise was used for further deception and criminal practices, the reaction was extremely negative. Considered the worst of these practices was the perversion of a relationship or even marriage with another woman" (74). According to Wheelwright, the reverse is also true. Women who renounced their sexuality altogether acquired male privileges in return (Wheelwright 116).

9. Lincken's case is similar to that of Barbara, alias Willem, Adriaens. During a stay in Amsterdam in 1632, the soldier Adriaens marries Hilletje Jans, the younger sister of his landlady. Negligent of his marital duties and given to alcohol, Adriaens meets with the wrath of the landlady, which ultimately leads to his discovery. He is exiled to Frisia, where he soon marries another woman (Dekker and van de Pol 6of.).

10. Cf. Stephan, who calls writing "a form of killing of a very particular nature" and art "a form of de-vivification" ("Weiblichkeit" 6–7).

11. Kreuzer, in referring to the man-woman duality as an "example of a natural polarity with metaphysical and ethical dimensions" (364), draws our attention to the fact that the gender dichotomy can be utilized for the stabilization of other systems of order.

12. Cf. Garber, who claims that transvestites, in addition to being signs of the constructedness of gender (9), also confront us with the possibility that there is no naturalness to signs (40).

13. Schiller was born in Marbach at the Neckar in 1759. His father, Johann Caspar Schiller, a surgeon, was married to Elisabetha Dorothea, née Kodweiß. From 1772 on, Schiller attended the Carlsschule, a boarding school founded by Duke Carl Eugen. After completing his degree in medicine, he took up work as a doctor in Stuttgart. The performance of his first drama *The Robbers* [Die Räuber] (January 13, 1782, in Mannheim) led to a severe disagreement with Carl Eugen. In order to avoid persecution, Schiller had to flee from Stuttgart. He spent some time with Frau von Wolzogen in Bauerbach/ Thuringia and finally accepted an engagement as poet-in-residence for the Mannheim theater. After a visit with his friend Körner in Leipzig and Dresden in 1785, Schiller moved to Jena where he was appointed professor of philosophy in 1789. In 1799 Schiller and his wife Charlotte von Lengefeld moved to Weimar, where they live until Schiller's death in 1805.

14. Schiller originally wrote *Fiesco* for the National Theater of Mannheim, where his *Räuber* had been performed with great success. But Wolfgang Heribert von Dalberg, the director of the Mannheim theater, refused to stage *Fiesco*. When the revised version of the play was also rejected, Schiller decided to sell the drama to the Mannheim bookseller Schwan. This revised version of 1783 provides the textual basis for the following interpretation, but the revised stage version of 1784, the so-called Mannheim stage version, will also be consulted. There is a third version, the so-called Leipzig-Dresden stage version of 1785, but it is generally assumed that Schiller did not author it. An adaptation of Schiller's drama by Carl Martin Plümicke was more successful on the contemporary stage than the Schillerian model from which it was derived. Schiller lambasted Plümicke's play and referred to it as "Plümike's bungle of my play" (to Körner, July 3 1785, *Nationalausgabe* XXIV: 3).

15. Readers are also likely to fall for Fiesco's pretense of an Epicurean life-style, which is meant to deflect attention away from his plans to overthrow the government. The eighth scene of the first act hints at Fiesco's true intentions, but it is not until the second act that Schiller enlightens readers about Fiesco's plans.

16. The fact that Fiesco's co-conspirators are motivated by lowly impulses also takes away from the Republican impetus of the play (cf. Meier 122).

17. The historical sources on which Schiller's work is based portray Andreas Doria as a just ruler who implements a constitution and recognizes the authority of an aristocratic assembly (Delinière 24). Schiller portrays Doria as a morally superior individual. Delinière pointed out that in Schiller's play Doria's only crime is that he has an unworthy nephew (25). This nephew Gianettino, however, is a far more nefarious character in Schiller's play than in the historical documents.

18. Phelps points out that a twentieth-century reading of the term "republic" leads to misinterpretations and suggests that republic should be interpreted as "res publica," that is, civic state. Lützeler also refers to the historical meaning of the term when he states that Doria is a republican in the Rousseauistic sense of the word (22). Jamison, on the other hand, draws attention to the fact that Doria's reinstatement constitutes a "victory of the aged" and is problematic as such (62).

19. This impression is confirmed by a report by Andreas Streicher, Schiller's companion on his flight from Ludwigsburg. Streicher claims that Schiller, who carried *Fiesco* in his luggage, had originally devised a tragic ending and that the revision did not come easily ("You may believe that the last scenes required far more deliberation than the entire play," qtd. in Hecht 43).

20. Other amazons in Schiller's work are the virgin of Orléans in the epony-

mous play [Jungfrau von Orléans] and a cross-dressed pirate in *Die Flibüstiers*.

21. The fact that Schiller placed great value on costumes suggests that one should take such details very seriously (cf. "With respect to the choice of clothing, let me add this unpresuming remark that it is a bagatelle in nature but never on the stage" [to Wolfgang Heribert Dalberg, 6. 8br. 81, XXIII: 4]).

22. In this respect, a comparison of the 1783 version with the Mannheim stage version proves particularly enlightening. Clearly, the structural pattern is the same in both versions. In the Mannheim version, in which Fiesco turns out to have been a true republican all along, that is, where the mask has always been just that, Leonore stays alive. Since appearance and reality remain separated, since Fiesco's performance never turns into reality, a violent solution is not necessary. In the version of 1783, on the other hand, Fiesco's attempt to substitute his own construct for the given reality sets a trap which leads to the unintentional murder of his wife and finally to Fiesco's own death. Ultimately, Fiesco falls victim to the deceptions that his own machinations brought into existence. (Some scholars might object that it is not Fiesco's performance but his thirst for power that brings about his downfall. This, however, neglects to account for the numerous metaphors of performance and masks that are of such central importance for Schiller's play; cf. also Hinderer who claims that Fiesco's failure is that he "loses himself in his role," 256).

23. Cf. Janz, who calls Fiesco a "creative genius" (40) and highlights his similarity to the promethean heroes of the Storm and Stress drama.

24. "I have written down all your parts; if everybody fulfills his, then nothing is left to say" (*Fiesco* IV: 90).

25. Fiesco's hubris, his ambition to be God-like (Mansouri 51), and Schiller's statement that *Fiesco* is "a whole, great portrait of active and overthrown ambition" (letter to Wolfgang Heribert von Dalberg, November 16, 1782, XXIII: 50), must be understood in the context of this parallel between artist and power-hungry politician.

26. "Heilig und feierlich war immer der stille der grose Augenblick in dem Schauspielhaus, wo die Herzen so vieler Hunderte, wie auf den allmächtigen Schlag einer magischen Ruthe, nach der Fantasie eines Dichters beben [. . .] wo ich des Zuschauers Seele am Zügel führe, und nach meinem Gefallen, einem Ball gleich dem Himmel oder der Hölle zuwerfen kann" (IV: 272).

27. Cf. Graham, who comments that "once again we are inclined to regard the imitation as more real than the real thing" (12).

28. "und eine einzige grose Aufwallung, die ich durch die gewagte Erdichtung

in der Brust meiner Zuschauer bewirke, wiegt bei mir die strengste historische Genauigkeit auf" (IV: 271).

29. "So trozig stehst du da, weil du *Leben* auf *todten* Tüchern heuchelst, und
    große Thaten mit kleinem Aufwand verewigst [. . .] Stürzest Tyrannen auf
    Leinwand;—bist selbst ein elender Sklave? Machst Republiken mit einem
    Pinsel frei;—kannst deine eigene Ketten nicht brechen? Voll und
    befehlend. Geh!—Deine Arbeit ist Gaukelwerk—der *Schein* weiche der
    That" (*Fiesco* IV: 61)

30. The dedicated republican Leonore would not have been driven to her
    "unnatural" action if not for Fiesco's thirst for power. Cf. Ueding, who
    claims that Fiesco himself "has created the conditions that lead to his
    downfall in that the result of his politics is an objective and all-encom-
    passing appearance by which he himself is affected in turn" (40).

31. Kieffer points out that the murder is Fiesco's first physical action and as
    such marks the transition from word to deed (130). However, I do not con-
    cur with his interpretation that "those who rely too exclusively on lin-
    guistic means are doomed to fail when they act in the material world"
    (130). Fiesco's failure is caused by the dissociation of language and moral-
    ity, not by linguistic hubris.

32. Thus, Jamison's insight that political arguments are formulated as laws of
    nature not only applies to Schiller's *Wilhelm Tell*, as Jamison claims, but
    also to *Fiesco*.

33. Interestingly, "the juxtaposition and opposition of courtly intrigues and
    family drama" (Janz 53) is often interpreted as yet another flaw of the
    drama.

34. "Genoa lost its hero—and I my husband" (IV: 9).

35. Hinderer calls Verrina's coupling of his daughter's happiness with the lib-
    eration of Genoa inhuman, because it condemns her to suffering until the
    liberation is achieved (41). Hinderer claims that Schiller's drama contains
    a critique of the concatenation of the public and private spheres. That
    Schiller intended to highlight the private-public dichotomy is also indi-
    cated by the fact that he eliminated all references to Genoa's foreign pol-
    icy, so prominent in the historical sources.

36. Interestingly, in the stage version, Berta is not raped and, consequently,
    does not don male attire.

37. For the linking together of truth and beauty see also Schiller's letter to
    Körner of December 25, 1788: "I am convinced that every work of art must
    answer only to itself, that is to its own rules of beauty, and is subject to no
    other demand. But I also believe firmly that it is in this way that it will not
    fail to satisfy all other demands as every form of beauty can ultimately be
    dissolved into objective truth" (XXV: 167).

38. That the contrast between "proper" masculinity and femininity is indis-

pensable for this stabilization is further corroborated by the fact that Schiller developed the rather complex character of Leonore from a passing remark in his sources.

39. Cf. Ueding, who claims that "Fiesco plays his different parts according to political needs, for none of them derives from the God-given system of world order, they are all based on reason and agreement and are thus of instrumental import only" (40).

40. It is not just Schiller's poetry that propagates a conservative ideal of femininity. His correspondence also contains misogynistic remarks. See for example his comment on Wieland's daughter who, as Schiller claims, has been raised "to be an excellent woman, extremely few needs and infinitely much economy" (to Körner, November 19, 1787, II: 178).

41. I do not agree with Mansouri who claims that Leonore is the first female character in Schiller's work who is actively engaged in politics (60). The fact that Leonore is both fanatical and dignified is no contradiction, as Mansouri claims, but is consistent with the contradictory definition of femininity itself which encompasses the extreme poles of whore and saint. Leonore embodies the contrary types of passive sufferer and raging fury that comprise the female repertory of eighteenth-century drama (cf. Huyssen 160).

42. Anthony Stephens, for example, lists "the collapse of a teleological view of the world, a loss of trust in language as a means of producing truth, and a skepticism about the efficacy of moral development in the genesis of the individual" (*The Dramas and Stories* 3). See also Helbling 88.

43. Interestingly, Raimar Zons has claimed that Kleist's texts are not addressed to souls, but to nerves and bodies ("Von der Not" 182).

44. Cf. Barbara Kennedy, who refers to "the literal destruction of the female body for the good of the nation" (17).

45. "Da ging ich, in mich gekehrt, durch das gewölbte Tor, sinnend zurück in die Stadt. Warum, dachte ich, sinkt wohl das Gewölbe nicht ein, da es doch keine Stütze hat? Es steht, antwortete ich, weil alle Steine auf einmal einstürzen wollen und ich zog aus diesem Gedanken einen unbeschreiblich erquickenden Trost, der mir bis zu dem entscheidenden Augenblicke immer mit der Hoffnung zur Seite stand, daß auch ich mich halten würde, wenn alles mich sinken läßt" (to Wilhelmine von Zenge, November 16, 1800, *Briefe* 125).

46. The figure of the Doppelgänger in *Amphytrion* might be cited as another example that proves the instability of the body as guarantor of truth.

47. Kleist was born on October 18, 1777, in Frankfurt an der Oder. He joined the Potsdam regiment at age 15 and served until 1799, when he took up the study of law. His subsequent engagement with Wilhelmine von Zenge lasted for several years but did not lead to matrimony. After several jour-

neys within Germany, to France and to Switzerland, Kleist accepted an administrative position in Königsberg. He was arrested as a spy during a journey to Berlin in 1807 and imprisoned in Fort des Joux. After his release in 1807, Kleist betook himself to Dresden, then to Berlin in 1810. In 1811, Kleist committed suicide at the Berlin Wannsee together with Henriette Vogler.

48. "Ihm war eines Tages die seltsame Auskleideszene des letzten Aktes, rein als Szene, in den Sinn gekommen, und da die Situation ihn anzog, hatte er sie wie eine zusammenhanglose Phantasie niedergeschrieben. Dann erst fiel ihm ein, sie mit andern Fäden der Erfindung, vielleicht auch mit einem zufällig entdeckten Stoff zusammenzuspinnen, und so wob sich allmählich um diese Szene die ganze Tragödie herum" (qtd. in Sembdner, *Lebensspuren* 45–46).

49. In Wieland's story, the rich Don Pedro promises his brother Don Felix that the latter's second child, provided it is a boy, would become his sole heir. When Felix's wife gives birth to a girl, the parents decide to conceal the gender of the child, call it Pedro, and raise it as a boy. After several intricacies of plot, "Pedro" finally marries Ferdinand, the relative who was deprived of his rightful inheritance by Pedro's gender masquerade.

50. The assumption that Kleist's first drama represents his attempt to come to terms with his sister's gender defiance would also explain why he did not want her to read this "miserable trashy book," that is, his first drama (*Briefe* 254).

51. "Ich wäre auf dieser Rheinreise sehr glücklich gewesen, wenn—wenn— Ach, gnädigste Frau, es giebt wohl nichts Großes in der Welt, wozu Ulrike nicht fähig wäre, ein edles, weises, großmüthiges Mädchen, eine Heldenseele in einem Weiberkörper, u ich müßte von Allem diesen nichts sein, wenn ich das nicht innig fühlen wollte. Aber—ein Mensch kann viel besitzen, vieles geben, es läßt sich doch nicht immer, wie Göthe sagt, an seinem Busen ruhen—Sie ist ein Mädchen, das orthographisch schreibt u handelt, nach dem Tacte spielt und denkt, ein Wesen, das von dem Weibe nichts hat, als die Hüften, und nie hat sie gefühlt, wie süß ein Händedruck ist—Aber Sie mißverstehen mich doch nicht—? O es giebt kein Wesen in der Welt, das ich so ehre, wie meine Schwester. Aber welchen Mißgrif hat die Natur begangen, als sie ein Wesen bildete, das weder Mann noch Weib ist, u gleichsam wie eine Amphibie zwischen zwei Gattungen schwankt?" (to Adolphine von Werdeck, July 28, 1801, *Briefe* 202).

52. "Ich weiß, Eustache, Männer sind die Rächer— / Ihr seid die Klageweiber der Natur. Doch nichts mehr von Natur. / Ein hold ergötzend Märchen ists der Kindheit, / Der Menschheit von den Dichtern, ihren Ammen, / Erzählt. Vertrauen, Unschuld, Treue, Liebe, / Religion, der Götter Furcht sind wie Die Tiere, welche reden.—Selbst das Band / Das heilige, der

Blutsverwandtschaft riß, [. . .] / Und weil doch alles sich gewandelt, Menschen / Mit Tieren die Natur gewechselt, wechsle / Denn auch das Weib die ihrige—" (40–59). This and all subsequent quotes from the *Family Schroffenstein* are taken from the Deutscher Klassiker Verlag edition and given in line numbers.

53. "—Sieh, wenn du mir sagtest, / Die Ströme flössen neben ihren Ufern / Bergan, und sammelten auf Felsenspitzen / In Seen sich, so wollt—ich wollts dir glauben; / Doch sagst du mir, ich hätt ein Kind gemordet, / Des Vetters Kind—" (629–633).

54. "RUPERT: Wer von euch beiden ist das Weib? / SANTING: Ich sage, Johann [wurde getötet, EK]; und ists der Herold, wohl, so steckt die Frau ins Panzerhemd, mich in den Weibsrock. / [. . .] SANTING: Hier ist der Wanderer, Herr, er kann dir sagen, Ob ich ein Weib, ob nicht" (1512–1514).

55. "Wie ich muß lachen, eh ich will, wenn einer / Sich lächerlich bezeigt, so muß ich weinen / Wenn einer stirbt. / [. . .] Zwar der Pater sagt, Er sei nicht in dem Grabe.—Nein, daß ichs Recht sag, er sei zwar in dem Grabe— Ach. / Ich kanns dir nicht so wiederbeichten. Kurz, / Ich seh es, wo er ist, am Hügel" (396–409).

56. Karoline Friederike Luise Maximiliane von Günderrode was born in Karlsruhe on February 11, 1780. She had five siblings. Her father, a ducal chamberlain and governmental councilor, died when she was 6 years old. Her mother, Louise, relocated the family to Hanau, where she assumed a position as lady-in-waiting at the court of Wilhelm of Hessen-Kassel. The monetary constraints of her family prompted Karoline to enter the Cronstettten-Hynspergische Damenstift, a Protestant institution for unmarried, aristocratic ladies, which provided financial security along with a moderate degree of personal independence, such as the permission to travel and receive visitors. Günderrode occupied herself with intensive studies and entertained an extended correspondence with her friends Lisette Nees von Esenbeck and Bettina Brentano. At age 19 she fell in love with the legal scholar Karl Friedrich von Savigny, who married Gunda Brentano. In 1804 Günderrode made the acquaintance of the married philologist Friedrich Creuzer. Even though he reciprocated her feelings, Creuzer did not want to leave his wife. The end of this relationship triggered Günderrode's suicide.

57. Günderrode stabbed herself in Winkel am Rhein in 1806.

58. Cf. Geiger, who claims that Günderrode's literary estate would be a "far more significant issue if one were really primarily concerned with Günderrode the writer, not Günderrode the woman. But as the latter is the case, her estate has little to offer in every respect" (*Günderrode* 2).

59. "Wir machten ein Reiseprojekt, wir erdachten unsre Wege und Abenteuer,

wir schrieben alles auf, wir malten alles aus, unsre Einbildung war so geschäftig, daß wir's in der Wirklichkeit nicht besser hätten erleben können; oft lasen wir in dem erfundenen Reisejournal und freuten uns der allerliebsten Abenteuer, die wir darin erlebt hatten, und die Erfindung wurde gleichsam zur Erinnerung, deren Beziehungen sich noch in der Gegenwart fortsetzten. Von dem, was sich in der Wirklichkeit ereignete, machten wir uns keine Mitteilungen" (*Goethes Briefwechsel mit einem Kinde* 81).

60. "Unsere Vorstellungen hingegen wären absolut leer, blose Formen, wenn es nicht ihnen entsprechende Dinge gäbe. Demnach sind Dinge ohne Vorstellungen für uns nicht gedenkbar, und Vorstellungen von Dingen, ohne die Dinge nichts, leere wesenlose Begriffe, damit aber die Dinge für uns Wirklichkeit, und unsere Vorstellungen Realität haben, sucht die Filosofie ihre absolute Einheit, die Identität des Objekts und Subjekts, sie kann aber hierzu keinen andern Weg einschlagen als den der Selbstbetrachtung" (qtd. in Hopp and Preitz 295–296).

61. Creuzer calls her "the friend" or "the saint" (Preisendanz 74, 124).

62. At times Creuzer and Günderrode encrypted their correspondence by using Greek letters in order to render it illegible for Creuzer's wife.

63. "Der Freund hat mir gesagt, wenn dieser Krieg ihm und seinen Wünschen gefährlich werden sollte, so wollte er Dir bewußt Kleidung anziehn, entlaufen und bei Ihnen Bedienter werden, wegjagen können Sie ihn doch nicht, und er wollte sich so fein verstellen, daß man ihn nicht erkennen sollte" (letter to Friedrich Creuzer, September 15, 1805, *Briefe* 240).

64. Cf. Sophie Creuzer to Friedrich Carl von Savigny: "But I found here that she had the idea to disguise herself with men's clothing and flee to Russia with Cr." (*Briefe der Karoline von Günderrode* 273).

65. "Das einzige, was man der ganzen Sammlung Böses vorwerfen könnte, wäre, daß sie zwischen dem Männlichen und Weiblichen schwebt, und hier und da nicht genug Gedichten, sondern sehr gelungen aufgegebenen Exerzitien oder Ausarbeitungen gleicht" (letter to Karoline von Günderrode, May 31–June 2, 1804, Vol. XXXI: 328).

66. "Hör!—und im Frühjahr nähmen wir unsre Stecken und wanderten, denn wir wären als Einsiedler und sagten nicht, daß wir Mädchen wären. Du mußt Dir einen falschen Bart machen, weil Du groß bist, denn sonst glaubt's niemand, aber nur einen kleinen, der Dir gut steht, und weil ich klein bin, so bin ich als Dein kleiner Bruder, da muß ich mir aber meine Haare abschneiden" (*Günderode* 318).

67. "Gestern las ich Ossians Darthula, und er wirkte so angenehm auf mich; der alte Wunsch, einen Heldentod zu sterben, ergriff mich mit großer Heftigkeit; unleidlich war es mir, noch zu leben, unleidlicher, ruhig und gemein zu sterben. Schon oft hatte ich den unweiblichen Wunsch, mich

in ein wildes Schlachtengetümmel zu werfen, zu sterben. Warum ward ich kein Mann! Ich habe keinen Sinn für weibliche Tugenden, für Weiberglückseligkeit. Nur das Wilde, Große, Glänzende gefällt mir. Es ist ein unseliges, aber unverbesserliches Mißverhältnis in meiner Seele; und es wird und muß so bleiben, denn ich bin ein Weib und habe Begierden wie ein Mann, ohne Männerkraft. Darum bin ich so uneins mit mir" (letter to Gunda Brentano, August 29, 1801, *Briefe der Karoline von Günderrode* 78–79).

68. Cf. Goozé, who claims that Günderrode's "desire to be a hero was tied to her own fascination with death" ("Seduction" 122). Hopp and Preitz maintain that the fusion of the desire for love and death constituted the dominant problematic of her poetry (273).

69. *Darthula According to Ossian* was written around 1800. It was the first poem in her collection *Poems and Fantasies* of 1804. Geiger points out that around 1800 the Ossian-fad had already faded and calls Günderrode's Ossian-poem a "strange latecomer" (*Günderrode* 69).

70. This constitutes an interesting parallel to the writing of British women novelists of the eighteenth century who, according to Craft-Fairchild, also "feminized their heroes, putting men into the powerless position of women and showing them sharing in the misery entailed by the law of the father" (21).

71. In Macpherson's text Colla advises Darthula to "keep thou near the arm of Colla; beneath the shadow of my shield" (142). Darthula is not depicted as a fighter; she merely stretches her buckler over her father's body when the latter lies slain (143).

72. "Nathos! Reiche mir das Schwerdt der Tapfern, / Vater! Ich will deiner würdig seyn, /In des Stahles Treffen werd' ich gehen, / Nimmer Caibars duster Hallen sehen, / Nein! Ihr Geister meiner Liebe! Nein! / Freude glänzt in Nathos bei den Worten, / Die das schöngelockte Mädchen sprach: / Caibar, meine Stärke kehret wieder! / Komm mit Tausenden Erins Gebieter! / Komm zum Kampfe! Meine Kraft ist wach!" (*Sämtliche Werke* I: 15).

73. Cf. Obermeier: "Most of her male characters undergo a process of feminization" (38). Her female characters, on the other hand, are exceptionally strong and heroic (cf. Kastinger Riley 93; Burwick, "Liebe und Tod" 209).

74. Cf. Obermeier: "Only in death do Mora and Darthula [. . .] attain heroism through the articulation and fulfillment of their love" (119).

75. "FROTHAL. Soll ich die Jagd vermeiden! Nimmer Mädchen, nimmer meid ich Gefahr, denn mir ward Liebe und Ruhm, so ist mein Sterben kein Tod, was fürcht' ich noch, Tochter von Torlat? MORA. Stirbst du mit Ruhm und Liebe, so starbst du doch Frothal für mich" (*Sämtliche Werke* I: 57).

76. "KARMOR. Er hat mir die Seele meines Busens geraubt, ich liebte die Tochter von Torlat, und sie wählt ihn. MORA. Sie wählt ihn, und nicht dich. Was nutzt dir der Kampf? Was hilft dir der Sieg" (*Sämtliche Werke* I: 57)

77. "FROTHAL: Sing, you bards, the praise of the beautiful daughter of Torlat! Sing the praise of the girl so that her brittle beauty may flower immortally. And call to the battle the dark Karmor, he shall die, and be his arm as powerful as the arm of Thor, his sword like that of Odin" [Singet ihr Barden, das Lob der schönen Tochter von Torlat! Singet den Ruhm des Mädchens, daß unsterblich blühe die leicht verwelkliche Schönheit. Und ruft mir zum Kampfe den finstern Karmor, fallen soll er, und ware sein Arm mächtig wie der Arm von Thor, sein Schwert wie Odins (*Sämtliche Werke* I: 58)].

78. "Mora! Mora dich erweckt nicht der blumige Frühling, nicht der Glanz des Morgens nicht der Purpur des Abends, nicht der Ruf der Liebe. Schön ists zu wandeln, im Lichte des Lebens, aber eng ist das Grab und finster, ewig der Schlummer, darum weinet um Mora, denn sie kehrt nicht wieder zum Lichte" (*Sämtliche Werke* I: 59).

CHAPTER 4

1. "unseliges Mitteldung zwischen Hofstadt und Dorf" (qtd. in Eberhardt 6).

2. "Weimar n'est pas une petite ville, mais un grand chateau" (qtd. in Kühn, *Weimar* 24).

3. Goethe's autobiography *Poetry and Truth* [Dichtung und Wahrheit, 1811] is filled with episodes in which the author masquerades as a person of a lower social standing (see, e.g., the encounter with Friederike Brion).

4. For a history of the Weimar theater see Meßner, Sichardt, Schrickel.

5. Other examples are Schiller's *Don Carlos* (Christiane Neumann and Malcolmi as boys), Schiller's *Wallenstein's Camp* (Malcolmi as a peasant boy), Schiller's *Wilhelm Tell* (Corona Becker as Walther Tell, Sophie Teller as Wilhelm Tell). At an amateur performance of Goethe's *Iphigenie* in von Stein's house, Orestes and Pylades were portrayed by Countess Egloffstein and Fräulein Wolfskeel. Von Stein also mentions Mme Schönberger's excellent portrayal of a man in the opera *Joseph*.

6. "selbst Knabenrollen spielte sie mit einer Vollendung, daß sie ein ganzes Publikum über ihr Geschlecht täuschen konnte" (Genast 49).

7. "Knabe schien ich, ein rührendes Kind, du nanntest mich Arthur."

8. For a discussion of Goethe and homosexuality see W. Wilson 126, Tobin, Gustafson.

9. "Denn dadurch daß Menschen diese Rollen spielen, werden zuletzt die Tugenden, deren Schein sie eine geraume Zeit hindurch gekünstelt haben,

nach und nach wohl wirklich erweckt, und gehen in die Gesinnung über"
(Kant 151).

10. "und man glaubt nicht, wie zu so viel tausend kleinen Geschäften des
Lebens, die wir besorgen müssen, mehr Geisteskraft muß aufgewendet werden, die uns für nichts angerechnet wird, als die eines Genies, das Ehre
und Ruhm einerntet" (qtd. in Düntzer I: 18).

11. "Ich glaube, daß wenn ebenso viel Frauen Schriftsteller wären, als Männer
es sind, und wir nicht durch so tausend Kleinigkeiten in unserer
Haushaltung herabgestimmt würden, man vielleicht auch einige gute
darunter finden würde; denn wie wenige gute gibt es nicht unter den
Autoren ohne Zahl" (qtd. in Düntzer II: 99).

12. Von Stein claims that even though Schiller's poem "Die Würde der
Frauen" praises women, it clandestinely reintroduces man as paragon of all
virtue (Düntzer II: 30).

13. Cocalis claims that *Dido* questions the "humanistic discourse and the social
construction of love" ("Acts" 89) while Kord recognizes in *Dido* the rejection of the myth of masculinity and femininity in general ("Image" 59).

14. If her works are mentioned, they are considered to lack any artistic values.

15. Unlike *Dido*, which von Stein did not want to publish in spite of Schiller's
encouragement because she feared that its publication might make enemies, she very much wanted to see *A New System of Freedom* in print.

16. In the introduction to his edition of *Ein neues* Freiheitssystem, Felix von
Stein claims that even though in revising the play he "condensed the five
acts into four, eliminated much that is considered 'dated' in our time, and
highlighted a couple of things that agree with our time [. . .] situations and
characters are true to the original, and out of piety much that should have
been deleted was left" (3).

17. An example of this is a passage in which a gambler, who has just lost all
his money, elaborates on the beneficent and virtuous nature of gambling:
"2. GAMBLER: Now dear friend, consider this matter calmly. All the virtues
that you develop when you gamble?—Patience, when your card does not
take the trick. Endurance, when you try to push your color. Moderation,
when you go home with a small prize; modesty, if others are luckier than
you. 1. GAMBLER: And compassion, if you take somebody home with you
whom the goddess of luck has just kicked out." [2. SPIELER: Alter Freund,
betrachte einmal die Sache mit ruhigem Blut. Was für Tugenden bringt
das Spiel nicht alle in Übung?—Die Geduld, wenn die Karte nicht ein-
schlägt; die Ausdauer, wenn man ein Blatt forciert; die Mäßigkeit, wenn
man mit einem kleinen Gewinn nach Hause geht; die Bescheidenheit,
wenn andere mehr Glück haben—1. SPIELER: Und die Barmherzigkeit,
wenn man einen, den die Glücksgöttin vor die Thür gesezt hat, mit nach
Hause nimmt, 5]

18. "MAJOR: Junker, you look like a woman yourself. MONTROSE: But my uniform gives the lie to my face." [MAJOR: Junker, Du siehst selbst noch wie ein Frauenzimmer aus. MONTROSE: Aber meine Uniform straft mein Gesicht lügen, 4].

19. "FRIEDRICH: Once and for all, I won't announce his sergeant Montrose.— He is already here and I don't want to make a fool of myself. CONRAD: But I tell him, there is only one sergeant Montrose and that is my master, and just arrived. FRIEDRICH: Then his spirit has traveled faster than he. He can go ahead and beat the dust out of his jacket. CONRAD: Heavenly father, I dread having to wait on the spirit as well." [FRIEDRICH: Ein für allemal, ich melde seinen Fähndrich Montrose nicht.—Er ist schon einmal da und ich will mich nicht zum Narren haben lassen. CONRAD: Aber ich sag' ihm ja, es giebt nur einen Fähndrich Montrose und das ist mein Herr und eben angekommen. FRIEDRICH: Dann ist sein Geist schneller gereist als er. Dem kann er gleich die Jacke ausklopfen. CONRAD: Himmlischer Vater, mir graust, wenn ich den Geist noch extra bedienen müßte, 26].

20. "THEODORA: Erst die Parole, daß du Susette bist.—Was für eine Heilige hängt zu Hause über meinem Schreibtische? SUSETTE: Das hab' ich rein vergessen. Da sehen Sie doch, daß ich Susette bin, die immer alles vergißt, selbst die Heiligen. MENONDA: Der Beweis ist untrüglich" (21).

21. See also Kord, who questions the validity of the obligatory happy ending and claims that, beneath the surface, "the spectator has been encouraged to ridicule the posturing of male superiority" ("Image" 62).

22. It was published anonymously by Cotta. The following new edition bore Schiller's name. Von Stein received an honorarium of 12 new Louisdors.

23. Petersen assumes that von Stein was not familiar with the English original but relied on the German translation by Friedrich von Oertel, which was published in 1799 (129).

24. "Ach! Ist denn wirklich eine unübersteigliche Kluft zu dem abgeschiedenen Freunde meines Herzens?—O! wenn er die zarten Bande treulos zerrissen hätte? Dann, dann wäre sie es!—Aber nein!—Es ist keine Täuschung, ich fühle mich noch in seiner Nähe [. . .] ich fühle ein schauervolles Vergnügen meinen geliebten Lenox wieder aus dem Grabe hervorzurufen—ich unterhalte mich mit ihm, ich drücke ihn an mein Herz! Kannst du überirdischer Freund meine Laute vernehmen? Gieb mir ein Zeichen, daß du mir nahe bist, wenn mein irdisches Auge dein himmlisches Bild nicht mehr erfassen kann!" (225–226).

25. The name Hypolith also hints at an unlawful passion. In Euripides' tragedy *Hippolytus*, the eponymous hero is not only the son of the Amazon Hippolyte but also the object of his stepmother's passionate desire.

26. "Mein Betrug war gerechte Rache.—Ja, es bleibt wahr und gewiß. Nie standen die Frauen an ihrem gehörigen Platze, weder nach der Ordnung

der Natur, noch nach dem Vertrag der gesellschaftlichen Einrichtung. Was der einen gelingt, stürzt die andere herab. Vorzügliche Eigenschaften schaden ihnen oft, oft nutzen ihnen ihre Fehler und tragen sie aus einer unbekannten Sphäre zu einer höhern Rolle empor. Einmal sind wir alles und bald darauf nichts—Aber ich habe eine Männerseele und will auf keine Art Fesseln tragen" (223).

27. His desire to distance himself from this pleasure which is as yet unknown to him ("mir noch unbekannte Vergnügen") is also evident in his efforts to locate it in a far-removed archaic realm. Forgotten everywhere else, it survived in Rome "where past times talk to the observer so immediately and with so many voices" (XXXI: 7). This claim, however, is contradicted by a following statement in which Goethe reminds his readers that it is an "antic in which we all found enjoyment during our childhood" (XXXI: 8).

28. "Der Jüngling hat die Eigenheiten des weiblichen Geschlechts in ihrem Wesen und Betragen studiert [. . .] er spielt nicht sich selbst, sondern eine dritte und eigentlich fremde Natur. Wir lernen diese dadurch nur desto besser kennen, weil sie jemand beobachtet, jemand überdacht hat, und uns nicht die Sache, sondern das Resultat der Sache vorgestellt wird" (XXXI: 9).

29. "Die Idee kann mir sehr bequem sein, ich kann andern zeigen, dass sie es Ihnen auch sein werde: aber es läßt sich nach meiner Vorstellung nur sehr schwer, und vielleicht gar nicht beweisen, daß sie wirklich mit den Objekten übereinkommen und mit ihnen zusammentreffen müsse" (XIX: 244–245).

30. See also Tobin, who claims that Goethe's essay "points to an eighteenth-century awareness of the arbitrariness of the signification of gender" (125).

31. "Meine Idee von den Frauen ist nicht von den Erscheinungen der Wirklichkeit abstrahiert, sondern sie ist mir angeboren, oder in mir entstanden, Gott weiß wie! Meine dargestellten Frauencharaktere sind daher auch alle gut weggekommen; sie sind alle besser, als sie in der Wirklichkeit anzutreffen sind" (*Conversation With Eckermann*, October 22, 1828, Artemis XXIV: 229).

32. One might claim that Goethe's attempt to locate the origin of gender in the desires of the individual, not in biology, is in conformity with a general characteristic of his age in which the arousal of wishes ["Wunscherweckung"] had become the predominant method of socialization (Kittler 41).

33. "Das Carneval hab ich satt! Es ist, besonders an den letzten schönen Tagen ein unglaublicher Lärm, aber keine Herzensfreude. Die Großen sind oekonomisch und zurückgehalten, der Mittelmann unvermögend und das Volck lahm" (letter to Herder, February 17, 1787, Weimar Ausgabe, *Herausgegeben* IV: 188).

34. There is a consensus that the *Italian Journey* [Italienische Reise], which was initially conceived as a part of Goethe's autobiography *Poetry and Truth*, is the product of a substantial editing process (cf. Boyle 21), in which the original letters and diary entries were changed substantially. Schulz recommends that the *Italian Journey* be read as a work of art, not as an authentic account of a journey (6).

35. "There is absolutely nothing to write about it; in an oral account it might be entertaining at best" [Zu schreiben ist davon gar nichts, bei einer mündlichen Darstellung möchte es allenfalls unterhaltend sein, XI: 190].

36. "das römische Karneval einem fremden Zuschauer, der es zum erstenmal sieht und nur sehen will und kann, weder einen ganzen noch einen erfreulichen Eindruck gebe" (XI: 533).

37. Cf. "Even serious people who sit in their coaches unmasked give permission to their coachmen and servants to mask themselves" (XI: 496).

38. Goethe himself, who traveled incognito as "Möller," made use of this kind of social disguise as he reports in a letter to Charlotte von Stein: "I observed how a certain middle class here deports itself and dressed up just like them. I derive unspeakable pleasure from this. Now I even imitate their manners" (*Tagebuch der Italienischen Reise für Frau von Stein* 65). Cf. also: The Italians "look at a person from head to toe and seem to have an excellent physiognomic eye for clothing. Now, it is my pleasure to confuse them with my stockings, which make it impossible for them to take me for a gentleman" (XXVI: 152).

39. According to Koselleck, the absolutist state is characterized by the endeavor to remove its subjects from the public-political realm and to relegate them to the private sphere. The enlightened bourgeois order, on the other hand, instrumentalizes the moral laws of the private sphere as a medium of critique of the political sphere.

40. Cf.: "The Roman Carnival is a festival which is not really given to the people but which the people give to themselves" (XI: 484).

41. The image of a world turned upside down culminates in the performance of a male cross-dresser who imitates the act of giving birth (XI: 503–504).

42. In light of this context, one begins to understand why Goethe is fascinated with the coaches on the corso. The description of the smooth order of the coaches, which collapses as soon as it gets dark, becomes a metaphor for the functioning of societal orders in general: "Schon alle Sonn- und Festtage eines Jahres ist der römische Korso belebt. Die vornehmern und reichern Römer fahren hier eine oder anderthalb Stunden vor Nacht in einer sehr zahlreichen Reihe spazieren; die Wagen kommen vom venezianischen Palast herunter, halten sich an der linken Seite [. . .] Die früher oder später Umkehrenden halten sich an die andere Seite; so ziehen die beiden Wagenreihen in der besten Ordnung aneinander hin [. . .] Sobald die

Nacht eingeläutet wird, ist diese Ordnung unterbrochen; jeder wendet, wo es ihm beliebt, und sucht seinen nächsten Weg, oft zur Unbequemlichkeit vieler andern Equipagen, welche in dem engen Raum dadurch gehindert und aufgehalten werden [. . .] Das Karneval ist, wie wir bald bemerken können, eigentlich nur eine Fortsetzung oder vielmehr der Gipfel jener gewöhnlichen sonn- und festtägigen Freuden" (XI: 486). Only the uninterrupted performance of this order by every individual can keep it alive. If the performance stops, the order ceases to exist.

43. Goethe conceived *Wilhelm Meister's Apprenticeship* in February 1777. He worked on it intermittently during the next ten years but did not finish it until 1794, when he took it up again after a pause of almost eight years.

44. Because his troupe consists of boys only, the young males have to take on some women's parts.

45. "Ich werde sorgen müssen, rief sie aus, daß sie wieder bald in lange Kleider kommt, wenn ich meines Lebens sicher sein will. Fort, zieht euch aus! Ich hoffe das Mädchen wird mir abbitten, was mir der flüchtige Junker Leids zugefügt hat; herunter mit dem Rock und immer so fort alles herunter! Es ist eine unbequeme Tracht, und für Euch gefährlich, wie ich merke. Die Achselbänder begeistern euch" (VII: 10).

46. Cf. Dick, who points out that Therese's life "revolves around the tasks that bourgeois society has assigned to women" (85).

47. "Ich kann Ihnen gar nicht sagen, wie lächerlich mir es vorkam, wenn die Menschen, die ich alle recht gut kannte, sich verkleidet hatten, da droben standen, und für etwas anders, als sie waren, gehalten sein wollten. Ich sah immer nur meine Mutter und Lydien, diesen Baron und jenen Sekretär, sie mochten nun als Fürsten und Grafen, oder als Bauern erscheinen, und ich konnte nicht begreifen, wie sie mir zumuten wollten zu glauben, daß es ihnen wohl oder wehe sei, daß sie verliebt oder gleichgültig, geizig oder freigebig seien, da ich doch meist von dem Gegenteile genau unterrichtet war. Deswegen blieb ich auch sehr selten unter den Zuschauern" (VII: 482).

48. "Zum erstenmal in meinem Leben fiel mir's ein zu scheinen, oder, daß ich mir nicht unrecht tue, in den Augen des trefflichen Mannes für das zu gelten, was ich war" (VII: 489).

49. The same phenomenon recurs in Wilhelm's second vision (VII: 315). Other passages note that in spite of an intense search Natalie's fleeting nature could not be found on any map or in any genealogy (VII: 256).

50. Cf. Schlechta, who claims that Wilhelm's relationship with Natalie signifies his connection with the Tower Society, not his union with a woman (69).

51. Though Irigaray deliberately obfuscates differences between the terms "homosexual" and "homosocial," I believe that the constellation in Goethe's novel is best characterized as homosocial.

52. See also Natalie's identification with the bride in the prominently featured portrait of the sick prince. In the beginning, Wilhelm is identified with the sick son who is connected to the generation of his father through the faceless and shapeless body of Natalie. By the end of the novel, however, Friedrich's interpretation of the portrait designates Wilhelm as father, whose connection to his son is brought about by Natalie (VII: 648–649).

53. Cf. Friedrich's remark, "I believe you won't marry until some day there is a bride missing somewhere, and you give yourself then, according to your usual kind-heartedness, as a supplement to some existence" [Ich glaube, du heiratest nicht eher, als bis einmal irgendwo eine Braut fehlt, und du gibst dich alsdann, nach deiner gewohnten Gutherzigkeit, auch als Supplement irgendeiner Existenz hin (VII: 606)].

54. The limitation to the role of an intermediary may be responsible for what a number of scholars refer to as Natalie's coldness and indifference (cf. Schlechta 57: "She is utterly uninvolved").

55. This peculiar usage was especially pronounced in the *Theatrical Mission*, as MacLeod ("Pedagogy" 401) has pointed out.

56. Even as a young child, Mignon had worn boy's clothing and climbed trees with her male companions (VII: 629).

57. "Man konnte auch hier wieder bemerken, dass bei einer grossen Anstrengung sie nur schwer und muehsam begriff. So war auch ihre Handschrift, mit der sie sich viele Muehe gab. Sie sprach noch immer sehr gebrochen Deutsch." (VII: 281); cf. also "Sie brachte ihre Antworten in einem gebrochnen Deutsch und mit einer sonderbar feierlichen Art vor" (VII: 105) and "Nur mit Worten konnte es sich nicht ausdruecken" (VII: 628).

58. Cf. Schlaffer, who claims that Mignon symbolizes "deep emotions which are unspeakable" (59) and Dick, who believes that Mignon and the harper embody "the inexplicable, unspeakable" (54). Schmitz has claimed that Mignon's songs are the embodiment of Goethe's construct of a "natural" but primitive kind of art which is unable to survive in the realm of culture.

59. Mignon has been interpreted as a symbol of Wilhelm's desires. Consequently, her dead body is read as the transformation of these desires into art: "Die Verobjektivierung eines im Innern des schaffenden Künstlers herangebildeten, mit allen Wünschen und Ahnungen seiner Seele genährten, mit den dunklen Reminiszenzen seines Lebens ausgestatteten und deshalb mit ihm lebenden Gestalt, die sich, nach Beendigung ihres Werdens im vollendeten Werk, von der Person ihres Schöpfers ablöst [. . .] Sie muß zum Kunstwerk werden, damit Wilhelm als Mensch frei ist zu neuem Leben" (Ammerlahn 26). MacLeod has drawn attention to the problematic consequences of this theory of art for Goethe's female characters, "who are so often the victims of the aesthetic realm with which they are identified" ("Pedagogy" 409).

60. Schlaffer claims that it is imperative within the logic of the text that this desire remain unspoken: "The destruction of Mignon and the harper begins as soon as the Turmgesellschaft, ostensibly in order to heal them, sets out to induce them to speak" (59).

61. In a conversation with Kanzler Müller (qtd. in Schlaffer 40); Wilhelm, on the other hand, is his "beloved dramatic mirror image" (qtd. in Wolff 28)

62. Cf. MacLeod, who claims that "the androgyne, with its dyadic oscillation between masculinity and femininity, properly belongs to the pre-Oedipal sphere of the imaginary, and indeed cannot survive in the triangulated world of Bildung and socialization" ("Pedagogy" 396).

CHAPTER 5

1. *Franz Sternbald's Migrations* features a cross-dressed countess, who is part of a group of hunters, and the male character Florestan who is disguised as an old woman.

2. Weigel claims that woman is "the instrument through which man finds wholeness" ("Romantische" 75).

3. Brendel, as she was initially called (she changed her name to Dorothea in 1794), was the second daughter of the famous philosopher Moses Mendelssohn and his wife Fromet (née Gugenheim). Born on October 24, 1764, she had 9 siblings, four of whom died early deaths. Her home was a center of Jewish emancipation and enlightenment. Her marriage with the unrefined businessman Simon Veit (April 3, 1783), whom her father selected for her, left Dorothea—who was used to an educated environment—unsatisfied. She gave birth to four children (Moses, 1787; Jonas, 1790; Abraham, 1790; Philipp, 1793), two of whom died in their first year. The two surviving sons, Jonas and Philipp, became painters and joined the famous Nazarener group in Rome, where Dorothea visited them from 1818 to 1820. In 1797, Dorothea met Friedrich Schlegel and decided to leave her husband. The divorce was finalized in 1799. Dorothea followed Friedrich to Jena (October 6, 1799, to January 1802), Paris, Cologne (1804–1808), Vienna and Frankfurt (April 27, 1817, to April 21, 1818). She converted and married Friedrich in 1804. Dorothea Schlegel translated numerous works and wrote articles for Friedrich's magazines in order to alleviate their financial misery. Her works are published under Friedrich's name. After Friedrich's death in 1829, the widow moved to Frankfurt to live with her son Philipp. She died on August 3, 1839. Among her friends were Henriette Herz, Friedrich Schleiermacher, Karoline Paulus, Caroline von Humboldt, Julie von Zichy, Fanny von Arnstein, and Helmina von Chezy.

4. There is a recent edition of Dorothea Schlegel's novel, *Florentin*, edited by Liliane Weissberg.

5. Huch's negative portrayal of Dorothea Schlegel has itself been the subject of criticism by recent scholars (cf. Frank; Schmitz; Stern).

6. Dorothea's initial decision not to remarry was influenced by the fact that she was likely to lose her son Philipp, who lived with her after the separation from Veit. Another consideration was Friedrich's aversion to "philistine conventions."

7. Aside from *Florentin*, Dorothea Schlegel's work consists mostly of translations and reviews, a fact which has often been interpreted as a confirmation of the claim that her talent was mostly reproductive. Among the works she translated are Juliane von Krüdener's *Valerie ou lettres de Gustave de Linar a Ernest de G . . .* , Madame de Stael's *Corinne ou de l'Italie*, a novel about the magician Merlin, and biographies of Joan of Arc and the wife of Henry VIII. Her reviews, mostly written for Friedrich Schlegel's magazine projects, comprise a variety of topics. She wrote a review of Ramdohr's *Moralische Erzählungen* and of Felicité de Genlis' *Voeux temeraires* for Schlegel's *Athenäum*, as well as the essays "About the State of Music in Paris" and "Conversation about the Most Recent Novels by French Women" for *Europa*. Dorothea Schlegel also composed poetry for the *Poetisches Taschenbuch für das Jahr 1806*. The publication dates demonstrate that her work on the story of Joan of Arc could not have influenced her portrayal of the transvestite in *Florentin*. She was, however, very impressed by the character of Joan of Arc (cf. letter by Theodor Körner, qtd. in Deibel 108).

8. *Florentin* was printed in November 1800 and appeared in February 1801.

9. Dorothea Schlegel did not object to this practice. However, she did protest when Friedrich wanted to include her translations in his completed works.

10. Some compared Florentin to Julius while others emphasized the similarity between the names Julius and Juliane.

11. Cf. Hibberd, who claims that *Florentin* is "not comparable in quality with *Wilhelm Meisters Lehrjahre* or with *Franz Sternbalds Wanderungen* though its indebtedness to these novels (among others) is so striking that such comparisons are inevitable" (198).

12. Schmitz has pointed out that many of these shared elements might be said to derive from a common "inventory of motives for the popular enlightened novel" (105). Among these similarities is the fact that, like *Wilhelm Meister*, *Florentin* is set in Italy and Germany. The protagonist Florentin, like the marchese in *Wilhelm Meister*, is destined to become a priest but wants to be a soldier. The name Florentin, on the other hand, is reminiscent of Florestan in Tieck's *Franz Sternbald's Migrations*.

13. I am, of course, aware of the fact that *Wilhelm Meister* itself could be and

has been described as an anti-Bildungsroman. However, the nature of this "anti" is different. In Goethe's novel the ostensible closure is undermined, while Schlegel's novel is left without an ending altogether.

14. Cf. her letter to Karoline Paulus of July 13, 1805: "By the way, I took up 'Florentin' again" (*Briefwechsel* I:155).

15. She expressed her doubts and anxieties even before *Florentin* was published, for example, in a letter to Friedrich Schleiermacher of August 22, 1800: "If truth be told, I would wish that no human being should read this Florentin because my feelings tell me that it is and remains an injustice that this growth of nature (in other words this weed) should appear under the auspices of an artist" (qtd. in Frank 148); see also her letter to August Wilhelm Schlegel of October 28, 1800: "Florentin is really being printed to my great fear" (*Briefwechsel* I:53).

16. Letters to Schleiermacher of October 31, 1800 (*Briefwechsel* I:56) and to Friedrich Schlegel of 1806 (*Briefwechsel* I:179).

17. The orphaned Florentin grew up on an island. A noble lady, whom he believes to be his mother, visits him regularly and finally takes him to her home. Florentin is supposed to become a priest, a profession that he loathes thoroughly and from which he escapes with the help of his neighbor Manfredi. His plan to do the same for his sister and rescue her from the monastery are foiled. Florentin learns that his true parents are unknown and flees to Italy. After numerous adventures in Rome and Venice he decides to fight in the American Revolution. It is on his way there that he meets the Schwarzenberg family.

18. Dorothea Schlegel's interest in literary cross-dressing might have been sparked by her acquaintance with several extravagant practitioners of gender-bending, among them Madame de Genlis and Countess Schlabrendorff.

19. "Da Juliane gut zu Pferde saß, und oft in Männerkleidung ausritt, so war sie ihrer nicht ungewohnt, sie ging so leicht und ungezwungen daher, als hätte sie nie eine andere Kleidung getragen, und auch so als Knabe sah sie wunderschön aus" (37).

20. "Er drückte Julianen mit Heftigkeit an seine Brust; die Gegenwart des Freundes vergessend hielt er sich nicht länger, seine Lippen waren fest auf die ihrigen gepreßt, seine Umarmung wurde kühner, er war außer sich.— Juliane erschrak" (38).

21. Cf. Weissberg: "*Florentin* desires very much to reconfirm and establish social order" (177).

22. "Bald war sie so dreist gemacht, daß sie sich einige zweideutige Späße über Julianen erlaubte, deren Stand sie weit entfernt war zu ahnden" (88).

23. "Da es nun einmal gegen die bürgerliche Ordnung ist, und es durchaus nicht erlaubt wird, romantische Poesie in das Leben zu führen, so bringt

man lieber sein Leben in die romantische Poesie hinein; dagegen kann keine Polizei und keine Erziehungsanstalt etwas haben" (*Briefwechsel* I:96).

24. "Seine Eigenthümlichkeit nicht verläugnen, nach seinem eignen Gemüth und Gewissen leben, ist unanständig und arrogant, als wenn man auf einer Maskerade ohne Maske erscheinen wollte" (*Briefwechsel* I:97).

25. Cf. her letter to Rahel Levin of June 2, 1800: "Who is going to make a masquerade his eternal constant occupation?" (*Briefwechsel* I:14).

26. Interestingly, she seems to have enjoyed the mystery that enveloped her authorship of *Florentin*. In a letter to Clemens Brentano, for example, she denies her authorship of *Florentin* with wanton irony ("Thus, all of Jena now claims, as we are told, that I, I made *Florentin*!" *Briefwechsel* 19) and includes a short but benevolent review of her novel: "Friedrich is publishing it under his name, but I truly don't know to whom we really are indebted. Be that as it may, it is a rather friendly, pleasant, delightful book which strives against weepiness with all might, in which the colors are at times put on rather garishly in a somewhat childish way but which because of this is rather funny in its perspective like a decoration and which tells most endearing little stories in a rather educated way" (*Briefwechsel* 20). The playful mood of Schlegel's letter suggests that her denial is not necessitated by a pretense of respect for feminine modesty.

27. "Ich hätte sie gern das Manuskript (Florentin) erst sehen lassen, Wilhelm meint aber, es wäre besser, wenn Sie gar nicht damit bekannt zu sein schienen. Ich könnte Ihnen zwar den ersten Brouillon schicken, aber ausser dass es Porto kostet, ist auch die rothe Dinte allenthalben zum Spektakel darin, denn der Teufel regiert immer an den Stellen, wo der Dativ oder Accusativ regieren sollte, und in dieser Gestalt sollen sie es nicht zuerst sehen, das thue ich dem humoristischen Taugenichts nicht zu leide. Gedulden Sie sich also, bis er Toilette gemacht und die Staatsuniform anhat, dann soll er sich hübsch präsentieren" (to Schleiermacher, January 1, 1800, *Briefwechsel* I:45).

28. "Ich bin nie ganz beruhigt, wenn mir der Dichter nichts hinzu zu denken oder zu träumen läßt. So kann ich mich mit einer einzigen Geschichte recht lange beschäftigen und freuen, indem ich ihr bald diesen bald jenen Ausgang gebe. Es geht mir damit wie den kleinen Mädchen, welche lieber mit einem nackten Puppenkörper spielen, den sie sich jede Stunde anders ankleiden und ihm eine ganz verschiedene Gestalt geben können, als mit der prächtigsten und aufs vollendetste angezogenen Puppe, der man die Kleidungsstücke und damit auf immer ihre vollendete Bestimmung aufgenäht hat" (158).

29. "Ach da in der Wirklichkeit, in der Gewißheit, da geht mir erst alle Wehmut und alle Unbefriedigung recht an. Meine Wirklichkeit und meine Befriedigung liegt in der Sehnsucht und in der Ahndung" (157).

30. "Oft lachen sie mich aus und fühlen sich recht über mich erhaben, wenn ich die schicklichen Worte, die modigen Ausdrücke, mit denen sie so leicht sich alles bezeichnen, zu entbehren scheine [. . .] Ach, ich kenne diese Worte ja wohl, es sind Worte! Aber ich scheue mich sie zu brauchen. Sie könnten von heute an etwas ganz anders bezeichnen, grade das Gegenteil, und man würde sich gar nicht darüber wundern. Das was man nicht nennen kann, ist ja doch immer das liebste und beste und eigentlich das, was man meint" (*Briefwechsel* I:81).

31. "Einmal scheint es, als verbände er mit den Worten noch einen andern Sinn, als den sie haben sollen; ein andermal macht er zu den schmeichel-haftesten Dingen, die ihm gesagt werden, ein gleichgültiges Gesicht, als müßte es eben nicht anders sein; dann freut ihn ganz wider Vermuten ein-mal ein absichtsloses Wort, das von ungefähr gesprochen wird; da weiß er immer einen ganz eignen Sinn, ich weiß nicht, ob hineinzulegen, oder her-auszubringen" (33–34).

32. Cf. the following statement by Schlegel: "In the old novels the heroes remained loyal and true to the character that had once been chosen for them while all events around them changed perpetually and destiny played with them violently [. . .] In the popular novels of our time, the events are simple, indeed one can barely call them events [. . .] Neither accident or providence guide them in their need; their confusions are brought about by a change inside them" (*Briefwechsel* I:88).

33. "Die Menschenkenntniss ist so tief, so mannichfach und so unausweich-bar in ihnen, dass es gar nicht fehlen kann: jeder gebildete oder sich bildende Mensch muss irgendwo in einer dieser Darstellungen der unendlich tiefen und feinen Psychologie sein Inneres aufgedeckt finden und kann sich allda wie in einem Spiegel vollkommen anschauen, ohne die Selbsterkenntniss mit eigner Erfahrung erkaufen zu dürfen" (*Briefwechsel* I: 89).

34. She insisted that every character was influenced by but cannot be reduced to a number of different people: "if you wanted I could show you a body to every one of my spirits that I found fitting at some point or other" (*Briefwechsel* I:71). She denied especially that Florentin was a portrait of her friend Eduard d'Alton, who had come to Berlin in the mid-1790s. There are speculations that he was Schlegel's lover at one point. Like Florentin, d'Alton's descent is unknown. He claimed to have been edu-cated in a Jesuit convent and to have attended the military academy in Vienna afterwards.

35. Bettina Brentano was born on April 4, 1785, as the seventh of twelve chil-dren. The family of her father, the businessman Peter Anton Brentano, came from Tremezzo near the Comer lake. Brentano's second wife, Maximiliane, Bettina's mother, died when Bettina was only 8 years old.

After her grandmother's death in 1807 she lived in Marburg with her sister Gunda (who was married to Savigny, a noted professor of law), with her brother Franz in Frankfurt, and with her sister Lulu in Kassel. She followed Savigny to Munich and Landshut in 1810 and married Achim von Arnim in 1811. She gave birth to seven children (Freimund, 1812; Siegmund, 1813; Friedmund, 1815; Kühnemund, 1817; Maximiliane, 1818; Armgard, 1821; Gisela, 1827). Bettina and the children spent a lot of time in Berlin, while Achim preferred the country estate at Wiepersdorf. Bettina's career as a writer began after the death of her husband in 1831. She published *Ilius Pamphilius und Ambrosia* (1848), an epistolary novel based on the correspondence with Philipp Nathusius; *This Book Belongs to the King* [Dies Buch gehört dem König, 1843], in which she makes detailed suggestions regarding censorship, religious freedom, and the death penalty; and *Conversations With Demons* [Gespräche mit Dämonen, 1852]. She also compiled the *Poor Book* [Armenbuch], which documented the social deprivation of the Silesian weavers. She befriended Schinkel, Pückler-Muskau, Schleiermacher, Rahel Varnhagen, and the brothers Grimm.

36. Very few of the actual letters have come down to us (cf. Bäumer 25). Brentano-von Arnim's brother Clemens had died in 1842, two years before the publication of the novel.

37. Schultz claims that even while writing her letters, Brentano-von Arnim had already planned to edit her correspondence as a book (324).

38. Some scholars found great fault with this technique. Heinrich Düntzer, for example, called Brentano-von Arnim's epistolary novels unscrupulous forgeries (cf. Hahn, *Bettina* 21).

39. There are affinities with both Romanticism and Neues Deutschland. Wyss therefore called her writing a "transitional phenomenon," "a bridge between two different epochs" (80).

40. The list goes on. Eduard Wiß, for example, calls her a "mephisto in female disguise" (qtd. in Wolf 541).

41. Contemporaries were impressed by the apparent ease with which Brentano-von Arnim flouted social conventions. She herself carefully contributed to this reputation (see, for example, her dry comment "they think of me as of a half-savage," *Günderode* 59).

42. I will use Bettina Brentano-von Arnim when referring to the writer, and Bettine when referring to the fictional character that Brentano-von Arnim created. It is apparent that this differentiation cannot always be made clearly for a writer who consciously obfuscates the border between fact and fiction.

43. Fritzlar was taken by the French under General Hoche in 1797. Bettina Brentano then spent some time with her half-brother Franz in Frankfurt before she moved to her grandmother's home. For biographical informa-

tion on Bettina Brentano-von Arnim see Hirsch, Hans von Arnim, Hetmann, Milch, and Drewitz.

44. "Ja, ich müßte Dir von meiner Verwundrung sprechen über alles, was ich sehe und höre in der Welt! Über die Lehren, die jene Leute mir geben, die mich zu einem angenehmen und liebenswürdigen Mädchen erziehen wollen. Das kommt mir aber gar nicht angenehm, sondern sehr horribel vor, was andre Leute wohlerzogen oder gebildet nennen" (*Frühlingskranz* 21).

45. "Melancholie allein aus dieser Quelle des Lebensdrangs fließt, der sich nirgends ergießen kann" (*Günderode* 249).

46. See also the following statement: "Melancholy takes hold of you because there is no world in which you could act" (*Briefwechsel mit einem Kinde* 282).

47. "Sein und Werden ist zweierlei, das sag ich mir auch, und Werden ist für das wirkliche Leben Kraft fühlen und diese anwenden, und nicht bloß zum Helden träumen. Und dies ist, was mich oft vor mir erschreckt, daß ich im Lande der Phantasie mir eine große rolle auserwählt habe, die ich zwar ohne Gefahr spiele, die aber nicht die Wirklichkeit berührt.—Wie mache ich's, daß ich aus dieser Verbannung des Wirklichen erlöst werde?" (*Frühlingskranz* 91–92). Cf. also her letter to Savigny from October 1804: "Daß ich traurig bin, kannst du Dir wohl leicht erklären. So viel Lebenskraft und Mut zu haben und keine Mittel, ihn anzuwenden. Wie mag es einem großen Krieger zu Mute sein, dem das Herz glüht zu großen Unternehmungen und Taten, und der in der Gefangenschaft ist, mit Ketten beladen, an keine Rettung denken darf. Mir überwältigt diese immerwährende rastlose Begierde nach Wirken oft die Seele und bin doch nur ein einfältig Mädchen, deren Bestimmung ganz anders ist" (*Die Andacht zum Menschenbild* 23).

48. "Sollt ich Deinen Charakter zusammenfassen, so würd ich Dir prophezeien, wenn Du ein Knabe wärst, Du werdest ein Held werden" (*Günderode* 501).

49. "Und so werden Flammen aufsteigen, bewegt vom Gesetz Deines Hauchs, aus Deiner Seele und zünden im Herzen jugendlicher Geschlechter, die, knabenhaft männlich sich deuchtend, nimmer es ahnen, daß der Jünglingshauch, der ihre Brust erglüht, niemals erstieg aus Männergeist" (*Günderode* 381).

50. "Du weißt nicht, wie glücklich ich bin, daß ich Dir dies durch die liebenswürdigste Frau sagen kann, die durch ihr Geschick schon über den gewöhnlichen Kreis der Menschen hinausragt, noch mehr aber durch ihre Selbständigkeit, durch den festen ernsten Willen, mit dem sie dies Geschick bekämpfte und heldenmäßig ertrug, indem sie ruhig und allein zwischen den Schrecken der Blutgerichte hindurchwandelte [. . .] Durch die Vendée ist sie oft auf wilden Pferden geritten, um mit den großen

Helden dort sich zu treffen, denen sie oft auf nächtlichen gefahrvollen
Wegen voraneilte, manchen jener armen Landleute (Chouans) hat sie
gerettet mit Gefahr ihres Lebens, ihre ganze Familie aber hat die Guillotine
gefressen" (*Frühlingskranz* 47).

51. "auch sollst Du sie lieben wie den geistreichen Menschen, doch nur ihren
Geist und Herz, die Narben aber, die ihr Erfahrung und Geschick geschlagen, das männliche Wilde ihres Seins und Verstandes sollst Du übersehen,
überhaupt Dich ihr nicht hingeben; mein bleiben und Gott"
(*Frühlingskranz* 48).

52. "Und immer noch von dieser de Gachet, aber Gott weiß, es jagt mich
wieder aus dem Bette heraus [. . .] Ich bereue es sehr, und es ist eine
Übereilung, daß ich ihr den Brief an Dich gab" (*Frühlingskranz* 48, 49).

53. "Von einem Tag zum andern hat die Welt hier in Offenbach einen
Purzelbaum geschlagen [. . .] Siehe, da kam im Sturm dahergebraust ein
Kabriolet wie ein abgeschoßner Pfeil vor die Haustür, herabspringt der
Wagenlenker, ein jugendlich voller schöner Mannjüngling mit klirrenden
Sporen, zwei Reiter, die ihn begleiten, treten mit ihm ein, ich war, ich weiß
nicht wie, nicht warum, von Schrecken durchgriffen, daß ich vergaß zu
reden, und besann mich nicht, die Großmama zu rufen, die im Garten war.
Der Herzog fragte, wer da sei, ich deutete den Fremden an, er sei blind,
und sagte: C'est un jeune cavalier, Monseigneur, avec deux messieurs.
sagte der Jüngling und näherte sich" (*Frühlingskranz* 50).

54. See for example her response to Clemens' advice to get married: "It is fore-
sight, dear Clemens, but I believe that I do not need a support in life, and
that I do not want to be the victim of such foolish prejudices. I know what
I need!—I need to keep my freedom. To what?—To execute and fulfill what
an inner voice tells me to do" (156).

55. Cf. "It would almost be my wish that you partake more in the usual
Frankfurt routine so that you suppress that which is conspicuous in your
behavior, for you might well once suffer much displeasure because of this
conspicuousness, not that it is bad per se because of that, no, it is simply
troublesome and often and for a woman almost always in the way of doing
good" (143). Or: "The life of a woman is more firm and immobile than the
life of a man; the woman touches human beings more closely and must be
a blessing to her surroundings" (143–144). Bettine's rejection of her
brother's advice is portrayed in *Die Günderode*, for example, when Bettine
complains that her brother laments her aversion to traditionally feminine
virtues (453).

56. "Die allerledernste Heuschrecke ist mir die, wo Du mich mit Gewalt willst
auf den großen Unterschied hinweisen zwischen einem vortrefflichen
Weib und einen braven Manne. Mögen sich diese zwei beiden zusam-
menfinden auf irgendeinem glücklichen Stern, nur das einzige bitte ich mir

aus, daß Du es mir nicht zu wissen tust; und ein für allemal will ich von diesem Heiligtum gänzlich ausgeschlossen sein!—Und zweitens—Deine Warnung vor aller männlichen Gesellschaft! Die Günderode sagt zu mir, sie kenne keine männliche Gesellschaft, außer die meine. Ich, lieber Clemens, kenne auch keinen männlichen Umgang, als den mit den Hopfenstecken, die mir die Milchfrau besorgt hat für den kommenden Frühling, sie sind die derbsten unter meine Bekannten [. . .] Die nice ingrata, die obschon sie Dein Universitätsfreund ist, und nachdem Du ihr den Doktorschmaus bezahlt hattest, mit Deinen besten Kleidern durchging, hat zwar einen Bart und möchte vielleicht auch für einen Mann gehalten sein; aber sie sieht in den Spiegel und singt nice bella, und wer zweifelt, daß sie eine Nice ist" (*Frühlingskranz* 159).

57. Brentano-von Arnim's concept of gender cannot be described as role reversal nor can it be characterized as androgyny (cf. Waldstein, *Bettine* 71). Rather, there is no predictable connection between body and gender (cf. Goodman, "Lens" 129).

58. The publication of this novel made Brentano-von Arnim famous. It consists of three parts: the correspondence with Goethe's mother, correspondence with Goethe from 1803 to 1813, and a diary. One might claim that the strangely inverted chronology of Brentano-von Arnim's novels mirrors the process of memory. That which is closest to one's immediate presence (that is, her memory of Goethe) is most easily accessible whereas the events of her youth (her relationship with Günderrode and, even earlier, with Clemens Brentano) needed to be unearthed in a lengthy process. The foundational memories of childhood are farthest removed.

59. In *Die Günderode*, Günderrode and Bettine also planned a journey in male disguise, wearing both male clothing and beards.

60. The journey led them from Kassel to Berlin. They stopped in Weimar on their way back. That the "gender police" was still active can be seen in a letter that Bettina received from her half-brother Franz in April 1807 as a reaction to her journey: "Du weißt, wie ich das Herumschwärmen von Mägden in der Welt hasse, welches in den Augen aller vernünftigen Menschen für unanständig gehalten wird" (qtd. in Bäumer 50). That Bettina herself had wished for this journey for a long time can be gathered from a letter by Goethe's mother, the Frau Rat: "Da hat den doch die kleine Brentano ihren Willen gehabt, und Goethe gesehen—ich glaube im gegen gesetzten fall wäre sie Toll geworden—denn so was ist mir noch nicht vorgekommen—sie wolte als Knabe sich verkleiden, zu Fuß nach Weimar laufen" (552).

61. According to Ockenfuß, cross-dressing was a way of protecting oneself against gangs of robbers and soldiers intent on rape ("Verkleidungsspiele" 122).

62. "Ein Paar Hosen?—Ja!—Vivat!—jetzt kommen andre Zeiten angerückt—
    und auch eine Weste und ein Überrock dazu. Morgen wird alles anpro-
    biert, es wird schon sitzen, denn ich hab' mir alles bequem und weit
    bestellt, und dann werf' ich mich in eine Chaise und reise Tag und Nacht
    Kurier durch die ganzen Armeen zwischen Feind und Freund durch; alle
    Festungen tun sich vor mir auf [. . .] Denk' Sie doch, Weimar schien mir
    immer so entfernt, als wenn es in einem andern Weltteil läg,' und nun ist's
    vor der Tür" (*Briefwechsel* 32). The concern that her new clothes may be
    too big and long, which is expressed later on, may be an indication that
    she is afraid of her new role.

63. Interestingly, the dissolution of one binary category, gender, affects
    another, nationality. Bystanders call Bettina "Savoyardenbube" and claim
    that she might render the French welcome services.

64. The authorities took Brentano-von Arnim's political engagement very
    seriously. Secret reports on her activities were filed in 1843 and 1847
    (Waldstein, *Bettine* 61).

65. See also *Briefwechsel mit einem Kinde:* "only I could no longer tell the dif-
    ference between the so-called real world, in which the other people
    claimed to be, from this dream- and fantasy world; I didn't know which
    was waking, which sleeping, yes at last I believed more and more that I
    only dreamt the everyday life" (85).

66. "Die Zukunft muß übertreten in das, was der Geist so lange schon in der
    Dichtung vorausbegründete; denn was wär der Dichter, wenn er nicht dem
    Geist der Wahrheit den Weg bahnte, der längst in ihm Fleisch und Blut
    geworden, nun auch zum sinnlichen Leib der Zukunft werde durch ihn"
    (qtd. in Betz 68).

Bibliography

Ackroyd, Peter. *Dressing Up: Transvestism and Drag: The History of an Obsession.* New York: Simon & Schuster, 1979.

Alternhofer, Norbert. *Der erschütterte Sinn: Hermeneutische Überlegungen zu Kleists Das Erdbeben in Chili.* Munich: Beck, 1985.

Ammerlahn, Hellmut. "Puppe—Tänzer—Dämon—Genius—Engel: Naturkind, Poesiekind und Kunstwerdung bei Goethe." *The German Quarterly* 54 (1981): 19–32.

Amrain, Susanne. "Der Androgyn: Das poetische Geschlecht und sein Aktus." *Frauen, Weiblichkeit, Schrift.* Ed. Renate Berger et al. Berlin: Argument Verlag, 1985. 119–129.

Annuß, Evelyn, and Robert Schmidt. "The Butler Boom: Queer Theory's Impact on German Women's/Gender Studies." *Queering the Canon: Defying Sights in German Literature and Culture.* Ed. Christoph Lorey and John L. Plews. Columbia: Camden House, 1998. 73–86.

Appell, J. W. *Die Ritter-, Räuber- und Schauerromantik: Zur Geschichte der deutschen Unterhaltungsliteratur.* Leipzig: Engelmann, 1959.

Ariès, Philippe. *The Hour of Our Death.* New York: Oxford University Press, 1981.

———. *Western Attitudes Toward Death from the Middle Ages to the Present.* Baltimore: Johns Hopkins University Press, 1975.

Arnim, Bettine von. *Clemens Brentanos Frühlingskranz: Aus Jugendbriefen geflochten, wie er selbst schriftlich verlangte.* Ed. Joachim Müller. Frechen: Barthmann, 1961.

———. *Die Andacht zum Menschenbild: Unbekannte Briefe von Bettine Brentano.* Ed. Friedrich Fuchs and Wilhelm Schellberg. Jena: Eugen Diederichs, 1942.

———. *Die Günderode.* Ed. Christa Wolf. Leipzig: Suhrkamp, 1994.

———. *Goethes Briefwechsel mit einem Kinde.* Ed. Waldemar Oehlke. Frankfurt am Main: Insel, 1984.

Arnim, Hans von. *Bettina von Arnim.* Berlin: Haude & Spenersche Verlagsbuchhandlung, 1963.

Arnold, Heinz Ludwig. *Heinrich von Kleist.* München: Edition Text und Kritik, 1993.

Bachtin, Michail M. *Literatur und Karneval: Zur Romantheorie und Lachkultur.* Frankfurt am Main: Fischer Wissenschaft, 1990.

Bakshi Gokhale, Vibha. *Walking the Tightrope: A Feminist Reading of Therese Huber's Stories.* Columbia: Camden House, 1996.

Bamberg, Eduard von, ed. *Die Erinnerungen der Karoline Jagemann.* Dresden: Sibyllen Verlag, 1926.

Bansa, Elfriede. *Bettina von Arnims Verhältnis zur Kunst.* Würzburg: Karl J. Triltsch, 1938.

Barth, Ilse-Marie. *Literarisches Weimar: Kultur, Literatur, Sozialstruktur im 16.–20. Jahrhundert.* Stuttgart: Metzler, 1971.

Batley, Edward M. "Das Römische Karneval oder Gesellschaft und Geschichte." *Goethe Jahrbuch* 105 (1988): 128–143.

Bäumer, Konstanze. *Bettine, Psyche, Mignon: Bettina von Arnim und Goethe.* Stuttgart: Hans Dieter Heinz, 1986.

Baur, Samuel. *Deutschlands Schriftstellerinnen (1790).* Ed. Uta Sadji and Hans-Dieter Heinz. Stuttgart: Hans Dieter Heinz, 1990.

Beaujeau, Marion. *Der Trivialroman in der zweiten Hälfte des 18. Jahrhunderts: Die Ursprünge des modernen Unterhaltungsromans.* Bonn: Bouvier, 1964.

Becker-Cantarino, Barbara. "'Die wärmste Liebe zu unsrer litterarischen Ehe': Friedrich Schlegels *Lucinde* und Dorothea Veits *Florentin.*" *Bi-Textualität. Inszenierungen des Paares.*" Ed. Annegret Heitmann, Sigrid Nieberle, Barbara Schaff, and Sabine Schütting. Berlin: Erich Schmidt, 2001. 131–141.

———. "Priesterin und Lichtbringerin: Zur Ideologie des weiblichen Charakters in der Frühromantik." *Die Frau als Heldin und Autorin: Neue kritische Ansätze zur deutschen Literatur.* Ed. Wolfgang Paulsen. Bern: Francke, 1979. 111–124.

———. "Revolution im Patriarchat: Therese Forster-Huber (1764–1829)." *Out of Line/Ausgefallen: The Paradox of Marginality in the Writings of 19th Century German Women.* Ed. Ruth-Ellen Boetcher Joeres and Marianne Burkhard. Amsterdam: Rodopi, 1989. 235–253.

———. "(Sozial)geschichte der Frau in Deutschland 1500–1800: Ein Forschungsbericht." *Die Frau von der Reformation zur Romantik: Die Situation der Frau vor dem Hintergrund der Literatur- und Sozialgeschichte.* Ed. Barbara Becker-Cantarino. Bonn: Bouvier, 1980. 243–281.

———. "Von der Prinzipalin zur Künstlerin und Mätresse: Die Schauspielerin im 18. Jahrhundert in Deutschland." *Die Schauspielerin: Zur Kulturgeschichte der weiblichen Bühnenkunst.* Ed. Renate Möhrmann. Frankfurt am Main: Insel, 1989. 88–116.

Berger, Renate, and Inge Stephan. *Weiblichkeit und Tod in der Literatur.* Köln: Böhlau, 1987.

Berkin, Carol R., and Clara M. Lovett, eds. *Women, War, and Revolution.* New York: Holmes & Meier, 1980.

Bettinger, Elfi, and Julika Funk. *Maskeraden: Geschlechterdifferenz in der literarischen Inszenierung.* Berlin: Erich Schmidt, 1995.

Betz, Otto. *Bettina von Arnim: Meine Seele ist eine leidenschaftliche Tänzerin.* Freiburg: Herder, 1982.

Bitzer, Hermann. *Goethe über den Dilettantismus.* Bern: Herbert Lang, 1969.

Blackwell, Jeannine. "An Island of Her Own: Heroines of the German Robinsonades from 1720 to 1800." *German Quarterly* 58 (1985): 5–26.

———. "Marriage by the Book: Matrimony, Divorce, and Single Life in Therese Huber's Life and Works." *In the Shadow of Olympus: German Women Writers Around 1800.* Ed. Katherine R. Goodman and Edith Waldstein. New York: State University of New York Press, 1992. 137–156.

Blackwell, Jeannine, and Susanne Zantop, eds. *Bitter Healing: German Women Writers from 1700 to 1880. An Anthology.* Lincoln: University of Nebraska Press, 1990.

Blankenagel, John C. *The Dramas of Heinrich von Kleist: A Biographical and Critical Study.* Chapel Hill: University of North Carolina Press, 1931.

Block, Peter André. *Walter Muschg. Pamphlet und Bekenntnis: Aufsätze und Reden.* Freiburg: Walter, 1968.

Blumberg, Horst. *Die deutsche Textilindustrie in der industriellen Revolution.* Berlin: Akademie Verlag, 1965.

Bode, Wilhelm. *Charlotte von Stein.* Berlin: Ernst Siegfried Mittler und Sohn, 1912.

———. *Damals in Weimar.* Weimar: Gustav Kiepenheuer, 1910.

Boehn, Max von. *Das Bühnenkostüm im Altertum, Mittelalter und Neuzeit.* Berlin: Bruno Cassirer, 1921.

———. *Die Mode: Menschen und Moden im achtzehnten Jahrhundert.* München: F. Bruckmann, 1939.

———. *Die Mode: Eine Kulturgeschichte vom Barock bis zum Jugendstil.* Munich: Bruckmann, 1976.

Bohm, Arnd. "Charlotte von Stein's *Dido, Ein Trauerspiel.*" *Colloquia Germanica* 22 (1989): 38–52.

Bolin, Anne. "Traversing Gender: Cultural Context and Gender Practices." *Gender Reversals and Gender Cultures: Anthropological and Historical Perspectives.* Ed. Sabrina Petra Ramet. London: Routledge, 1996. 22–51.

Bollacher, Martin. *Der junge Goethe und Spinoza: Studien zur Geschichte des Spinozismus in der Epoche des Sturms und Drangs.* Tübingen: Max Niemeyer, 1969.

Bolten, Jürgen. *Friedrich Schiller: Poesie, Reflexion und gesellschaftliche Selbstdeutung.* München: Wilhelm Fink, 1985.

———. "Zur Genese des bürgerlichen Selbstverständnisses im ausgehenden 18. Jahrhundert: Schillers Frühdramen als Beispiel." *Germanistik— Forschungsstand und Perspektiven. 2. Teil: Ältere Deutsche Literatur, Neuere*

Deutsche Literatur. Ed. Georg Stötzel. Berlin: Walter de Gruyter, 1985. 492–504.

Boy-Ed, Ida. *Das Martyrium der Charlotte von Stein: Versuch ihrer Rechtfertigung.* Stuttgart: Cotta, 1916.

Boyle, Nicholas. "Goethe in Paestum: A Higher-Critical Look at the *Italienische Reise*." *Oxford German Studies* 20/21 (1991–92): 18–31.

Brentano, Clemens. *Sämtliche Werke und Briefe.* Ed. Lieselotte Kinskofer. Stuttgart: Kohlhammer, 1991–.

Brinker-Gabler, Gisela. "Das weibliche Ich: Überlegungen zur Analyse von Werken weiblicher Autoren mit einem Beispiel aus dem 18. Jahrhundert: Sidonia Hedwig Zäunemann." *Die Frau als Heldin und Autorin: Neue kritische Ansätze zur deutschen Literatur.* Ed. Wolfgang Paulsen. Bern: Francke, 1979. 55–81.

Bronfen, Elisabeth. *Over Her Dead Body: Death, Femininity and the Aesthetic.* New York: Routledge, 1992.

———. "The Body and Its Discontents." *Body Matters: Feminism, Textuality, Corporeality.* Ed. Avril Horner and Angela Keane. Manchester: Manchester University Press, 2000. 109–123.

Brown, Jane K. "The Theatrical Mission of the Lehrjahre." *Goethe's Narrative Fiction: The Irvine Goethe Symposium.* Ed. William J. Lillyman. Berlin: Walter de Gruyter, 1983. 69–84.

———. "The Renaissance of Goethe's Poetic Genius in Italy." *Goethe in Italy, 1786–1986: A Bi-Centennial Symposium November 14–16, 1986.* Ed. Gerhart Hoffmeister. Amsterdam: Rodopi, 1988. 77–93.

Bruford, W. H. *Culture and Society in Classical Weimar 1775–1806.* Cambridge: Cambridge University Press, 1962.

Bullough, Vern L., and Bonnie Bullough. *Cross-Dressing, Sex, and Gender.* Philadelphia: University of Pennsylvania Press, 1993.

Bulst, Neithard. "Kleidung als sozialer Konfliktstoff: Probleme kleidergesetzlicher Normierung im sozialen Gefüge." *Saeculum* 43 (1992): 32–46.

Burdorf, Dieter. "Diese Sehnsucht ist ein Gedanke, der ins Unendliche starrt: Über Karoline von Günderrode—aus Anlaß neuer Ausgaben ihrer Werke und Briefe." *Wirkendes Wort* 1 (1993): 49–67.

Bürger, Christa. *Der Ursprung der bürgerlichen Institution Kunst im höfischen Weimar: Literatursoziologische Untersuchungen zum klassischen Weimar.* Frankfurt am Main: Suhrkamp, 1977.

———. *Leben Schreiben: Die Klassik, die Romantik und der Ort der Frauen.* Stuttgart: Metzler, 1990.

Burshatin, Israel. "Elena Alias Eleno: Genders, Sexualities, and 'Race' in the Mirror of Natural History in Sixteenth-Century Spain." *Gender Reversals and Gender Cultures: Anthropological and Historical Perspectives.* Ed. Sabrina Petra Ramet. London: Routledge, 1996. 105–122.

Burwick, Roswitha. "Bettina von Arnim's *Die Günderrode*: Zum Selbstverständnis der Frau in der Romantik." *Frauensprache—Frauenliteratur? Für und wider eine Psychoanalyse literarischer Werke*. Ed. Inge Stephan and Carl Pietzcker. Tübingen: Max Niemeyer, 1986. 62–67.

———. "Liebe und Tod in Leben und Werk der Günderode." *German Studies Review* 3 (1980): 207–223.

Butler, Judith. *Bodies That Matter: On the Discursive Limits of "Sex."* New York: Routledge, 1993.

———. *Gender Trouble: Feminism and the Subversion of Identity*. New York: Routledge, 1990.

Calvert, George. *Charlotte von Stein: A Memoir*. Boston: Lee and Shepard, 1886.

Campe, Joachim Heinrich. *Briefe aus Paris während der Französischen Revolution geschrieben*. Ed. Helmut König. Berlin: Rütten & Loening, 1961.

Carlson, Marvin. *Goethe and the Weimar Theatre*. Ithaca: Cornell University Press, 1978.

Carson, James. "Narrative Cross-Dressing and the Critique of Authorship in the Novels of Richardson." *Writing the Female Voice*. Ed. Elizabeth Goldsmith. Boston: Northeastern University Press, 1989. 95–113.

Castle, Terry. *Masquerade and Civilization: The Carnivalesque in Eighteenth-Century English Culture and Fiction*. Stanford: Stanford University Press, 1986.

———. *The Female Thermometer: 18th-Century Culture and the Invention of the Uncanny*. New York: Oxford University Press, 1995.

Cerati, Marie. *Le Club des Citoyennes Républicaines Révolutionnaires*. Paris: Editions Sociales, 1966.

Cocalis, Susan L. "Acts of Omission: The Classical Dramas of Caroline von Wolzogen and Charlotte von Stein." *Thalia's Daughters: German Women Dramatists from the Eighteenth Century to the Present*. Ed. Susan L. Cocalis and Ferrel Rose. Tübingen: Francke, 1996. 77–98.

———. "Around 1800: Reassessing the Role of German Women Writers in Literary Production of the Late Eighteenth and Early Nineteenth Centuries: Review Essay." *Women in German Yearbook* 8 (1992): 159–77.

———. "Der Vormund will Vormund sein: Zur Problematik der weiblichen Unmündigkeit im 18. Jahrhundert." *Gestaltet und Gestaltend: Frauen in der deutschen Literatur*. Ed. Marianne Burkhard. Amsterdam: Rodopi, 1980. 33–55.

———, ed. *The Defiant Muse: German Feminist Poems from the Middle Ages to the Present. A Bilingual Anthology*. New York: Feminist Press, 1986.

Cocalis, Susan L., and Ferrel Rose, eds. *Thalia's Daughters: German Women Dramatists from the Eighteenth Century to the Present*. Tübingen: Francke, 1996.

Cocalis, Susan L., and Kay Goodman, eds. *Beyond the Eternal Feminine: Critical Essays on Women and German Literature*. Stuttgart: Hans Dieter Heinz, 1982.

Cohen, Daniel A., ed. *The Female Marine and Related Works: Narratives of Cross-Dressing and Urban Vice in America's Early Republic*. Amherst: University of Massachusetts Press, 1997.

Craft-Fairchild, Catherine. *Masquerade and Gender: Disguise and Female Identity in Eighteenth-Century Fictions by Women*. University Park: Pennsylvania State University Press, 1993.

Craig, Charlotte. "Fiesco's Fable: A Portrait in Political Demagoguery." *Modern Language Notes* 86 (1971): 393–399.

Crawford, Kathleen Vivienne. *The Transvestite Heroine in Seventeenth-Century Popular Literature*. Diss. Harvard University, 1984.

Cullens, Chris, and Dorothea von Mücke. "Love in Kleist's *Penthesilea* and *Käthchen von Heilbronn*." *Deutsche Vierteljahresschrift für Literaturwissenschaft und Geistesgeschichte* 63.3 (1989). 461–493.

Cyrus, Helga. "Von erlaubter und unerlaubter Frauenart, um Freiheit zu kämpfen: Freiheitskämpferinnen im 19. Jahrhundert und die Freie Hansestadt Bremen." *Grenzgängerinnen: Revolutionäre Frauen im 18. und 19. Jahrhundert: Weibliche Wirklichkeit und männliche Phantasien*. Ed. Helga Grubitzsch, Hannelore Cyrus, and Elke Haarbusch. Düsseldorf: Schwann, 1985. 19–69.

Dascher, Otfried. *Das Textilgewerbe in Hessen-Kassel vom 16. bis 19. Jahrhundert*. Marburg: Elwert Verlag, 1968.

De Erauso, Catalina. *Lieutenant Nun: Memoir of a Basque Transvestite in the New World*. Trans. Michelle Stepto and Gabriel Stepto. Boston: Beacon Press, 1996.

Dege, Martha. *Bettina von Arnim*. Kiel: Handorff, 1904.

Deibel, Franz. *Dorothea Schlegel als Schriftstellerin im Zusammenhang mit der romantischen Schule*. Berlin: Mayer & Müller, 1905.

DeJean, Joan. "Amazonen und literarische Frauen: Weibliche Kultur während der Regierungszeit des Sonnenkönigs." *Frauen im Frankreich des 18. Jahrhunderts: Amazonen, Mütter, Revolutionärinnen*. Ed. Jutta Held. Hamburg: Argument Verlag, 1989. 19–34.

Dekker, Rudolf M., and Lotte C. van de Pol. *The Tradition of Female Transvestism in Early Modern Europe*. New York: St. Martin's Press, 1989.

De Lauretis, Teresa. "Upping the Anti in Feminist Theory." *The Cultural Studies Reader*. Ed. Simon During. New York: Routledge, 1993. 74–89.

Delinière, Jean. "Le Personnage d'Andreas Doria dans *Die Verschwörung des Fiesco zu Genua*." *Etudes Germaniques* 40 (1985): 21–32.

Dick, Anneliese. *Weiblichkeit als natürliche Dienstbarkeit: Eine Studie zum klassischen Frauenbild in Goethes Wilhelm Meister*. Frankfurt am Main: Peter Lang, 1986.

Dischner, Gisela. *Bettina von Arnim: Eine weibliche Sozialbiographie aus dem 19. Jahrhundert*. Berlin: Klaus Wagenbach, 1977.

Dittberner, Hugo. "Der Sensationsdichter: Zu Kleist." *Heinrich von Kleist*. Ed. Heinz Ludwig Arnold. Munich: Text und Kritik, 1993.

Docter, Richard F. *Transvestites and Transsexuals: Toward a Theory of Cross-Gender Behavior*. New York: Plenum Press, 1988.

Doniger, Wendy. *The Bedtrick: Tales of Sex & Masquerade*. Chicago: University of Chicago Press, 2000.

Dotzler, Bernhard J. "Seht doch wie ihr vor Eifer schäumt: Zum männlichen Diskurs über Weiblichkeit um 1800." *Jahrbuch der deutschen Schillergesellschaft* 30 (1986): 339–382.

Dreger, Alice Domurat. *Hermaphrodites and the Medieval Invention of Sex*. Cambridge: Harvard University Press, 1998.

Drewitz, Ingeborg. *Bettine von Arnim: Romantik, Revolution, Utopie*. Düsseldorf: Eugen Diederichs, 1969.

———. "Karoline von Günderode (1780–1806)." *Letzte Tage: Sterbegeschichten aus zwei Jahrtausenden*. Ed. Hans Jürgen Schultz. Stuttgart: Kreuz, 1983. 87–100.

Duden, Barbara. *The Woman Beneath the Skin: A Doctor's Patients in Eighteenth-Century Germany*. Trans. Thomas Dunlap. Cambridge: Harvard University Press, 1991.

Dugaw, Dianne. *Warrior Women and Popular Balladry, 1650–1850*. Chicago: University of Chicago Press, 1996.

Düntzer, Heinrich. *Charlotte von Stein: Goethes Freundin, ein Lebensbild*. 2 vols. Stuttgart: Cotta, 1874.

During, Simon. "Introduction." *The Cultural Studies Reader*. Ed. Simon During. New York: Routledge, 1993. 1–25.

Dusinberre, Juliet. "As Who Liked It?" *Shakespeare Survey: An Annual Survey of Shakespeare Studies and Production* 46 (1994): 9–21.

Eberhardt, Hans. *Weimar zur Goethezeit: Gesellschafts- und Wirtschaftsstruktur*. Weimarer Schriften Heft 31, 1988.

Entwistle, Joanne. *The Fashioned Body: Fashion, Dress, and Modern Social Theory*. Cambridge: Polity Press, 2000.

Exner, Richard. "Die Heldin als Held und der Held als Heldin: Androgynie als Umgehung oder Lösung eines Konflikts." *Die Frau als Heldin und Autorin: Neue kritische Ansätze zur deutschen Literatur*. Ed. Wolfgang Paulsen. Bern: Francke, 1979. 17–54.

Fausto-Sterling, Anne. *Sexing the Body: Gender Politics and the Construction of Sexuality*. New York: Basic Books, 2000.

Ferris, Lesley. *Crossing the Stage: Controversies on Cross-Dressing*. London: Routledge, 1993.

———. "The Legacy of Goethe's Mimetic Stance." *Crossing the Stage: Controversies on Cross-Dressing*. Ed. Lesley Ferris. London: Routledge, 1993. 51–57.

Finke, Heinrich. *Über Friedrich und Dorothea Schlegel*. Köln: Bachem, 1918.

Fischer, Ernst. "Heinrich von Kleist." *Heinrich von Kleist: Aufsätze und Reden*. Ed. Walter Müller-Seidel. Darmstadt: Wissenschaftliche Buchgesellschaft, 1967.

Flieger, Jerry Aline. "Proust, Freud, and the Art of Forgetting." *Sub-Stance* 29 (1980): 66–82.

Foldenauer, Kurt. "Karoline von Günderrode (1780–1806)." *Kostbarkeiten: Essays und Laudationes zur Literatur des 19. und 20. Jahrhunderts im Namen der literarischen Gesellschaft (Scheffelbund) Karlsruhe*. Ed. Beatrice Steiner. Waldkirch: Waldkircher Verlagsgesellschaft, 1981. 81–111.

Fowler, Frank M. "Schiller's *Fiesco* Re-Examined." *Publications of the English Goethe Society* XL (1969–1970): 1–29.

Frank, Heike. *Die Disharmonie, die mit mir geboren ward, und mich nie verlassen wird: Das Leben der Brendel/Dorothea Mendelssohn-Veit-Schlegel (1764–1839)*. Frankfurt am Main: Peter Lang, 1988.

Frederiksen, Elke, and Katherine R. Goodman, eds. *Bettina Brentano-von Arnim: Gender and Politics*. Detroit: Wayne State University Press, 1995.

Frederiksen, Elke, and Monika Shafi. "Sich im Unbekannten suchen gehen: Bettina von Arnim's *Die Günderode* als weibliche Utopie." *Frauensprache— Frauenliteratur? Für und wider eine Psychoanalyse literarischer Werke*. Ed. Inge Stephan and Carl Pietzcker. Tübingen: Max Niemeyer, 1986. 54–61.

French, Loreley. "Strategies of Female Persuasion: The Political Letters of Bettina Brentano-von Arnim." *Bettina Brentano-von Arnim: Gender and Politics*. Ed. Elke P. Frederiksen and Katherine R. Goodman. Detroit: Wayne State University Press. 71–94.

Fricke, Gerhard. *Gefühl und Schicksal bei Heinrich von Kleist: Studien über den inneren Vorgang im Leben und Schaffen des Dichters*. Darmstadt: Wissenschaftliche Buchgesellschaft, 1975.

Friedrichsmeyer, Sara. *The Androgyne in Early German Romanticism: Friedrich Schlegel, Novalis, and the Metaphysics of Love*. Bern: Peter Lang, 1983.

Frühwald, Wolfgang. "Die Not der schlesischen Weber: Zu Bettine von Arnims Armenbuch 1844." *Herzhaft in die Dornen der Zeit greifen: Bettine von Arnim 1785–1859*. Ed. Christoph Perels. Frankfurt am Main: Freies Deutsches Hochstift, 1985. 269–280.

Fuhrmann, Helmut. "Revision des Parisurteils: Bild und Gestalt der Frau im Werk Friedrich Schillers." *Jahrbuch der deutschen Schillergesellschaft* 25 (1981): 316–366.

Gajek, Bernhard. "Das rechte Verhältnis der Selbständigkeit zur Hingebung: Über Karoline von Günderrode (1760–1806)." *Frankfurt aber ist der Nabel dieser Erde: Das Schicksal einer Generation der Goethezeit*. Ed. Christoph Jamme and Otto Pöggeler. Stuttgart: Klett-Cotta, 1983. 206–226.

Garber, Marjorie. *Vested Interests: Cross-Dressing and Cultural Anxiety*. New York: Harper Perennial, 1993.

Gauster, Hannelore. "Zu Hermaphroditen-Darstellungen in der Antike." *Frauen, Weiblichkeit, Schrift*. Ed. Renate Berger et al. Berlin: Argument Verlag, 1985. 79–98.

Geiger, Ludwig. *Karoline von Günderrode und ihre Freunde*. Stuttgart: Deutsche Verlags-Anstalt. 1895.

———. *Therese Huber 1764 bis 1829: Leben und Briefe einer deutschen Frau*. Stuttgart: Cotta, 1901.

Geitner, Ursula. "Die eigentlichen Enragé ihres Geschlechts: Aufklärung, Französische Revolution und Weiblichkeit." *Grenzgängerinnen: Revolutionäre Frauen im 18. und 19. Jahrhundert: Weibliche Wirklichkeit und männliche Phantasien*. Ed. Helga Grubitzsch, Hannelore Cyrus, and Elke Haarbusch. Düsseldorf: Schwann, 1985. 181–217.

———. "Passio Hysterica: Die alltägliche Sorge um das Selbst: Zum Zusammenhang von Literatur, Pathologie und Weiblichkeit im 18. Jahrhundert." *Frauen, Weiblichkeit, Schrift*. Ed. Renate Berger et al. Berlin: Argument Verlag, 1985. 130–144.

Genast, Eduard. *Aus Weimars klassischer und nachklassischer Zeit: Erinnerungen eines alten Schauspielers*. Ed. Robert Kohlrausch. Stuttgart: Robert Lutz, n.d.

Gilbert, O. P. *Men in Women's Guise: Some Historical Instances of Female Impersonation*. London: John Lane, 1926.

———. *Women in Men's Guise*. London: Jarrold & Sons, 1932.

Gilbert, Sandra M., and Susan Gubar. "Cross-Dressing and Re-Dressing: Transvestism as Metaphor." *No Man's Land: The Place of the Woman Writer in the Twentieth Century*. Ed. Sandra Gilbert and Susan Gubar. New Haven: Yale University Press, 1989. 324–376.

———. *The Madwoman in the Attic*. New Haven: Yale University Press, 1988.

Goethe, Catharina Elisabeth. *Die Briefe von Goethes Mutter*. Ed. Mario Leis et al. Frankfurt am Main: Insel, 1996.

Goethe, Johann Wolfgang von. *Gedenkausgabe der Werke, Briefe, Gespräche, 29 August 1949*. 25 vols. Ed. Ernst Beutler. Zürich: Artemis, 1965.

———. *Goethes Werke: Hamburger Ausgabe in 14 Bänden*. Ed. Erich Trunz. Munich: Beck, 1981.

———. *Sämtliche Werke nach Epochen seines Schaffens, Münchner Ausgabe*. Ed. Karl Richter and Gerhard Sauder. Munich: Hanser, 1985.

———. *Tagebuch der Italienischen Reise für Frau von Stein*. Stuttgart: Cotta, 1953. *Werke*. Weimar Edition. 143 vols. Munich, 1987.

———. *Werke: Herausgegeben im Auftrage der Großherzogin Sophie von Sachsen*. Weimar: Hermann Böhlaus Nachfolger, 1887–1919. 147 vols.

———. *Wilhelm Meisters Lehrjahre*. Ed. Erich Schmidt. Frankfurt am Main: Insel, 1980.

Goodman, Katherine R. "The Sign Speaks: Charlotte von Stein's Matinees." *In the Shadow of Olympus: German Women Writers Around 1800*. Ed.

Katherine R. Goodman and Edith Waldstein. Albany: State University of New York Press, 1992. 71–93.

———. "Through a Different Lens: Bettina Brentano-von Arnim's Views on Gender." *Bettina Brentano-von Arnim: Gender and Politics.* Ed. Elke Frederiksen and Katherine R. Goodman. Detroit: Wayne State University Press, 1995. 115–141.

Goodman, Katherine R., and Edith Waldstein. *In the Shadow of Olympus: German Women Writers Around 1800.* Albany: State University of New York Press, 1992.

Goozé, Marjanne E. "A Language of Her Own: Bettina Brentano-von Arnim's Translation Theory and Her English Translation Project." *Bettina Brentano-von Arnim: Gender and Politics.* Ed. Elke Frederiksen and Katherine R. Goodman. Detroit: Wayne State University Press, 1995. 278–303.

———. "The Reception of Bettina Brentano-von Arnim as Author and Historical Figure." *Bettina Brentano-von Arnim: Gender and Politics.* Ed. Elke Frederiksen and Katherine R. Goodman. Detroit: Wayne State University Press, 1995. 349–401.

———. "The Seduction of Don Juan: Karoline von Günderrode's Romantic Rendering of a Classic Story." *The Enlightenment and Its Legacy: Studies in German Literature in Honor of Helga Slessarev.* Ed. Sara Friedrichsmeyer and Barbara Becker-Cantarino. Bonn: Bouvier, 1991. 117–129.

Gottsched, Johann Christoph. *Die vernünftigen Tadlerinnen 1725–1726.* Ed. Helga Brandes. 2 vols. Hildesheim: Georg Olms, 1993.

Graham, Ilse. *Schiller: A Master of the Tragic Form: His Theory in His Practice.* Pittsburgh: Duquesne University Press, 1975.

Grawe, Christian. *Friedrich Schiller: Die Verschwörung des Fiesco zu Genua: Erläuterungen und Dokumente.* Stuttgart: Philipp Reclam, 1985.

———. "Zu Schillers *Fiesco:* Eine übersehene frühe Rezension." *Jahrbuch der deutschen Schillergesellschaft* 26 (1982): 9–30.

Greenfield, Kent Roberts. *Sumptuary Law in Nürnberg: A Study in Paternal Government.* Baltimore: Johns Hopkins University Press, 1918.

Gresky, Wolfgang. "Gast bei Charlotte von Stein 1794: Aus dem Reise-Tagebuch des Schweizers Ludwig Zeerleder (1772–1840)." *Im Bannkreis des klassischen Weimar: Festschrift für Hans Tümmler zum 75. Geburtstag.* Ed. Herbert Hörnig and Dietrich Pfaeler. Bad Neustadt a. d. Saale: Dietrich Pfaehler, 1982. 41–50.

Grimm, Reinhold, and Klaus L. Berghahn. *Schiller: Zur Theorie und Praxis der Dramen.* Darmstadt: Wissenschaftliche Buchgesellschaft, 1972.

Gross, Heinrich. *Deutschlands Dichterinnen und Schriftstellerinnen: Eine literarhistorische Skizze.* Wien. 1882.

Grubitzsch, Helga, Hannelore Cyrus, and Elke Haarbusch, eds. *Grenzgängerinnen:*

Revolutionäre Frauen im 18. und 19. Jahrhundert: Weibliche Wirklichkeit und männliche Phantasien. Düsseldorf: Schwann, 1985.

Gubar, Susan. "Blessings in Disguise: Cross-Dressing as Re-Dressing for Female Modernists." *Massachusetts Review* 22 (1981): 476–508.

Günderrode, Karoline von. *Der Schatten eines Traums: Gedichte, Prosa, Briefe, Zeugnisse von Zeitgenossen*. Ed. Christa Wolf. Frankfurt am Main: Sammlung Luchterhand, 1989.

———. *Dichtungen*. Ed. Ludwig v. Pigenot. München: Hugo Bruckmann, 1922.

———. *Gesammelte Werke*. Ed. Leopold Hirschberg. Bern: Herbert Lang, 1970.

———. *Ich sende Dir ein zärtliches Pfand: Die Briefe der Karoline von Günderrode*. Ed. Birgit Weißenborn. Frankfurt am Main: Insel, 1992.

———. *Sämtliche Werke und ausgewählte Studien*. Ed. Walter Morgenthaler. 3 vols. Basel: Stroemfeld/Roter Stern, 1990.

Günzler, Claus. *Bildung und Erziehung im Denken Goethes: Philosophische Grundlagen und aktuelle Perspektiven einer Pädagogik der Selbstbeschränkung*. Köln: Böhlau, 1981.

Gustafson, Susan E. "Male Desire in Goethe's *Gotz von Berlichingen*." *Outing Goethe & His Age*. Ed. Alice Kuzniar. Stanford: Stanford University Press, 1996. 111–124.

Gutmann, Myron P. *Toward the Modern Economy: Early Industry in Europe 1500–1600*. New York: Knopf, 1988.

Haas, Rosemarie. *Die Turmgesellschaft in Wilhelm Meisters Lehrjahren: Zur Geschichte des Geheimbundromans und der Romantheorie im 18. Jahrhundert*. Bern: Herbert Lang, 1975.

Haberland, Helga, and Wolfgang Pehnt. *Frauen der Goethezeit in Briefen, Dokumenten und Bildern*. Stuttgart: Philipp Reclam, 1960.

Hahn, Karl-Heinz. *Bettina von Arnim in ihrem Verhältnis zu Staat und Politik*. Weimar: Hermann Böhlaus Nachfolger, 1959.

———, ed. *Briefe an Goethe: Gesamtausgabe*. Weimar: Hermann Böhlaus Nachfolger, 1980.

Hamm, Heinz. *Der Theoretiker Goethe: Grundpositionen einer Weltanschauung, Philosophie und Kunsttheorie*. Berlin: Akademie Verlag, 1980.

Hanstein, Adalbert von. *Die Frauen in der Geschichte des deutschen Geisteslebens des 18. und 19. Jahrhunderts*. Leipzig: Freund & Wittig, 1899.

Harms, Ingeborg. "Wie fliegender Sommer: Eine Untersuchung der 'Höhlenszene' in Heinrich von Kleists *Familie Schroffenstein*." *Jahrbuch der deutschen Schillergesellschaft* 28 (1984): 270–314.

Harte, N. B., and K. G. Ponting. *Textile History and Economic History: Essays in Honor of Miss Julia de Lacy Mann*. Manchester: Manchester University Press, 1973.

Hecht, Wolfgang. "Aufstieg und Fall des Grafen zu Lavagna: *Die Verschwörung des Fiesco zu Genua*." *Schiller: Das dramatische Werk in Einzelinterpretationen*.

Ed. Hans-Dietrich Dahnke and Bernd Leistner. Leipzig: Philipp Reclam, 1982. 42–63.

Hecker, Kristine. "Die Frauen in den frühen Commedia dell'Arte-Truppen." *Die Schauspielerin: Zur Kulturgeschichte der weiblichen Bühnenkunst.* Ed. Renate Möhrmann. Frankfurt am Main: Insel, 1989. 27–58.

Helbling, Robert E. *The Major Works of Heinrich von Kleist.* New York: New Directions Publishing Corporation, 1975.

Held, Jutta, ed. *Frauen im Frankreich des 18. Jahrhunderts: Amazonen, Mütter, Revolutionärinnen.* Hamburg: Argument Verlag, 1989.

Helfer, Martha. "Dorothea Veit-Schlegel's *Florentin*: Constructing a Feminist Romantic Aesthetic." *German Quarterly* 69 (1996): 144–160.

Herdt, Gilbert, ed. *Third Sex, Third Gender: Beyond Sexual Dimorphism in Culture and History.* Cambridge: MIT Press, 1993.

Hetmann, Frederik. *Bettina und Achim: Die Geschichte einer Liebe.* Weinheim: Beltz & Gelberg, 1984.

———. *Drei Frauen zum Beispiel: Die Lebensgeschichte der Simone Weil, Isabel Burton und Karoline von Günderrode.* Weinheim: Beltz & Gelberg, 1980.

Heuschele, Otto. *Karoline von Günderrode.* Halle: Werkstätten der Stadt Halle, 1932.

Heuser, Magdalene. "Spuren trauriger Selbstvergessenheit: Möglichkeiten eines weiblichen Bildungsromans um 1800: Friederike Helene Unger." *Kontroversen, alte und neue. Akten des VII. Internationalen Germanisten-Kongresses.* Vol. 6. Ed. Albrecht Schöne. Tübingen: Niemeyer, 1985. 30–42.

———. "Stationen einer Karsch-Nachfolge in der Literatur von Frauen des 18. Jahrhunderts: Caroline von Klencke, Helmina von Chézy und Therese Huber." *Anna Louisa Karsch (1722–1791): Von schlesischer Kunst und Berliner "Natur:" Ergebnisse des Symposiums zum 200. Todestag der Dichterin.* Ed. Anke Bennholdt-Thomsen and Anita Runge. Göttingen: Wallstein, 1992. 149–161.

Hibberd, J. "Dorothea Schlegel's *Florentin* and the Precarious Idyll." *German Life and Letters* XXX (1977): 198–207.

Hinderer, Walter. "Ein Augenblick Fürst hat das Mark des ganzen Daseins verschlungen: Zum Problem der Person und der Existenz in Schillers *Die Verschwörung des Fiesco zu Genua.*" *Jahrbuch der deutschen Schillergesellschaft* 14 (1970): 230–274.

Hirsch, Helmut. *Bettine von Arnim mit Selbstzeugnissen und Bilddokumenten dargestellt.* Reinbek: Rowohlt, 1987.

Hirschfeld, Magnus. *Transvestites: The Erotic Drive to Cross-Dress.* Trans. Michael A. Lombardi-Nash. Buffalo: Prometheus Books, 1991.

Hirschfeld, Walter. *Goethe und Charlotte von Stein.* Frankfurt: Insel, 1979.

Hoff, Dagmar von. *Dramen des Weiblichen: Deutsche Dramatikerinnen um 1800.* Opladen: Westdeutscher Verlag, 1989.

Hoffmeister, Gerhart, ed. *Goethe in Italy 1786–1986: A Bi-Centennial Symposium.* Amsterdam: Rodopi, 1988.

Hohoff, Curt. *Heinrich von Kleist in Selbstzeugnissen und Dokumenten.* Hamburg: Rowohlt, 1958.

Hollander, Anne. *Sex and Suits: The Evolution of Modern Dress.* New York: Kodansha International, 1995.

Holtmont, Alfred. *Die Hosenrolle: Variationen über das Thema das Weib als Mann.* München: Meyer & Jessen, 1925.

Holz, Hans Heinz. *Macht und Ohnmacht der Sprache: Untersuchungen zum Sprachverständnis und Stil Heinrich von Kleists.* Frankfurt am Main: Athenäum, 1962.

Honegger, Claudia. *Die Ordnung der Geschlechter: Die Wissenschaften vom Menschen und das Weib 1750–1850.* München: dtv, 1996.

Hopp, Doris, and Max Preitz. "Karoline von Günderrode in ihrer Umwelt III: Karoline von Günderrodes Studienbuch." *Jahrbuch des Freien Deutschen Hochstifts.* Ed. Detlev Lüders. Tübingen: Max Niemeyer, 1975. 223–298.

Horn, Peter. *Heinrich von Kleists Erzählungen.* Königstein: Scriptor, 1978.

Hotchkiss, Valerie R. *Clothes Make the Man: Female Cross-Dressing in Medieval Europe.* New York: Garland Publishing, 1996.

Howard, Jean E. "Cross-Dressing, the Theater, and Gender Struggle in Early Modern England." *Crossing the Stage: Controversies on Cross-Dressing.* Ed. Lesley Ferris. London: Routledge, 1993. 20–46.

Howe, George M. "The Possible Source of Kleist's *Familie Schroffenstein.*" *Modern Language Notes* 38 (1923): 148–153.

Hubbs, V.C. "The Concept of Fate in Kleist's *Schroffenstein.*" *Monatshefte* LXI (1964): 339–345.

Huber, Therese. *Die Familie Seldorf.* Ed. Magdalene Heuser. 2 vols. Hildesheim: Georg Olms, 1989.

———. *Die reinste Freiheitsliebe, die reinste Männerliebe: Ein Lebensbild in Briefen und Erzählungen zwischen Aufklärung und Romantik.* Ed. Andrea Hahn. Berlin: Henssel, 1989.

Huch, Ricarda. *Die Romantik: Blütezeit, Ausbreitung und Verfall.* Hamburg: Rowohlt, 1985.

Hunt, Alan. *Governance of the Consuming Passions: A History of Sumptuary Laws.* New York: St. Martin's Press, 1996.

Huyssen, Andreas. "Das leidende Weib in der dramatischen Literatur von Empfindsamkeit und Sturm und Drang: Eine Studie zur bürgerlichen Emanzipation in Deutschland." *Monatshefte* 69 (1977): 159–173.

Irigaray, Luce. *Das Geschlecht, das nicht eins ist.* Berlin: Merve, 1979.

Jameson, Frederic. *Postmodernism Or, The Cultural Logic of Late Capitalism*. Durham: Duke University Press, 1999.

Jamison, Robert L. "Politics and Nature in Schiller's *Fiesco* and *Wilhelm Tell*." *Friedrich Schiller: Kunst, Humanität und Politik in der späten Aufklärung. Ein Symposium*. Ed. Wolfgang Wittkowski. Tübingen: Max Niemeyer, 1982. 59–68.

Janz, Rolf-Peter. *Die Verschwörung des Fiesco zu Genua: Schillers Dramen: Neue Interpretationen*. Ed. Walter Hinderer. Stuttgart: Philipp Reclam, 1979. 37–57.

Jeep, Ernst. *Karoline von Günderrode: Mittheilungen über ihr Leben und Dichten*. Wolfenbüttel: Julius Zwißler, 1859.

Johnson, Mary Durham. "Old Wine in New Bottles: The Institutional Changes for Women of the People During the French Revolution." *Women, War, and Revolution*. Ed. Carol R. Berkin and Clara M. Lovett. New York: Holmes & Meier, 1980. 107–143.

Kahn, Madeleine. *Narrative Transvestism: Rhetoric and Gender in the Eighteenth-Century Novel*. Ithaca: Cornell University Press, 1991.

Kaiser, Gerhard, and Friedrich A. Kittler. *Dichtung als Sozialisationsspiel: Studien zu Goethe und Gottfried Keller*. Göttingen: Vandenhoeck & Ruprecht, 1978.

Kammler, Eva. *Zwischen Professionalisierung und Dilettantismus: Romane und ihre Autorinnen um 1800*. Opladen: Westdeutscher Verlag, 1992.

Kant, Immanuel. *Kants gesammelte Schriften*. Ed. Königlich Preußische Akademie der Wissenschaften. Vol. 7: *Der Streit der Fakultäten. Anthropologie in pragmatischer Hinsicht*. Berlin: Georg Reimer, 1917.

Kastinger Riley, Helene M. *Die weibliche Muse: Sechs Essays über künstlerisch schaffende Frauen der Goethezeit*. Columbia: Camden House, 1986.

Kates, Gary. *Monsieur d'Eon Is a Woman: A Tale of Political Intrigue and Sexual Masquerade*. New York: Basic Books, 1995.

Kelly, Veronica, and Dorothea von Mücke, eds. *Body and Text in the Eighteenth Century*. Stanford: Stanford University Press, 1994.

Kennedy, Barbara. "For the Good of the Nation: Woman's Body as Battlefield in Kleist's *Die Hermannsschlacht*." *Seminar* 30.1 (1994): 17–31.

Kieffer, Bruce. "Schiller: The Tragedy of Ideal Language." *The Storm and Stress of Language: Linguistic Catastrophe in the Early Works of Goethe, Lenz, Klinger, and Schiller*. University Park: Pennsylvania State University Press, 1986. 115–138.

Kisch, Herbert. *From Domestic Manufacture to Industrial Revolution: The Case of the Rhineland Textile Districts*. New York: Oxford University Press, 1989.

———. "The Impact of the French Revolution on the Lower Rhine Textile Districts—Some Comments on Economic Development and Social Change." *Economic History Review* 15 (1962): 304–27.

Kittler, Friedrich A. "In den Wind schreibend, Bettina." *Dichter—Mutter—Kind.* München: Wilhelm Fink, 1991. 219–255.

Kittler, Wolf. "Militärisches Kommando und tragisches Geschick: Zur Funktion der Schrift im Werk des preußischen Dichters Heinrich von Kleist." *Heinrich von Kleist: Studien zu Werk und Wirkung.* Ed. Dirk Grathoff. Opladen: Westdeutscher Verlag, 1988. 56–68.

Klauss, Jochen. *Alltag im "klassischen" Weimar 1750–1850.* Weimar: Nationale Forschungs- und Gedenkstätten der klassischen deutschen Literatur, 1990.

Kleinschnieder, Manfred. *Goethes Naturstudien: Wissenschaftstheoretische und -geschichtliche Untersuchungen.* Bonn: Bouvier, 1971.

Kleist, Heinrich von. *Briefe 1805–1811.* Vol. 6 of *Sämtliche Werke und Briefe in sieben Bänden.* Ed. Helmut Sembdner. Munich: dtv, 1964.

———. *Die Familie Schroffenstein: Ein Trauerspiel in fünf Aufzügen.* Ed. Curt Hohoff. Stuttgart: Reclam, 1988.

———. *Gesamtausgabe.* Ed. Helmut Sembdner. München: dtv, 1964.

Kleßmann, Eckart. *Goethe aus der Nähe: Berichte von Zeitgenossen.* München: Artemis & Winkler, 1985.

Kluge, Gerhard. "Der Wandel der dramatischen Konzeption von der *Familie Ghonorez* zur *Familie Schroffenstein.*" *Kleists Dramen: Neue Interpretationen.* Ed. Walter Hinderer. Stuttgart: Philipp Reclam, 1981. 52–72.

Kontje, Todd. "Under the Father's Spell: Patriarchy versus Patriotism in Therese Huber's *Die Familie Seldorf.*" *Seminar* 28.1 (1992): 17–32.

Koopmann, Helmut. *Schiller: Eine Einführung.* München: Artemis, 1988.

Köpke, Wulf. "Die emanzipierte Frau in der Goethezeit und ihre Darstellung in der Literatur." *Die Frau als Heldin und Autorin: Neue kritische Ansätze zur deutschen Literatur.* Ed. Wolfgang Paulsen. Bern: Francke, 1979. 96–110.

———. "Immer noch im Schatten der Männer? Therese Huber als Schriftstellerin." *Der Weltumsegler und seine Freunde: Georg Forster als gesellschaftlicher Schriftsteller der Goethezeit.* Ed. Detlef Rasmussen. Tübingen: Günter Narr, 1988. 116–132.

Kord, Susanne. *Ein Blick hinter die Kulissen: Deutschsprachige Dramatikerinnen im 18. und 19. Jahrhundert.* Stuttgart: Metzler, 1992.

———. "Performing Genders: Three Plays on the Power of Women." *Monatshefte* 86.1 (1994): 95–115.

———. "Eternal Love or Sentimental Discourse? Gender Dissonance and Women's Passionate Friendships." *Outing Goethe and His Age.* Ed. Alice Kuzniar. Stanford: Stanford University Press, 1996. 228–249.

———. "Not in Goethe's Image: The Playwright Charlotte von Stein." *Thalia's Daughters: German Women Dramatists From the Eighteenth Century to the Present.* Ed. Susan L. Cocalis and Ferrel Rose. Tübingen: Francke, 1996. 53–75.

————. *Sich einen Namen machen: Anonymität und weibliche Autorschaft 1700–1900.* Stuttgart: Metzler, 1996.

Koselleck, Reinhart. *Kritik und Krise: Eine Studie zur Pathogenese der bürgerlichen Welt.* Frankfurt am Main: Suhrkamp, 1989.

Kraus Worley, Linda. "The Body, Beauty, and Woman: The Ugly Heroine in Stories by Therese Huber and Gabriele Reuter." *German Quarterly* 64.3 (1991): 368–378.

Kreuzer, Helmut. "Die Jungfrau in Waffen: Hebbels Judith und ihre Geschwister von Schiller bis Sartre." *Untersuchungen zur Literatur als Geschichte: Festschrift für Benno von Wiese.* Ed. Vincent J. Günther et al. Berlin: Erich Schmidt, 1973. 363–384.

Kuhn, Anna K. "Peter Hacks' *Ein Gespräch im Hause Stein über den abwesenden Herrn von Goethe:* A Feminist Reinterpretation of the Geniebegriff." *Germanic Review* 60 (1985): 91–98.

————. "The Failure of Biography and the Triumph of Women's Writing: Bettina von Arnim's *Die Günderode* and Christa Wolf's *The Quest for Christa T.*" *Revealing Lives: Autobiography, Biography, and Gender.* Eds. Susan Groag Bell and Marilyn Yalom. Albany: State University of New York Press, 1990. 13–28.

Kühn, Paul. *Die Frauen um Goethe.* Leipzig: Klinkhardt, 1911.

————. *Weimar.* Leipzig: Klinkhardt & Biermann, n.d.

Küther, Carsten. *Räuber und Gauner in Deutschland: Das organisierte Bandenwesen im 18. und frühen 19. Jahrhundert.* Göttingen: Vandenhoeck & Ruprecht, 1976.

Kuzniar, Alice A., ed. *Outing Goethe and His Age.* Stanford: Stanford University Press, 1996.

Labhardt, Robert. *Metapher und Geschichte: Kleists dramatische Metaphorik bis zur Penthesilea als Widerspiegelung seiner geschichtlichen Position.* Kronberg: Scriptor, 1976.

Lacan, Jacques. *On Feminine Sexuality. The Limits of Love and Knowledge.* Ed. Jacques-Alain Miller. Trans. Bruce Fink. New York: Norton, 1998.

Laermann, Klaus. "Die riskante Person in der moralischen Anstalt: Zur Darstellung der Schauspielerin in deutschen Theaterzeitschriften des späten 18. Jahrhunderts." *Die Schauspielerin: Zur Kulturgeschichte der weiblichen Bühnenkunst.* Ed. Renate Möhrmann. Frankfurt am Main: Insel, 1989. 127–153.

Lahnstein, Peter. *Schillers Leben.* München: List, 1981.

Lange, Sigrid, ed. *Ob die Weiber Menschen sind: Geschlechterdebatten um 1800.* Leipzig: Reclam, 1992.

————. *Spiegelgeschichten: Geschlechter und Poetiken in der Frauenliteratur um 1800.* Frankfurt am Main: Ulrike Helmer, 1995.

————. "Über epische und dramatische Dichtung Weimarer Autorinnen:

Überlegungen zu Geschlechterspezifika in der Poetologie." *Zeitschrift für Germanistik* 2 (91): 341–351.

Laqueur, Thomas. *Making Sex: Body and Gender from the Greeks to Freud.* Cambridge: Harvard University Press, 1990.

Lavater-Sloman, Mary. *Wer sich der Liebe vertraut: Drei Abschnitte aus Goethes Leben.* Zürich: Artemis, 1960.

Lehnert, Gertrud. *Maskeraden und Metamorphosen: Als Männer verkleidete Frauen in der Literatur.* Würzburg: Königshausen & Neumann, 1994.

Leuschner, Brigitte. *Schriftstellerinnen und Schwesterseelen: Der Briefwechsel zwischen Therese Huber (1764–1829) und Karoline Pichler (1769–1843).* Marburg: Tectum, 1995.

Levy, Darline Gay, Harriet Branson Applewhite, and Mary Durham Johnson, eds. *Women in Revolutionary Paris 1789–1795.* Urbana: University of Illinois Press, 1980.

Levy, Darline Gay, and Harriet Branson Applewhite. "Women of the Popular Classes in Revolutionary Paris 1789–1795." *Women, War, and Revolution.* Ed. Carol R. Berkin and Clara M. Lovett. New York: Holmes & Meier, 1980. 9–35.

Liebertz-Grün, Ursula. *Ordnung im Chaos: Studien zur Poetik der Bettine Brentano von Arnim.* Heidelberg: Carl Winter, 1989.

Lipping, Margita. "Bürgerliche Konzepte zur weiblichen Sexualität in der zweiten Hälfte des 18. Jahrhunderts: Rekonstruktionsversuche am Material medizinischer und pädagogischer Texte." *Frauenkörper, Medizin, Sexualität: Auf dem Wege zu einer neuen Sexualmoral.* Ed. Johanna Geyer-Kordesch and Annette Kuhn. Düsseldorf: Schwann, 1986. 28–42.

Loschek, Ingrid. *Reclams Mode- und Kostümlexikon.* Stuttgart: Reclam, 1998.

Lukacs, Georg. *Deutsche Realisten des 19. Jahrhunderts.* Berlin: Aufbau, 1956.

Lüthi, Kurt. *Feminismus und Romantik: Sprache, Gesellschaft, Symbole, Religion.* Wien: Hermann Böhlaus Nachfolger, 1985.

Lützeler, Paul Michael. "Die grosse Linie zu einem Brutuskopfe: Republikanismus und Cäsarismus in Schillers *Fiesco*." *Monatshefte* 70 (1978): 15–28.

Lyncker, Karl Freiherr von. *Am Weimarischen Hofe unter Amalien und Karl August.* Ed. Marie Scheller. Berlin: Ernst Siegfried Mittler und Sohn, 1912.

Maas, Joachim. *Kleist: Die Geschichte seines Lebens.* Bern: Scherz, 1977.

MacKenzie, Gordene Olga. *Transgender Nation.* Bowling Green: Bowling Green State University Press, 1994.

MacLeod, Catriona. *Embodying Ambiguity: Androgyny and Aesthetics from Winckelmann to Keller.* Detroit: Wayne State University Press, 1998.

———. "Pedagogy and Androgyny in *Wilhelm Meisters Lehrjahre*." *MLN* 108 (1993): 389–426.

Macpherson, James. *The Poems of Ossian and Related Works.* Ed. Howard Gaskill. Edinburgh: Edinburgh University Press, 1996.

Mander, Gertrud. *Bettina von Arnim*. Berlin: Stapp, 1982.

Mansouri, Rachid Jan. *Die Darstellung der Frau in Schillers Dramen*. Frankfurt am Main: Peter Lang, 1988.

Maurer, Doris. *Charlotte von Stein: Ein Frauenleben der Goethezeit*. Bonn: Keil, 1985.

McClintock, Anne. *Imperial Leather: Race, Gender and Sexuality in the Colonial Contest*. New York: Routledge, 1995.

McGlathery, James M. *Desire's Sway: The Plays and Stories of Heinrich von Kleist*. Detroit: Wayne State University Press, 1983.

Meier, Albert. "Des Zuschauers Seele am Zügel: Die ästhetische Vermittlung des Republikanismus in Schillers *Die Verschwörung des Fiesco zu Genua*." *Jahrbuch der deutschen Schillergesellschaft* 31 (1987): 117–136.

Meise, Helga. *Die Unschuld und die Schrift: Deutsche Frauenromane im 18. Jahrhundert*. Berlin: Guttandin & Hoppe, 1983.

Meßner, Paul. *Das Deutsche Nationaltheater Weimar: Ein Abriß seiner Geschichte von den Anfängen bis Februar 1945*. Weimarer Schriften Heft 17, 1985.

Meyer, Kayserling. *Die jüdischen Frauen in der Geschichte, Literatur und Kunst*. Hildesheim: Georg Olms, 1991.

Meyer-Hepner, Gertrud. *Der Magistratsprozess der Bettina von Arnim*. Weimar: Arion, 1960.

Milch, Werner. *Die junge Bettine 1785–1811*. Heidelberg: Lothar Stiehm, 1968.

Miller, Daniel, ed. *Material Cultures: Why Some Things Matter*. Chicago: University of Chicago Press, 1998.

Möhrmann, Renate, ed. *Die Schauspielerin: Zur Kulturgeschichte der weiblichen Bühnenkunst*. Frankfurt am Main: Insel, 1989.

Montrose, Louis. "The Work of Gender in the Discourse of Discovery." *Representations* 33 (1991): 1–41.

Mosse, George L. *Nationalism and Sexuality: Middle-Class Morality and Sexual Norms in Modern Europe*. Madison: University of Wisconsin Press, 1985.

Motte-Fouqué, Caroline de la. *Das Heldenmädchen aus der Vendée*. 2 vols. Wien: Haas'sche Verlagsbuchhandlung, 1816.

———. *Geschichte der Moden 1785–1829: Als Beytrag zur Geschichte der Zeit*. Ed. Dorothea Böck. Hanau: Werner Dausien, 1988.

Mottek, Hans. *Wirtschaftsgeschichte Deutschlands: Ein Grundriss*. Vol. 2. Berlin: VEB Deutscher Verlag der Wissenschaften, 1971.

Müller, F. C. "Ein weiterer Fall von conträrer Sexualempfindung." *Friedreich's Series for Forensic Medicine: Criminal Investigation*. Nürmberg (1891): 91–112.

Müller, Joachim. "Liebe, Umwelt und Landschaft in Goethes Briefen an Charlotte von Stein." *Goethe-Jahrbuch* 25 (1963): 70–96.

———. *Von Schiller bis Heine*. Halle: Max Niemeyer, 1972.

Müller-Fraureuth, Carl. *Die Ritter- und Räuberromane.* Hildesheim: Georg Olms, 1965.

Müller-Harang, Ulrike. *Das Weimarer Theater zur Zeit Goethes.* Weimar: Verlag der Klassikerstätten, 1991.

Müller-Seidel, Walter, ed. *Heinrich von Kleist: Aufsätze und Essays.* Darmstadt: Wissenschaftliche Buchgesellschaft, 1967.

———, ed. *Kleists Aktualität: Neue Aufsätze und Essays 1966–1978.* Darmstadt: Wissenschaftliche Buchgesellschaft, 1981.

Muschg, Walter. "Erschrecken vor der Welt: Zu Kleists *Familie Schroffenstein.*" *Pamphlet und Bekenntnis: Aufsätze und Reden.* Ed. Peter André Bloch. Freiburg im Breisgau: Walter, 1968. 356–361.

Narweleit, Gerhard. "Die Standortverteilung des Textilgewerbes der Niederlausitz in der Mitte des 18. Jh. und Tendenzen der Entwicklung um 1800." *Jahrbuch für Wirtschaftsgeschichte.* 1 (1984): 157–194.

Neumann, Gerhard. "Das Stocken der Sprache und das Straucheln des Körpers: Umrisse von Kleists kultureller Anthropologie." *Heinrich von Kleist: Kriegsfall-Rechtsfall-Sündenfall.* Ed. Gerhard Neumann. Freiburg im Breisgau: Rombach, 1994. 13–29.

———, ed. *Heinrich von Kleist: Kriegsfall-Rechtsfall-Sündenfall.* Freiburg im Breisgau: Rombach, 1994.

———. "Skandalon: Geschlechterrolle und soziale Identität in Kleists *Marquise von O* und in Cervantes Novelle *La Fuerza de la sangre.*" *Heinrich von Kleist: Kriegsfall-Rechtsfall-Sündenfall.* Ed. Gerhard Neumann. Freiburg im Breisgau: Rombach, 1994.

Newton, Esther. *Mother Camp: Female Impersonators in America.* Chicago: University of Chicago Press, 1979. 149–192.

Nobel, Alphons. *Frau von Stein: Goethes Freundin und Feindin.* München: Münchner Verlag, 1939.

Noel, Major z.D. *Die deutschen Heldinnen in den Kriegsjahren 1807–1815.* Berlin: Julius Köppen, 1912.

Obermeier, Karin. *Private Matters Made Public: Love and the Sexualized Body in Karoline von Günderrode's Texts.* Diss. University of Massachusetts, 1995.

Ockenfuß, Solveig. *Bettine von Arnims Briefromane: Literarische Erinnerungsarbeit zwischen Anspruch und Wirklichkeit.* Opladen: Westdeutscher Verlag, 1992.

———. "Verkleidungsspiele." *Neue Horizonte: Eine Reise durch die Reisen.* Ed. Klaus Bergmann and Solveig Ockenfuß. Reinbek: Rowohlt, 1984. 117–143.

Oehlke, Waldemar. *Bettina von Arnims Briefromane.* Berlin: Mayer & Müller, 1905.

Oellers, Norbert, ed. *Schiller—Zeitgenosse aller Epochen: Dokumente zur Wirkungsgeschichte Schillers in Deutschland. Teil 1: 1782–1859.* Frankfurt am Main: Athenäum, 1970.

Ohnesorg, Stephanie. *Mit Kompaß, Kutsche und Kamel: (Rück-) Einbindung der Frau in die Geschichte des Reisens und der Reiseliteratur.* Stuttgart: Röhrig, 1996.

Opitz, Claudia. "Der Bürger wird Soldat—und die Bürgerin? Die Revolution, der Krieg und die Stellung der Frauen nach 1789." *Sklavin oder Bürgerin? Französische Revolution und neue Weiblichkeit 1760–1830.* Ed. Viktoria Schmidt-Linsenhoff. Frankfurt am Main: Jonas, 1989. 38–54.

———. "Die vergessenen Töchter der Revolution—Frauen und Frauenrechte im revolutionären Frankreich von 1789–1795." *Grenzgängerinnen: Revolutionäre Frauen im 18. und 19. Jahrhundert: Weibliche Wirklichkeit und männliche Phantasien.* Eds. Helga Grubitzsch, Hannelore Cyrus, and Elke Haarbusch. Düsseldorf: Schwann, 1985. 287–312.

Orgel, Stephen. *Impersonations: The Performance of Gender in Shakespeare's England.* Cambridge: Cambridge University Press, 1996.

Patterson, Rebecca. "Emiliy Dickinson's Debt to Günderode." *Midwest Quarterly* 8 (1967): 331–354.

Paulus, Karoline. *Wilhelm Dumont: Ein einfacher Roman.* Lübeck: Friedrich Bohn, 1805.

Peitsch, Helmut. "Die Revolution im Familienroman: Aktuelles politisches Thema und konventionelle Romanstruktur in Therese Huber's *Die Familie Seldorf.*" *Jahrbuch der Deutschen Schiller Gesselschaft* 28 (1984): 248–69.

Pelz, Annegret. *Reisen durch die eigene Fremde: Reiseliteratur von Frauen als auto-geographische Schriften.* Böhlau: Köln, 1993.

Perels, Christoph, ed. *Herzhaft in die Dornen der Zeit greifen: Bettine von Arnim 1785–1859.* Frankfurt am Main: Freies Deutsches Hochstift, 1985.

Petersen, Susanne. *Marktweiber und Amazonen: Frauen in der Französischen Revolution. Dokumente. Kommentare. Bilder.* Köln: Pahl-Rugenstein, 1987.

Pfister, Kurt. *Frauenschicksale aus acht Jahrhunderten.* München: Nymphenburger Verlagshandlung, 1949.

Phelps, Reginald H. "Schiller's *Fiesco*—A Republican Tragedy?" *PMLA* 89 (1974): 442–453.

Pratt, Mary Louise. *Imperial Eyes: Travel Writing and Transculturation.* New York: Routledge, 1992.

Preisendanz, Karl, ed. *Die Liebe der Günderrode: Friedrich Creuzers Briefe an Caroline von Günderrode.* Bern: Herbert Lang, 1975.

Price, Janet, and Margrit Shildrick, eds. *Feminist Theory and the Body: A Reader.* New York: Routledge, 1999.

Prill, Vera. *Caroline de la Motte-Fouqué.* Berlin: Kraus, 1933.

Purdy, Daniel. *The Tyranny of Elegance: Consumer Cosmopolitanism in the Era of Goethe.* Baltimore: Johns Hopkins University Press, 1998.

Püschel, Ursula. *Mit allen Sinnen: Frauen in der Literatur.* Halle: Mitteldeutscher Verlag, 1980.

Ramet, Sabrina Petra, ed. *Gender Reversals and Gender Cultures: Anthropological and Historical Perspectives.* London: Routledge, 1996.

Ratz, Norbert. *Der Identitätsroman: Eine Strukturanalyse.* Tübingen: Niemeyer, 1988.

Reddy, William M. *The Rise of Market Culture: The Textile Trade and French Society, 1750–1900.* London: Cambridge University Press, 1984.

Rieger, Bernhard. *Geschlechterrollen und Familienstrukturen in den Erzählungen Heinrich von Kleists.* Frankfurt am Main: Peter Lang, 1985.

Ritter, Naomi. "Poet and Carnival: Goethe, Grillparzer, Baudelaire." *Grillparzer's Der arme Spielmann: New Directions in Criticism.* Ed. Albrecht Bernd Clifford. Columbia: Camden House, 1988. 337–351.

Röder, Gerda. *Glück und glückliches Ende im deutschen Bildungsroman: Eine Studie zu Goethes Wilhelm Meister.* München: Max Hueber, 1968.

Rückert, Friedrich. *Werke.* Ed. Edgar Groß and Elsa Hertzer. Vol. 1. Hildesheim: Georg Olms, 1979.

Ruhl-Anglade, Gabriele. "Goethes *An den Mond*—nach Charlotte von Steins Manier." *Goethe-Jahrbuch* 109 (1992): 23–30.

Runte, Annette. "Androgynie als Pathos und Travestie als Satire: Zum literarischen Einsatz von Geschlechts-Umkehrung und Geschlechts-Umwandlung." *Frauen—Literatur—Politik.* Ed. Annegret Pelz et al. Hamburg: Argument, 1988. 94–109.

Satori-Neumann, Bruno. "Goethe und die Einrichtung der Weimarischen Redouten." *Festgabe der Gesellschaft für Deutsche Literatur zum siebzigsten Geburtstag ihres Vorsitzenden Max Herrmann.* Langensalza: Julius Belz, 1935. 47–60.

Scarry, Elaine. *The Body in Pain: The Making and Unmaking of the World.* New York: Oxford University Press, 1985.

Schanze, Helmut. "Dorothea geb. Mendelssohn, Friedrich Schlegel, Philipp Veit—ein Kapitel zum Problem Judentum und Romantik." *Judentum, Antisemitismus und europäische Kultur.* Ed. Hans Otto Horch. Tübingen: Francke, 1988. 133–150.

Schieth, Lydia. *Die Entwicklung des deutschen Frauenromans im ausgehenden 18. Jahrhundert: ein Beitrag zur Gattungsgeschichte.* Frankfurt am Main: Lang, 1987.

Schiller, Friedrich. *Werke. Nationalausgabe.* Ed. Julius Petersen and Gerhard Fricke. 43 vols. Weimar: Hermann Böhlaus Nachfolger. 1942.

Schlaffer, Hannelore. *Wilhelm Meister: Das Ende der Kunst und die Wiederkehr des Mythos.* Stuttgart: Metzler, 1980.

Schlechta, Karl. *Goethes Wilhelm Meister.* Frankfurt am Main: Vittorio Klostermann, 1953.

Schlegel, August Wilhelm. *Vorlesungen über dramatische Kunst und Litteratur:*

Vorlesungen von August Wilhelm Schlegel. 2 vols. Stuttgart: Kohlhammer, 1967.

Schlegel, Dorothea. *Dorothea von Schlegel, geb. Mendelssohn und deren Söhne Johannes und Philipp Veit: Briefwechsel im Auftrage der Familie Veit herausgegeben*. Ed. J. M. Raich. 2 vols. Mainz: Kirchheim, 1881.

———. *Florentin: Roman, Fragmente, Varianten*. Ed. Liliane Weissberg. Berlin: Ullstein, 1987.

Schlegel, Friedrich. *Sammlung von Memoiren und romantischen Dichtungen des Mittelalters aus altfranzösischen und deutschen Quellen*. Ed. Liselotte Dieckmann. Paderborn: Ferdinand Schöningh, 1980.

Schlegel-Schelling, Caroline. *Briefe an ihre Geschwister, ihre Tochter Auguste, bei Familie Gotter, F. L. W. Meyer, A. W. und Fr. Schlegel, J. Schelling u.a.* Ed. G. Waitz. Leipzig: Hirzel, 1871.

———. *Caroline und Dorothea Schlegel in Briefen*. Ed. Ernst Wieneke. Weimar: Kiepenheuer, 1914.

Schmidt-Linsenhoff, Viktoria, ed. *Sklavin oder Bürgerin? Französische Revolution und neue Weiblichkeit, 1760–1830*. Frankfurt am Main: Jonas, 1989.

Schmitz, Walter. "Nur eine Skizze, aber durchaus in einem großen Stil: Dorothea Schlegel." *Autoren damals und heute: Literaturgeschichtliche Beispiele veränderter Wirkungshorizonte*. Ed. Gerhard Knapp. Amsterdam: Rodopi, 1991. 91–131.

Schopenhauer, Johanna. *Im Wechsel der Zeiten, im Gedränge der Welt Jugenderinnerungen, Tagebücher, Briefe*. Düsseldorf: Artemis, 2000.

Schneider, Manfred. "Die Inquisition der Oberfläche: Kleist und die juristische Kodifikation des Unbewußten." *Heinrich von Kleist: Kriegsfall-Rechtsfall-Sündenfall*. Ed. Gerhard Neumann. Freiburg im Breisgau: Rombach, 1994. 107–126.

Scholl, John William. "The Cave Scene in *Die Familie Schroffenstein*." *Modern Philology* 18 (1921): 137–143.

Schormann, Sabine. *Bettine von Arnim: Die Bedeutung Schleiermachers für ihr Leben und Werk*. Tübingen: Niemeyer, 1993.

Schrickel, Leonhard. *Geschichte des Weimarer Theaters von seinen Anfängen bis heute*. Weimar: Pauses Verlag, 1928.

Schulte, Bettina. *Unmittelbarkeit und Vermittlung im Werk Heinrich von Kleists*. Göttingen: Vandenhoeck & Ruprecht, 1988.

Schulz, Gerhard. "Goethes Italienische Reise." *Goethe in Italy 1786–1986: A Bi-Centennial Symposium, November 14–16, 1986, University of California, Santa Barbara*. Ed. Gerhart Hoffmeister. Amsterdam: Rodopi, 1988. 5–19.

Schultz, Hartwig. "Bettine-Blüten: Ein Fund zu Clemens Brentanos Frühlingskranz." *Wirkendes Wort* 39.3 (1989): 323–326.

Schumacher, Martin. "Wirtschafts- und Sozialverhältnisse der Rheinischen

Textilindustrie im frühen 19. Jahrhundert." *Rheinische Vierteljahresblätter* 35 (1971): 301–34.

Schwarz, Gudrun. "Mannweiber in Männertheorien." *Frauen suchen ihre Geschichte: Historische Studien zum 19. und 20. Jahrhundert*. Ed. Karin Hausen. München: Beck, 1983.

Schweitzer, Antonie, and Simone Sitte. "Tugend—Opfer—Rebellion: Zum Bild der Frau im weiblichen Erziehungs- und Bildungsroman." *Frauen Literatur Geschichte. Schreibende Frauen vom Mittelalter bis zur Gegenwart*. Ed. Hiltrud Gnüg and Renate Möhrmann. Stuttgart: Metzler, 1985.

Schweitzer, Christoph E. "Dorothea Schlegel's Clementina (*Florentin*) und Goethe's Makarie (*Wilhelm Meisters Wanderjahre*)." *Analogon Rationis: Festschrift für Gerwin Marahrens zum 65. Geburtstag*. Ed. Marianne Henn and Christoph Lorey. Edmonton: University of Alberta Press, 1994. 209–218.

Secker, Wilfried. *Wiederholte Spiegelungen: Die klassische Kunstauffassung Goethes und Wilhelm von Humboldts*. Frankfurt am Main: Peter Lang, 1985.

Seeba, Hinrich C. "Der Sündenfall des Verdachts: Identitätskrise und Sprachskepsis in Kleists *Familie Schroffenstein*." *Deutsche Vierteljahresschrift für Literaturwissenschaft und Geistesgeschichte* 44 (1970): 64–100.

Seillière, Ernest. *Charlotte von Stein und ihr antiromantischer Einfluß auf Goethe*. Berlin: Hermann Barsdorf, 1914.

Sembdner, Helmut, ed. *Heinrich von Kleists Lebensspurn: Dokumente und Berichte der Zeitgenossen*. Bremen: Carl Schünemann Verlag, 1957.

Sichardt, Gisela. *Das Weimarer Liebhabertheater unter Goethes Leitung: Beiträge zu Bühne, Dekoration und Kostüm unter Berücksichtigung der Entwicklung Goethes zum späteren Theaterdirektor*. Weimar: Arion, 1957.

Sieg, Katrin. *Exiles, Eccentrics, Activists: Women in Contemporary German Theater*. Ann Arbor: University of Michigan Press, 1994.

Simpson, Patricia Anne. "Letters in Sufferance and Deliverance: The Correspondence of Bettina Brentano-von Arnim and Karoline von Günderrode." *Bettina Brentano-von Arnim: Gender and Politics*. Ed. Elke Frederiksen and Katherine R. Goodman. Detroit: Wayne State University Press, 1995. 247–277.

Slide, Anthony. *Great Pretenders: A History of Female and Male Impersonation in the Performing Arts*. Lombard: Wallace Homestead, 1986.

Soboul, Albert. *Understanding the French Revolution*. New York: International Publishers, 1988.

Spickernagel, Ellen. "Helden wie zarte Knaben oder verkleidete Mädchen: Zum Begriff der Androgynität bei Johann Joachim Winckelmann und Angelika Kauffmann." *Frauen, Weiblichkeit, Schrift*. Ed. Renate Berger et al. Berlin: Argument Verlag, 1985. 99–118.

Spiero, Heinrich. *Geschichte der deutschen Frauendichtung seit 1800*. Leipzig: B.G. Teubner, 1913.

Stahl, E. L. *Heinrich von Kleist's Dramas*. Oxford: Basil Blackwell, 1948.

Staiger, Emil. "Rasende Weiber in der deutschen Tragödie des 18. Jahrhunderts." *Stilwandel: Studien zur Vorgeschichte der Goethezeit*. Zürich: Atlantis, 1963. 25–74.

Stein, Charlotte von. *Dido: Ein Trauerspiel in fünf Aufzügen*. Ed. Heinrich Düntzer. Frankfurt am Main: Freies Deutsches Hochstift, 1867.

———. *Die zwey Emilien: Drama in vier Aufzügen*. Tübingen: Cotta, 1803.

———. *Ein neues Freiheitssystem: Lustspiel in vier Akten: Nach einem Lustspiel gleichen Namens aus dem Nachlaß der Frau Charlotte von Stein, geb. Von Schardt neu bearbeitet von Felix Freiherr von Stein-Kochberg. Deutsche Schaubühne* 8 Nr. 10 & 11 (1867): 1–31.

Steinsdoff, Sibylle von. "Bettine und Goethe." *Herzhaft in die Dornen der Zeit greifen: Bettine von Arnim 1785–1859*. Ed. Christoph Perels. Frankfurt: Freies Deutsches Hochstift, 1985. 233–252.

Stephan, Inge. "Revolution und Konterrevolution: Therese Hubers Roman *Die Familie Seldorf* (1795–96)." *Der deutsche Roman der Spätaufklärung: Fiktion und Wirklichkeit*. Ed. Harro Zimmermann. Heidelberg: Winter, 1990. 171–194.

Stephens, Anthony. "Das nenn ich menschlich nicht verfahren: Skizze zu einer Theorie der Grausamkeit im Hinblick auf Kleist." *Heinrich von Kleist: Studien zu Werk und Wirkung*. Ed. Dirk Grathoff. Opladen: Westdeutscher Verlag, 1988. 10–39.

———. *Heinrich von Kleist: The Dramas and Stories*. Oxford: Berg, 1994.

———. "The Illusion of a Shaped World: Kleist and Tragedy." *Aumla* 60 (1983): 197–219.

———. "Verzerrungen im Spiegel: Das Narziß-Motiv bei Heinrich von Kleist." *Heinrich von Kleist: Kriegsfall-Rechtsfall-Sündenfall*. Ed. Gerhard Neumann. Freiburg im Breisgau: Rombach, 1994. 249–297.

Stern, Carola. *Ich möchte mir Flügel wünschen: Das Leben der Dorothea Schlegel*. Reinbek: Rowohlt, 1990.

Stone, Sandy. "The Empire Strikes Back: A Posttranssexual Manifesto." *Writing on the Body: Female Embodiment and Feminist Theory*. Ed. Katie Conboy, Nadia Medina, and Sarah Stanbury. New York: Columbia University Press, 1997. 337–359.

Straayer, Chris. "Redressing the 'Natural:' The Temporary Transvestite Film." *Wide Angle* 14 (1992): 36–55.

Stuebben Thornton, Karin. "Enlightenment and Romanticism in the Work of Dorothea Schlegel." *German Quarterly* 39 (1966): 162–172.

Sullivan, Louis. *From Female to Male: The Life of Jack Bee Garland*. Boston: Alyson Publications, 1990.

Susman, Margarete. *Deutung einer großen Liebe: Goethe und Charlotte von Stein.* Zürich: Artemis, 1951.

———. *Frauen der Romantik.* Jena: Eugen Diederichs, 1929.

Szondi, Peter. *Versuch über das Tragische.* Frankfurt am Main: Insel, 1964.

Tanneberger, Irmgard. *Die Frauen der Romantik und das soziale Problem.* Kiel: Schulzesche Hofbuchdruckerei, 1928.

Thorn, Eduard. *Frauen um Dichter.* Stuttgart: Deutsche Verlags-Anstalt, 1933.

Timms, Edward. "The Matrix of Love: Warum gabst du uns die tiefen Blicke." *German Life and Letters* 36 (1982–83): 49–65.

Tobin, Robert. *Warm Brothers: Queer Theory and the Age of Goethe.* Philadelphia: University of Pennsylvania Press, 2000.

Toelpe, Elisabeth. *Frauen von Weimar.* Berlin: F. A. Herbig, 1927.

Torjesen, Karen Jo. "Martyrs, Ascetics, and Gnostics: Gender-Crossing in Early Christianity." *Gender Reversals and Gender Cultures: Anthropological and Historical Perspectives.* Ed. Sabrina Petra Ramet. London: Routledge, 1996. 79–91.

Touaillon, Christine. *Der deutsche Frauenroman des 18. Jahrhunderts.* Bern: Peter Lang, 1979.

Tümmler, Hans. *Goethe als Staatsmann.* Göttingen: Musterschmidt, 1976.

Ueding, Gert. *Friedrich Schiller.* München: C. H. Beck, 1990.

Unger, Friederike Helene. *Albert und Albertine.* Berlin: Unger, 1804.

———. *Bekenntnisse einer schönen Seele: Von ihr selbst geschrieben.* Berlin: Unger, 1806.

———. *Rosalie und Nettchen.* Berlin: Unger, 1801.

Varnhagen von Ense, Karl August. *Biographische Portraits.* Leipzig: F.A. Brockhaus, 1871.

———. *Denkwürdigkeiten und vermischte Schriften.* Leipzig: F.A. Brockhaus, 1843.

Veeser, Aram H. "The New Historicism." *The New Historicism Reader.* Ed. Aram H. Veeser. New York: Routledge, 1994. 1–32.

Vohland, Ulrich. *Bürgerliche Emanzipation in Heinrich von Kleist's Dramen und theoretischen Schriften.* Frankfurt am Main: Peter Lang, 1976.

Voß, Lena. *Goethes unsterbliche Freundin (Charlotte von Stein): Eine psychologische Studie an der Hand der Quellen.* Leipzig: Klinkhardt, 1922.

Wägenbaur, Birgit. *Die Pathologie der Liebe: Literarische Weiblichkeitsentwürfe um 1800.* Berlin: Erich Schmidt, 1996.

Waldstein, Edith. *Bettine von Arnim and the Politics of Romantic Conversation.* Columbia: Camden House, 1988.

———. "Goethe and Beyond: Bettine von Arnim's *Correspondence with a Child* and *Günderode.*" *In the Shadow of Olympus: German Women Writers Around 1800.* Ed. Katherine R. Goodman and Edith Waldstein. Albany: State University of New York Press, 1992. 95–113.

Walter, Eva. *Schrieb oft, von Mägde Arbeit müde: Lebenszusammenhänge deutscher*

Schriftstellerinnen um 1800—Schritte zur bürgerlichen Weiblichkeit. Düsseldorf: Schwann, 1985.

Warner, Marina. *Joan of Arc: The Image of Female Heroism.* Berkeley: University of California Press, 1981.

Weichberger, Alexander. *Goethe und das Komödienhaus in Weimar 1779–1825: Ein Beitrag zur Theaterbaugeschichte.* Leipzig: Leopold Voß, 1928.

Weigel, Sigrid. "Der schielende Blick: Thesen zur Geschichte weiblicher Schreibpraxis." *Die verborgene Frau: Sechs Beiträge zu einer feministischen Literaturwissenschaft.* Ed. Inge Stephan and Sigrid Weigel. Hamburg: Argument Verlag, 1988. 83–137.

———. "Wider die Romantische Mode: Zur ästhetischen Funktion des Weiblichen in Friedrich Schlegels *Lucinde.*" *Die verborgene Frau: Sechs Beiträge zu einer feministischen Literaturwissenschaft.* Ed. Inge Stephan and Sigrid Weigel. Hamburg: Argument Verlag, 1988. 67–82.

Weiner, Annette, and Jane Schneider, eds. *Cloth and Human Experience.* Washington: Smithsonian Institution Press, 1991.

Weissberg, Liliane. "The Master's Theme and Some Variations: Dorothea Schlegel's *Florentin* as Bildungsroman." *Michigan Germanic Studies* 13 (1987): 169–181.

Weißenborn, Birgit. *Bettina von Arnim und Goethe: Topographie einer Beziehung als Beispiel weiblicher Emanzipation zu Beginn des 19. Jahrhunderts.* Frankfurt am Main: Peter Lang, 1987.

Welch, J. L. "Cross-Dressing and Cross-Purposes." *Gender Reversals and Gender Cultures: Anthropological and Historical Perspectives.* Ed. Sabrina Petra Ramet. London: Routledge, 1996. 66–78.

Werner, Hans Georg. "Goethes Reise durch Italien als soziale Erkundung." *Goethe Jahrbuch* 105 (1988): 27–41.

Wertheim, Ursula. *Schillers Fiesco und Don Carlos: Zu Problemen des historischen Stoffes.* Berlin: Aufbau, 1967.

Wetzels, Walter D. "Schauspielerinnen im 18. Jahrhundert—Zwei Perspektiven: *Wilhelm Meister* und die Memoiren der Schulze-Kummerfeld." *Die Frau von der Reformation zur Romantik: Die Situation der Frau vor dem Hintergrund der Literatur- und Sozialgeschichte.* Ed. Barbara Becker-Cantarino. Bonn: Bouvier, 1980. 195–216.

Wheelwright, Julie. *Amazons and Military Maids: Woman Who Dressed as Men in the Pursuit of Life, Liberty and Happiness.* London: Pandora, 1989.

Wichmann, Thomas. *Heinrich von Kleist.* Stuttgart: Metzler, 1988.

Wilde, Jean T. *Caroline de la Motte-Fouqué: The Romantic Realist.* New York: Brookman Associates, 1955.

Wilson, W. Daniel. "Amazon, Agitator, Allegory: Political and Gender Cross-(Dress)ing in Goethe's *Egmont.*" *Outing Goethe and His Age.* Ed. Alice A. Kuzniar. Stanford: Stanford University Press, 1996. 125–146.

Wilson, Elizabeth. *Adorned in Dreams: Fashion and Modernity*. Berkeley: University of California Press, 1987.

Wolf, Christa, ed. "Anhang." *Bettina von Arnim: Die Günderode*. Ed. Christa Wolf. Darmstadt: Suhrkamp, 1994. 525–544.

Wolff, Eugen. *Mignon: Ein Beitrag zur Geschichte des Wilhelm Meister*. München: Beck, 1909.

Wolfson, Susan. "Teaching Don Juan from the Perspective of Cross-Dressing and the Politics of Gender." *Approaches to Teaching Byron's Poetry*. Ed. Frederick Shilstone. New York: MLA, 1991. 142–147.

Woodhouse, Annie. *Fantastic Women: Sex, Gender and Transvestism*. New Brunswick: Rutgers University Press, 1989.

Wurst, Karin A., ed. *Frauen und Drama im achtzehnten Jahrhundert*. Köln: Böhlau, 1991.

Wyss, Hilde. *Bettina von Arnims Stellung zwischen der Romantik und dem jungen Deutschland*. Bern: Paul Haupt, 1935.

Yalom, Marilyn. *Blood Sisters: The French Revolution in Women's Memory*. New York: Basic Books, 1993.

Zachmann, Karin. "Die Durchsetzung des kapitalistischen Fabriksystems in der deutschen Textilindustrie des 19. Jh. aus der Sicht der Verdrängung vorindustrieller Produktionsformen." *Jahrbuch für Wirtschaftsgeschichte* 3 (1991): 31–52.

Zantop, Susanne. "Aus der Not eine Tugend . . . Tugendgebot und Öffentlichkeit bei Friederike Helene Unger." *Untersuchungen zum Roman von Frauen um 1800*. Ed. Magdalene Heuser and Helga Gallas. Tübingen: Niemeyer, 1990. 132–147.

———. *Colonial Fantasies: Conquest, Family, and Nation in Precolonial Germany 1770–1870*. Durham: Duke University Press, 1997.

———. "The Beautiful Soul Writes Herself: Friederike Helene Unger and The Große Göthe." *In the Shadow of Olympus: German Women Writers Around 1800*. Ed. Katherine R. Goodman and Edith Waldstein. Albany: State University of New York Press, 1992. 29–51.

Zimmerman, Susan, ed. *Erotic Politics: Desire on the Renaissance Stage*. New York: Routledge, 1992.

Zobeltitz, Fedor von, ed. *Briefe deutscher Frauen*. Berlin: Ullstein, 1936.

Zons, Raimar. "Der Tod des Menschen: Von Kleists *Familie Schroffenstein* zu Grabbes *Gothland*." *Grabbe und die Dramatiker seiner Zeit: Beiträge zum II. Internationalen Grabbe-Symposium 1989*. Ed. Detlev Kopp and Michael Vogt. Tübingen: Max Niemeyer, 1990. 75–102.

———. "Von der Not der Welt zur absoluten Feindschaft: Kleist's *Hermannsschlacht*." *Zeitschrift für Deutsche Philologie* 109.2 (1990). 75–102.

Index